NICEY AND WIFEY'S

nice
cup of
tea and
a sit
down

TIME WARNER
BOOKS

TIME WARNER BOOKS

First published in Great Britain in October 2004 by Time Warner Books
This paperback edition published in September 2005 by Time Warner Books
Reprinted 2005

A CIP catalogue record for this book is available
from the British Library.

ISBN 0 7515 3765 9

Typeset in Frutiger by M Rules
Printed and bound in Great Britain by
The Bath Press, Bath

Time Warner Books
An imprint of
Time Warner Book Group UK
Brettenham House
Lancaster Place
London WC2E 7EN

www.twbg.co.uk

For Dad
who liked a decent biscuit

Contents

A Little Bit of Cake

And a Sit Down

Introduction

Put a cup of tea in your hand and what else can you do but sit down?

There can be few more relaxing things in life than a nice cup of tea and a sit down. A good hot bath is one, but that's not always an option, especially if you are at work or doing your shopping.

Or maybe like us your bath is fairly short and small, and you have to sit bolt upright in it. If you do lie down in it then your legs have to stick out at the tap end, halfway up the wall, and they get cold. Playing loud music and drinking a glass of brandy or whiskey go some way to diverting us from the fact that our bath was designed for a lost race of people with an average height of 4ft 6ins, but it's far from ideal.

Anyway, a nice cuppa while sitting down is the cornerstone of British society, possibly even more important to us than television or queuing up for things. The cultural accoutrements of tea and sitting down are everywhere in our daily life, from cups, pots, cosies and bags to whole ladies equipped with urns given over to the service of tea. Not to mention sofas, armchairs, kitchen stools, corners of desks and sitting up against a nice plumped-up pillow in bed.

When moving house the first item to be unpacked is the electric kettle. Tea in conjunction with sitting down is so important in British culture that its consumption after unifying and world-shaping events (such as moon landings, cup finals and the shooting of J. R. Ewing) results in millions of extra kilowatts of electricity being generated to cope with ten million British households putting the kettle on. Indeed, during half-time in the recent 2003 Rugby World Cup Final there was a power spike equivalent to 850,000 kettles being simultaneously switched on.

The vast majority of sitting-down-with-a-cup-of-tea engagements would, however, be incomplete without biscuits. Indeed, tea without biscuits is a missed opportunity. Like all great double acts, the whole is greater than the sum of its parts. On its own, the cup of tea will of course bring warmth and comforting refreshment to you but add, say, three or four Digestives and one is reinvigorated, ready to face the world anew. We can now perhaps achieve such great things as a little light housework, reading the paper, or potting on some geraniums.

Finding the perfect biscuit for the occasion is as much an art as it is a science, and has occupied most, if not all, of my tea-drinking life. In a similar way, the French have made a national pastime of choosing the right wine to go with the right dish. However, if you've ever read the labels on the wine bottles you'll see that they all seem to go with cheese, but that's probably because the French make an awful lot of that as well. There is obviously some kind of duopoly set up between the cheese makers and the vineyards. Perhaps science will eventually come up with a cheese that doesn't go with wine and a wine that doesn't go with cheese. This could then be combined to form a sauce that doesn't go well with itself, let alone anything else.

Like most of the British populace, biscuits have played a part in my life from my earliest memories. During the 1930s and 1940s, my grandparents had a small shop in the East End of London, which like all others at the time sold biscuits loose from large drums. As a young boy, my dad would help himself to the broken biscuits and developed his own keen biscuit skills, which he eventually passed on to me. Through my school years he would often discuss the merits of one biscuit over another during our daily four o'clock cuppa. So biscuit appraisal is in my blood.

I haven't set out to cover every classic biscuit in this book, or even every important biscuit that there is. Nevertheless, I seem to have covered quite a lot of them and I'm sure you'll find some of your favourites here. We all have our personal preferences for highly individual reasons and it's not just the way that they taste. Often it's to do with a time or place that they accompany us to while we munch away. To mark them out of ten would be undignified and meaningless, so I'll just share my personal thoughts on them. You might not always agree with me but then that is to be expected. I hope you will think that many have a curious personality that is worth a second look.

Tea drinkers don't tend to have moderate and liberal views on tea. We all like it the way we like it, whatever way that may be. I'm certainly not about to come up with something as doomed to failure as a pronouncement on how to make the ideal cup. If you've ever made tea for somebody else, chances are that they politely complained about it being too weak, too strong, too milky or in the wrong sort of cup. When it comes to tea, one size does not fit all. So it's not the recipe for the perfect cup of tea that I'll be discussing here but some of the obstacles that are placed in our personal path towards it.

Although it is biscuits that most often accompany our cuppas, from time to time cake pops up. So I've left space for a little bit of cake near the end as a special treat. Cake would like a much bigger bit, as it can be quite full of itself, but I've kept it down to a few slices of my favourites.

Finally, I'll take a look at some of the many and varied ways in which we pursue that relaxing sit down so crucial to a successful cup of tea. From not sitting down at a stand-up buffet to sitting on your coat while sipping tea from your vacuum flask, when tea is at hand the sit down is sought after; if we are already sitting down, then the need for tea increases. I'll look at some of the situations in which we risk scalded fingers, wet clothes, puncture wounds and instant tea, just to capitalise on our sedentary circumstances.

So here it is: forty years of biscuit eating, tea drinking and the occasional slice of cake condensed into a handy book. Much like on our website, Wifey is going to have her say, so watch yourselves. If you know the website then you'll find plenty that is new here, not least finally getting round to my thoughts on the Pink Wafer. If you don't know the site, then I hope you'll enjoy what is a personal and affectionate look at some of the simple pleasures that feature in most of our daily lives.

A Nice Cup of Tea

Tea

My Worst Cup of Tea Ever

San Jose, California, May 1999. My worst cup of tea, ever, really.

This was my first visit to the USA, and my first experience of jet lag. It was also my first time filling in one of those bizarre green cards, required by American Immigration, on which you are required to declare whether or not you have ever been a member of the Nazi Party or have committed acts of genocide. Now obviously these are very important and serious questions, but how often do they actually catch people out this way? If I were a genocidal sort of character, then not ticking a box asking me to own up to it would probably be something I was capable of too. Nevertheless, I couldn't help but glance at the green cards of other passengers near to me.

On the way to America we passed over Greenland, Baffin Island (named after an old Geography teacher of mine, or it may have been the other way round) and northern Canada. None of these places seemed like anywhere where we should have tried to make a quick stop for a cuppa and a little stretch of the legs.

After eleven hours' flying we touched down in San Francisco, three hours after taking off, or something like that. It quickly became apparent that, having dealt with the Nazis, fruit and snails were the next most pressing issues for the authorities. I immediately started to feel guilty and shifty, having freely associated with both. Indeed, a couple of days earlier while digging over the vegetable patch, I had filled the bottom of a bucket with snails that had been overwintering in the garden. Had any of these hidden themselves in the seams of my clothing? When asked by the official why I was visiting the United States, it was as much as I could do to remember, given that it was way past midnight at teatime. 'For business,' I replied. 'What sort of business?' he asked. Being a *Dallas* fan, I wanted to reply, 'Da oil business', but thought it best to say I was off to a computer development convention. This did the trick and they let me in. It was a good job I didn't mention the fifty bags of PG Tips stashed in my luggage.

We stayed up until what must have been technically half past five in the morning. After a wholesome tea of melted cheese chilli sticks, washed down with carbonated brown stuff and several other things that might have been chips we retired to our beds. I awoke the next day bright and early about 6.30 a.m. local time.

After showering, there really was only one thing on my mind. Tea. Whether it was ignorance, blind optimism or a misplaced faith in the kindness of my fellow man, I left my tea bags in my hotel room and headed down for breakfast. I met my colleagues in the dining room, all seasoned visitors to the US. They were seated around a table with starched white tablecloths, napkins, silver cutlery and a large bowl of freshly prepared Californian fruit. When the waiter appeared, everyone else ordered coffee. I asked for tea; 'a nice one please'. I should have picked up on his slightly confused expression.

Pots of coffee soon arrived. In my case, however, the waiter approached carrying a large wooden box, very much like the sort one keeps one's duelling pistols in. He opened the lid to show me the contents but rather than guns, it contained an array of unlikely and very dud-looking tea bags. Trying to take control over my general state of disorientation I carefully scanned the contents, which had names like 'blackcurrant leaf and sticks', and 'rosehip and herring'. I continued to scour the box for anything that might be related to conventional tea. English Breakfast seemed to be the best fit for my predicament, even if the tea bag looked to be filled with the soot scraped from the top of burnt toast.

A short while later the waiter returned with a small metal pot of warm water and half a lemon in a netting bag. Close to tears, I asked if they had any milk. Again, I was met by confused looks: perhaps the waiter thought I had completely changed my mind about which beverage I wanted. I explained it was for the tea. The waiter took my word for it and said that they didn't have any milk. I tried not to imagine what they were using in the kitchens to make all the batter needed for the huge mounds of pancakes being devoured around me. I also did a quick mental recap on how the process of dairy farming works, to see if there was something obvious I had forgotten. They did, the waiter ventured, have something called half and half. I decided to take my chances, as perhaps half of it would be milk.

The warm water did its best to leach some of the dark colouring from the ash-like substance in the tea bag. The tea bag, though, failed to swell up in that jolly steam-filled way and float to the top of the cup. It dropped forlornly to the bottom instead, as if wounded. Driven on by an almost pathological tea craving, I removed it and added a dash of the half and half, creating a dark brown and greasy mixture, similar to that obtained when washing out a roasting tin after a piece of beef has become stuck to the bottom.

The 'tea' was wet.

The next morning I brought down my own tea bags, and asked for 'very hot water' and some half and half.

The next morning I settled for coffee.

Learning to Love Tea

It's a beguiling idea to think that tea drinking is an innate skill that we are born with. It therefore comes as a bit of a surprise to find that we actually have to learn to drink tea. Just as a child learns to crawl, walk, ride a bike or open those little cartons of juice without squirting it all over themselves, so we all have to learn to drink tea. Here is Wifey, to explain how she developed her craving for the hallowed stuff.

The Importance of Mrs Brown

I was raised in a household where coffee was the drink of choice. Tea was reserved for having with the occasional meal, like a greasy fry-up, or with toast at breakfast-time. When I left home at the tender age of eighteen to become a nurse, I was innocent of its importance in the outside world.

The place I chose to do my training was a very traditional hospital on the outskirts of Belfast. It was run with rods of iron by matrons in starched uniforms, and consultants who were seen, but definitely not spoken to by lowly student nurses. My first placement was in a ward run by as old school a sister as you could ever come across. On my first day she took me aside to tell me that my role for the next six weeks would be to ensure the tidiness and cleanliness of the place, to test urine and to make beds. In that order. To this day, when I make a bed I cringe at the memory of how I was accused of 'slovenly placement of pillows', and carefully arrange them with the open end facing away from the door.

This is where Mrs Brown comes into the story. Patients were not allowed to think of the possibility that staff were actually human beings, who would need to have breaks and possibly a sit down every now and then. This presented a problem, as staff could not possibly go to the ward staffroom without the permission of Sister, at the exact time she had decided it was appropriate for you to do so. Sister, for all her gruff manner, was a fair woman, and she saw it as one of her duties that everyone had an adequate tea intake during the day, whether they liked the stuff or not. So in order to get people into the staffroom for their allocation of tea, they were called to see Mrs Brown. She was treated with reverence. The patients knew that when she called, she could not be kept waiting, despite what their needs were. They never even questioned who Mrs Brown was, despite the fact that this was a male ward.

The tea was made by senior members of staff, who knew how Sister liked it, and this was the way that everyone had it. It was made in a huge pot, with at least five or six heaped teaspoons of special, nameless NHS tea, and wasn't right unless it was thick enough for the spoon to stand upright in the cup. Alternatives, such as increasing or decreasing the amount of sugar or milk in one's cup, were tolerated, although it was accepted that those who drank tea the same way as Sister were most likely to get a favourable report at the end of the placement.

My first week there I hated Mrs Brown, and I had to wonder if nursing was really the career for me. After the second week I began to get used to the taste, found that Sister wasn't really so bad, and the ward really did need to be kept spotless. By the end of my six weeks I couldn't properly function unless I'd been to see Mrs Brown. In short, I'd been turned into a tea addict.

Later in my training I began to appreciate the other skills of Mrs Brown. She made a regular appearance in the ward for the patients at the end of visiting time in the evenings. This was seen as a bedtime treat, and a sign that patients were expected to settle down for the night in time for the arrival of the night staff, who despised patients being awake and talking to them. Mrs Brown also made special appearances in times of bad news. Patients quickly learnt that if they were offered a cup of tea outside normal hours, then they were about to be told something serious. And if their relatives were offered a cup of tea, well, they should make sure all their affairs were in order as quickly as possible.

These days, of course, wards have water coolers and students drink whatever they like, often while having a chat with the patients about how drunk they were the night before (sometimes even with their arms folded). I do wonder what Mrs Brown would have thought of it all, and whether the place isn't quite so spotlessly clean as it was in her day. Not that it's just the NHS which has been changed by the demise of Mrs Brown. All aspects of society are changing, and not necessarily for the better. There are often surveys done about how difficult it is to get a hold of a good builder or plumber, while avoiding the 'cowboys'. I don't remember these problems years ago when builders where famous for their tea with milk, two sugars and a nice Digestive.

But back to the tea. After years of visiting Mrs Brown my taste buds became used to it and now I can't drink anything else. I've tried the herbal teas and the fruit teas and the Earl Greys, but I can't get on with any of them. They just don't have the kick that I now depend on. To me Earl Grey tastes like tea made in a cup that's been washed with far too much washing-up liquid, and then not properly rinsed. I want to tip it into a clean cup and try again. In fact, I've tried this. It didn't work. I've experimented with herbal teas on and off over the years, but they just don't do it for me. When I was pregnant I was told by my sister to drink raspberry leaf tea, as this would help during labour. I really wanted to like it, but it just made me want to vomit. I gave up after about a week and have now had two boys without its help. I would like to like these exotic teas, much in the same way that I would like to like olives, but I don't.

So I've given up on the tea experimentation. I'll happily change brands of standard tea, and experiment with different types of tea bags, but that's as far as it goes.

Sorry.

Projected Tea Enjoyment

Of course, we mostly learn how to drink tea from our parents, and this results in a quite peculiar and universal phenomenon, that of 'projected tea enjoyment'. In this, the tea drinker imagines that everybody else on the planet likes tea made just the way they like it.

In a well-adjusted family most members enjoy their tea made in the same way: same strength, same temperature, same amount of milk and so forth. This shared family 'tea policy' is most often seen in families that use a teapot. When there is a difference of opinion between parents one or other usually wins out, and the other gradually learns to drink their tea differently. This very act of capitulation only fuels our idea that everyone not only *could* be made to drink tea as we like it but *should* drink tea as we like it. There are many common consequences of this:

- **People don't bother asking how you like your tea**, assuming you'll drink whatever they give you with relish.

- **They do ask you how you like your tea but then totally ignore anything you tell them**, thinking that you're bound to enjoy their tea better.

- **They ask you and then violently disagree**, pointing out all the reasons why you are wrong and misguided.

- **They try to make it as you have requested but get it all wrong**, either maliciously or through ineptitude.

- **They tell you to make your own tea**, not from compassion but because they can't stand to make it in the degenerate way you have suggested.

This explains why you rarely get a nice cup of tea when visiting other people. Of course, it is easy to endear yourself to your host simply by uttering the line, 'That's the best cup of tea I've had in ages', preceded by a sort of gasped '*Ahhhh*' for maximum effect. Your congratulations will bolster your host's already firmly held belief that they do in fact make the best cup of tea on the planet. If you have been sufficiently fawning they might even be moved to get out their really good biscuits.

Our Tea Policy

Well, the thing about tea is that everyone just drinks it the way they like it. Generally, we make it in mugs, one tea bag – PG Pyramids – for every two mugs. Put the hot water in first, then give it a bit of a stir before adding the milk. Simple. Oh and we don't add sugar. If you drink any other sort of tea, that's fine. If you put the milk in with the bag first, that's OK too. Just so long as you know that it's wrong. Sugar is good too, especially if you're a builder. Occasionally we use a pot, when we can be bothered. That's all we have to say on the subject. Cheers.

Tea Bags

The One Per Cup Misunderstanding

A few years ago, while in the employment of a large company, I found myself in the kitchen making a couple of mugs of tea for a colleague and myself. As I did so the company handyman watched me. A chap in his mid-sixties, he was replacing a fluorescent tube, I believe. For making two mugs of tea one bag is of course more than sufficient, yet as I dunked the bag into the second mug I heard him say, 'I've seen everything now! Two mugs with one bag.'

Despite living through World War Two, seeing mankind take their first steps on the moon and the everyday medical miracles of organ transplants, the most startling thing the handyman had witnessed in his life was the sight of me making two mugs of tea with one tea bag. I was sorely tempted to deliver a caustic remark. However, as he was a fairly elderly chap and on top of a ladder I thought better of it. His mistake, though, is all too common. Those used to using tea bags straight in a cup or mug often lose sight of the tea bag's original intended purpose.

Technology

The tea bag was introduced as a miraculous labour-saving device to a nation that for nearly three hundred years had made tea from loose leaves brewed in a pot. Although this produces a lovely cuppa, it is a slight chore getting shot of the used tea leaves. The traditional method was to swill some water inside the teapot, wander into the back garden and eject the lot under the roses. Obviously this is a problem for those who live in flats. Those without rose bushes in their gardens also have to improvise. Even those with rose bushes don't always want to see a heap of gently decomposing tea leaves underneath them. There is the option of chucking the whole lot down the sink, but eventually this will probably block it up. It's also a bit of an unnecessary burden on the poor old water works.

The real problem with the used tea leaves in the pot is that it's one more hurdle to jump before you have your much-needed cup of tea. To some it may be part of the ritual, but none the less it is a fairly irksome task. So let's cast our minds back to the 1960s. The Americans were planning on sending a man to the moon and inventing lots of things along the way. The very least the British could do was come up with some way of streamlining their tea-making process. This would also free up invaluable time that could be put to good use, inventing stuff for the 1970s like flared jeans and Raleigh Choppers. The stage was set.

Enter the tea bag, or rather re-enter the tea bag.

At the turn of the twentieth century, the American tea importer Thomas Sullivan sent out some samples of his tea in protective silk bags. His somewhat unorthodox customers assumed that rather than opening up the small sachets (as Sullivan intended), they should just throw the whole thing into their pots. It's ironic that that most British of items, the tea bag, was invented by accident through the actions of some well-meaning but mostly clueless Americans. The tea bag was refined again in America during the 1920s and eventually would be made from paper.

I receive a lot of correspondence on the technicalities of tea brewing, mainly from those who wish to justify their personal tea policies through some form of scientific deduction. If they can show that there is a scientific advantage to their chosen methods then their tea policy will have to be accepted as the one true way, or at the very least an aspect of it. From time to time a popular science story occurs in the media about an aspect of tea and biscuits and this just fans the flames. So don't be scared if you see the word 'molecular' in the next paragraph, it's unavoidable.

The tea used in these early tea bags was intended for pot brewing, and as such could release its flavour, aroma and colour at a gentle and restrained pace. People were used to waiting for the tea to 'mash' for a few minutes and there wasn't any special reason for the tea bag to speed this up. The leaves used were large compared to today: their fibrous structure acted as a natural filter, holding back the bitter, high-molecular-weight tannins (the ones that account for the stewed taste in tea) and allowing the more desirable low-weight tannins to move out of the leaves into the liquid. In other words, the early tea bags produced a cuppa that compared perfectly favourably to that made from loose tea. To ensure that people had a satisfying brew of proper strength, the amount of tea was sufficient to make two cups (the basic assumption being that a bag is sufficient for one person and that person will want two cups of decent tea). Those who adopted tea bags soon found that between two to three bags were ample for a full pot of average size.

As the pace of daily life has increased we have become ever more impatient, and as a result the tea bag has found itself brewing tea outside the teapot. It is commonplace now to make tea in the mug and we don't really care for waiting three or four minutes while it brews. In fact, the modern tea bag needs to do its job in a matter of seconds: the majority of people leave the bag for thirty seconds, while one in four people allow no more than ten seconds. Tea snobs are quick to dismiss tea bags as being filled with 'sweepings'. This is clearly completely ludicrous as 85% of all tea sold in the UK is in the form of bags. The process that produces the 15% loose tea would have to be incredibly wasteful to create enough 'sweepings' to make five times the amount of tea bags. The reality is that much of the tea in bags is now finer to allow for a very quick 'release'. However, this also means the tea is quicker to stew, to the detriment of those using the pot.

Over the years we have seen a pace of innovation in the area of tea bag design so rapid that it is only a few orders of magnitude less than that of washing detergent. After playing about with the contents, manufacturers then began to make the holes or pores in the bags bigger. Then some bags changed shape from square-ish to round and now pyramidal. The format also evolved; now you can get special bags with tags and strings to be whipped out of cups, drawstrings that wring out the bag, and the 'one cup bag', with just enough tea to make one nice cup. Oi! You up the ladder! Did you hear that? If tea bags had been meant for only one cup then why did they have to invent the one cup bag? And what about those little stainless-steel teapots, the ones you get at motorway service stations that empty the tea all over the table? They only have one bag in them, yet do they not contain about two and a half cups of tea? I rest my case.

All of this bag technology could have presented the rose bushes which had acquired a taste for a couple of pots of tea a day with quite a problem. Most of the used tea bags were finding their way straight into the rubbish bin, ultimately to be buried in landfills. Not a very dignified end for all those little leaf tips that started life under the sunshine of an Indian or African sky. However, in recent times it has dawned upon most of us that we need to take a bit of individual responsibility for our environment, and home composting is a great way of helping out. Used tea bags make excellent compost and not only do the roses benefit but so does the rest of the garden, particularly the marrows and courgettes. One of the most relaxing ways to pass a warm summer's afternoon is to sit in the garden, admiring your crop of Cucurbitaceae flourishing on composted tea bags. While drinking a mug of tea and munching on a biscuit, of course.

Sugar

Tea tastes bitter, and many tea drinkers when starting out take theirs with a spoonful of sugar to offset this taste. As we get older our tastes change and we start to enjoy flavours such as tea, beer, olives and tonic water. However, we still don't enjoy those dreadful local speciality liquors you get given on holiday in the Alps, the ones that taste like a solution of paracetamol filtered through old carpet soaked in petrol. The sugar in tea also provides a little energy lift that can be quite welcome. I took sugar in my tea right up to going to university. However, once there I quickly gave it up. This wasn't because I wanted to establish my sophisticated adult credentials, but because my cupboard in the shared kitchen was so tiny I couldn't fit a bag of sugar in it. That and the fact I was totally broke.

But perhaps the most meaningful part of giving up sugar is the fact that it is one less thing to bother with when making tea. Having grown used to this extra level of convenience, most non-sugar people find it galling to have to dig some out for those who still require it. They are often still quite smug about the ten days' self-sacrifice they had to endure while giving up, and are keen for others to share that pain. Their agenda now is to get everybody else to stop taking sugar, and they have a number of well-known approaches when making tea for a sugar user:

🫖 **Deny the sugar-user direct access to the sugar bowl**, insisting that they put it in and then deliberate give less sugar than requested. The expectation is that rather than complain about the lack of sweetness, the sugar person will declare that this is the nicest cup of tea they have ever had, and enquire how it was made so extra especially nice.

🫖 **Dig out a really ancient bag of sugar which has a few ounces left at the bottom.** Here one can find all the accumulated brown and yellow lumps where people have been forced to stick their damp tea-spoons in, and possibly the odd toast crumb. The bag itself has begun to yellow with age, and where one would normally expect to see a bar-code there is a competition to win some 45r.p.m. vinyl singles. There may even be grubby marks where it has become embroiled in some post-bicycle-chain-mending hand-cleansing. Of course, the hardened sugar user will be undeterred and somehow retrieve pristine spoonfuls.

🫖 **Pretend that they don't have any sugar at all in the house, and force the sugar person to have it without.** Of course, they won't like this at all but the ex-sugar person will know that it is in fact good for them both physically and mentally. For good measure they'll probably want to insist that the sugar person has a second cup.

🫖 **Pretend that they have no proper sugar and offer them some form of derivative sugar such as icing sugar, demerara or, most degradingly of all, golden syrup.** Again the sugar person isn't meant to like this and should resolve to drink their tea without any sort of sweetening. Annoyingly, they will willingly take the dodgy sugar without apparently realising that such behaviour is sordid and demeaning.

🫖 **Genuinely not have any sugar in the house, and derive some sort of sick pleasure from watching the poor sugar user suffer as they are forced to drink 'proper' tea.**

🫖 **The ultimate cruelty: give them some form of artificial sweetener**, because the non-sugar user is also a recovering sugar addict and has managed to persuade themself that they actually enjoy the taste of saccharine. Only now they've become hooked on the sweeteners, and are starting to use more and more as they don't seem to be quite as sweet as they once were. Perhaps they can lure the sugar user into their twisted world where they too will have to carry their own personal supply of sweeteners in their jacket pocket. Oh yes, they know only too well what can happen if they're deprived of their tablets and forced to take up the offer of the sugar bowl. You might as well give a bottle of vodka to a recovering alcoholic.

There are times in life when we are not too choosy about our tea. At such times even the most out-of-kilter brew can become divine nectar. Anything handed out by the emergency services tends to be simultaneously both of these opposites and often contains a good helping of sugar.

Teapots

A Potted History

The Chinese invented tea, and probably about twenty minutes later the teapot to make some in. There are teapots that date back to the early Ming dynasty, which is nice as that is most people's favourite dynasty. These earliest pots were fairly selfish affairs as you were meant to drink the tea directly from the spout. (Mind you, how many of us can honestly say that we haven't done that ourselves at times?) Teapots as we know them were really a seventeenth-century European invention, most likely based directly on the Islamic coffee pots which were already well known in the coffee houses of Europe's great cities. Early models were ropey old affairs due to the poor quality of ceramics used to make them. In fact, one early design even featured a replaceable spout as they broke so often.

So it was back to China to get some proper porcelain ones made to European specifications. The East India Company, who ran the tea business back then, commissioned teapots directly from Chinese artisans. These teapots were incredibly expensive, having been brought halfway round the world in a trip that could take a total of three years there and back. As such, they were as much a status symbol of the well to do as they were a functional object. But the desire by the middle classes to take part in the elite and fashionable ritual of afternoon tea fuelled a huge new market for teapots, and European alternatives to porcelain began to appear.

It's ironic that today most of the upper classes have had to turn their stately homes in to tea rooms, their gardens into car parks and their stables into public conveniences in order to attract the working classes into their estates. If they also laid on bingo and chicken in a basket, I'm sure they'd soon be back in the lap of luxury.

Now in the twenty-first century we have 300 years of European teapot tradition and innovation to draw upon. Our teapot heritage runs from Josiah Wedgwood's Creamware, through the many and varied influences on Victorian teapots, to the modernists and the postmodernists. Let's see if we can find one that doesn't pour its contents all over our feet.

Form and Function

The pen and the car: two commodities at opposite ends of the spectrum of costs. A new pen may cost only a matter of pence and yet you get to try it out on a little jotter pad. You can write your name, do some squiggles or your favourite doodle before deciding whether to splash out 70 pence on it. Equally, when buying a car, even a bottom-of-the-range model, you get to take it out for a test drive. You might keep it only a year or two, but you still get to make your choice safe in the knowledge that at least it went OK the day you bought it.

So why don't you get to do the same with teapots?

There are two primary mission objectives that any teapot should fulfil: holding enough tea and being able to get it into your cup without spilling it everywhere. A teapot test-drive zone in your local department store would be a boon to those in need of a new pot. Health and Safety might not like people boiling kettles, so cold tea would need to be used. No doubt it would have a slightly different viscosity to proper hot tea which could affect the results, but let's be realistic and not set our sights unattainably high.

No, I've changed my mind. Let's aim high. One could sign a disclaimer, indemnifying the store from your possible self-harm. Then you could enter a special teapot-testing cubicle with little bulletproof Plexiglas view ports, through which your loved ones could look on. Alternatively, you could take out a short-term insurance policy covering the store against possible breakage, carpet staining and total catastrophic destruction of their teapot-testing cubicles. It could also cover you against scalds, tea-stained clothes and trench foot.

Obviously one is after a good clean pouring action which starts and stops without any nasty surprises. The ability to pour well is prized above all else, including capacity, as it's no good how much your pot can hold if it then pours most of it over your feet and table. There should be no dribbling or trickling. Spout pressure should not drop away too prohibitively towards the last cups. Finally, the pot should feel balanced and pouring from it should be comfortable no matter how full it is.

Having said all that, the capacity issue cannot be glossed over and there really is only one way to test it: with a row of mugs or cups which closely match or, better still, replicate your domestic drinking vessel set-up. It's going to be easier if you have matching sets and a bit more tricky if you have to simulate a variety of personal mugs and cups. Perhaps you could select them from a laminated illustrated catalogue, via a code number: the test-zone personnel could then fetch them from a large system of racks using little trays. The mugs should all be glazed white, possibly with those little black and yellow quarter-circle thingies that crash-test dummies have all over them, placed at strategic points. If you are intending to use tea bags then it's imperative that you use your own brand as they will no doubt have their own volumetric signature when they swell up.

When using leaf tea the shape of the pot becomes even more crucial. Clearly the tea brewing is going to be affected by the convection currents in your pot, even after you've given it a good stir. No, the real issue with pot shape is spout clogging. The placing of the spout, its width, taper and extra moulded-in paraphernalia to catch the leaves all contribute. The shape of some pots can also cause annoying cubby holes in which limescale and wayward tea leaves can congregate. They will hide here and then spring out at you when you least expect it, black and scaly or bleached and insipid.

The next most important issue is lid retention. Even some of the most potentially nice pots can suffer from premature lid loss right in the middle of a good pour. This can be acutely embarrassing for all concerned. It's a great shame as there really is no excuse for it. It can even lead to some pots becoming virtual recluses, living out their days at the back of kitchen cupboards.

Apart from a nice comfy handle and a good stable 'footprint', that's most of the practical considerations out of the way. Now you are free to make purely aesthetic decisions such as will it go with the curtains and does it complement your tea service. But if you find a teapot that really does deliver in the vital areas I've outlined then it might be easier just to get new curtains and redecorate the house around it.

Work Tea Making

When The Tea Bags Run Out

There are certain events that can have a dramatic impact on productivity in the modern office environment, effectively bringing any useful work to a standstill. Power cuts, fire drills, World Cup matches and Wimbledon fortnight can all be crippling, but none is as damaging as running out of tea bags. A form of mild mass-hysteria soon sets in, with employees wandering aimlessly with empty mugs, moaning bitterly about the lack of tea.

An all too common mistake in an office is to put the most junior member of staff in charge of the task of ordering stationery and kitchen supplies. An even bigger error is to put the visiting foreign work experience student in charge. Not only will their youth and inexperience count against them but their cultural background will make them unaware of the gravity and responsibility of keeping a good stock of tea bags. Even if such matters are made plain to them they may actually not drink tea (it *is* possible) and thus be completely unaware of tea bag levels and any impending 'no tea bag' calamities.

A responsible managing director will take steps to ensure that the company places somebody trustworthy in charge of tea bags, such as the lady in accounts who does the payroll. Often these unsung heroes can stave off a crisis situation by popping to the local shop to get a box of tea bags when supplies are low. Such occasions are when their spreadsheet model of tea bag consumption has been thrown into disarray by a late delivery of the catering-size sacks of tea bags from the suppliers, or a surge in tea drinking due to a particularly dull workload.

Tea Notation

There are various things in this world of ours which require some form of notation to describe their composition or make-up. For example, the chemical notation for sodium bicarbonate, a common raising agent in biscuits, is:

$$NaHCO_3$$

From this we learn that there is one atom of sodium, one of hydrogen, one of carbon and three of oxygen per molecule of sodium bicarbonate. You might have thought that noting how people take their tea would be a much simpler task than recording the chemical composition of compounds. Well, it's not.

Most people will hastily invent a drinks notation on the spot when making tea for a group of people. A typical approach might be 'T' for tea and 'C' for coffee. Of course, the next most important fact to note is sugar, and this is simply dealt with by the addition of a number. 'T2' is thus not a film staring Arnold Schwarzenegger, but tea with two sugars. Just as you think you have that part under control, somebody pipes up that they like a level, not heaped, teaspoon. Somebody else adds that they actually just like half a level teaspoonful, unless it's coffee, when they like one heaped.

Then there are those who take their drinks black, which being the exception to the rule is denoted by a 'B'. However, those who take it with milk will typically like it with 'a dash', 'normal' (by far the most difficult one to get right) or 'milky', so we might get a third column with 'B', 'D', or 'M' in it. Not that this is the end of it: somebody always wants something odd like Earl Grey, for which you'll need to write down 'Earl Grey' in full. By rights this should be it, but it's not. Some like it weak, some strong, some 'normal' again. So you may need a fourth column with 'W' and 'S' in it.

Surely we must be done by now? Well, normally, yes, at this point good manners should prevail and people should drink whatever is put in front of them. However, there may also be the occasional person who will insist that you track down their personal mug. This might require you to take a description or even possibly a small sketch of the intended mug with you. In extreme cases, you may be forced to do their dirty work and retrieve it for them from the dishwasher, or worse still the sales department.

Still, armed with a semi-accurate list of people's preferences, you can not only get the drinks in, but might gain insight into their personalities. For instance:

T3MW	–	Immature
T	–	Very normal
T1L	–	Normal sugar user
Earl Grey 0.5 B Lemon Peter Rabbit Mug	–	Very annoying
CBS Large Mug	–	Party animal / New parent

This provides a welcome bit of light relief as making drinks for a dozen or more people is going to keep you in the kitchen for the next ten minutes of your life. Effectively this is like taking a small fire-safety course: by the time you make it out of there, boredom will have driven you to read the instructions on the fire extinguisher and the fire blanket, and you'll also know where to congregate in case of an emergency. You may also be wondering why the egg tray in the fridge door has managed to collect some small deposits of a semi-solid, yellow, waxy substance despite never seeing an egg in its entire existence.

Studying people's preferences can also prove useful for gauging who is going to object to whatever they are given. See if you can spot the troublemaker from the list above. You may have thought it was the Earl Grey drinker, but they will be quite happy with what you give them as it all tastes the same regardless of what you do to it. It's actually the first one, who will claim that there isn't enough sugar in it, and they are probably right, aren't they?

Kettle Etiquette

We tend to think that our values as a society are being constantly eroded. The things that we value, such as respect for others and orderly behaviour, seem to be put under increasing strain in our overcrowded and busy world. However, queuing for things in an orderly way is something that the British have always taken pride in. In fact, one of the most repugnant social crimes of all is queue jumping. Anyone committing this heinous act is subjected to withering stares and even the occasional indirect jibe, discussed between two law-abiding queue members and designed to be overheard by the queue jumper.

The imported American idea of a 'water cooler culture' in the UK is of course a falsehood. We drink tea, not little paper cups of water, even if the weather is hot. All the discussion on the latest and greatest reality TV show takes place over the electric kettle, in the office kitchen. The water cooler, if one exists, is actually regarded with a degree of suspicion and mistrust. Most people don't like to be seen using it as somebody is obviously having a joke at our expense, and making the company pay for cold water when the taps are full of it.

As such, the office kettle is the place where our social skills are challenged to the limit as we gather round it and struggle not to disgrace ourselves. When to fill the kettle and when to use the boiled water are matters on which our peers will judge us, and nobody likes a queue jumper. Here are some guidelines that you might care to memorise:

 Social ranking. Everybody is an equal in the sight of the kettle. Company directors and their guests enjoy no special privileges, waiting their turn along with everybody else.

 The water in the kettle should only be boiled once, as repeated boiling drives off the dissolved oxygen that is considered essential for good tea. It is therefore better to use any boiled water left in the kettle than to add more cold and boil it again.

 Big jobs. If somebody is making tea for a large number of people, say in excess of three, then they will require exclusive use of the kettle and probably a time-consuming full boil from cold. Their right to do this should be respected. However, if there is enough freshly boiled water in the kettle to meet the needs of the people directly behind them in the queue, then it should be offered to them.

 Abandoned tea makings. Sometimes you will encounter an abandoned teacup or mug containing a tea bag and next to a recently boiled kettle with only sufficient water to make one cup of tea. Under no circumstances should you attempt to finish the job, as this will probably result in a stewed cold cup of tea with that shiny film on top. Whatever they may think, by leaving their mug the owner has forfeited any rights to the kettle. You should make your own tea then refill the kettle and switch it on again.

 Catastrophic kettle failure. Any technical problems with a kettle, such as a blown fuse or dead element, should be immediately notified to the correct authorities (usually the lady in accounts). A yellow Post-It note with the word 'Dead' written on it should be affixed to the kettle. A company email memo should be circulated advising of the crisis and the actions that are being taken to remedy it. It is better that people learn of these things first hand rather than via ugly rumours.

Mugs

Mug Menagerie

The average workplace kitchen has five distinct forms of drinking vessel, intended for deployment with hot beverages, such as soup, hot chocolate, coffee and of course tea:

- **Proper plain white cups and saucers that get used in meetings with visitors.**

- **Generic mugs that are slightly oddly shaped, typically no more than six, that were bought from a department store as the cheapest thing they had.** These are intended for everybody's use. Unfortunately the mugs were seconds – that's why they were cheap – and those that still have handles compensate with strange glazed warts.

- **A seemingly unlimited supply of some form of promotional mug, which somebody in marketing had made to give away as freebies.** If one of these ever breaks then somebody can always pop down to the store cupboard and get another box of fifty. Such mugs are intrinsically embarrassing as they often commemorate a hopelessly out of date or discontinued product or perhaps a marketing campaign that was widely accepted to be the most expensive and least effective yet. It's not uncommon for the more subversive employees to use these mugs in some form of obtuse political statement. (They are often the reason why the lady from accounts had to go out and buy the nice set of cups and saucers for meetings with visitors.)

Samples. Hiding among the personal mugs is a small community of one-off samples that were made for the people in marketing. These feature horrendous colour schemes, defunct logos, and incorrect postcodes and telephone numbers.

 Personal mugs. These are brought in by the employees themselves and are characterised by the fact that they are meant to be repellent to other people.

Personal Mugs Explained

If an Englishman's home is his castle, then his mug is what he drinks his tea out of. This also applies to other nations and to the ladies. So it's little wonder that most of us go off the deep end when somebody uses our personal mug. They might as well complete the job by pinching our toothbrush and putting on our underwear.

There are a number of reasons why people turn to the loathsome criminal activity that is mug theft. The most common excuse is that there are no clean mugs. This is a malaise that, perversely, affects kitchens that have a dishwasher, leading to a climate of diminished social responsibility in which people simply don't bother to clean their mugs. Instead, huge filthy colonies build up on work surfaces: occasionally these are put in the dishwasher, which is able to warehouse vast quantities. As most people don't know how to use the dishwasher, or consider themselves to have insufficient authority to switch it on, clean mugs quickly become scarce. People may even resort to using the warty no-handle mug.

Driven by desperation, the unscrupulous mug thief turns to what is obviously somebody's personal mug. They justify their actions by reasoning that it is almost lunchtime and that person hasn't used their mug so far today so maybe they have become disaffected with it or simply abandoned it. The people most at risk here are those who have been out of the office for the morning, anybody off sick or those on holiday. It's not uncommon to return from a long weekend to find that your mug has gone missing, to say nothing of your swivel chair and computer keyboard.

Of course, there is always the possibility that your mug isn't languishing on the culprit's desk alongside your keyboard but has in fact found its way into the dishwasher. Not only that, but uncharacteristically this has been switched on, thus presenting you with three choices:

- **Patiently wait the forty-five minutes it takes for the dishwasher to remove the graphics or design from the outside of your mug and identifies it as yours** (how they manage to do this using hot water and a bit of soap is a wonder of the modern world).

- **Open up the dishwasher and take your life in your hands as you rummage around in a scalding-hot hell of mugs and partially cleaned bowls of tomato soup.**

- **Use the warty no-handle mug.** You may have to remove eight months' worth of dust from the bottom of it. In some situations it may have gone completely native and be sporting a small bunch of flowers, helping to brighten up the place. Or maybe it's languishing inside the fridge door half full of curry sauce.

Personal Mug Types

Twee. Anything with flowers, bunnies, kittens, puppies, pictures of cottages or those flat-headed teddies with the line down the middle of their face.

Pottery class. Lopsided and ugly dark blue monstrosities that weigh as much as a small family car.

Giant. Enormous mugs about the size of a small saucepan, usually with something written on the side about how much caffeine this person requires just to function. Never follow this person into the kitchen, as they might have to boil two kettlefuls before they are done.

Rustic. These look like they have been made from reformed roof tiles, plant pots or the same stuff that they use to make those brown glazed pipes at the bottom of manholes.

Impractical. Novelty-shaped mugs might seem like a terrific Christmas-present idea to some, but to the poor recipient they provide weeks of unsatisfactory tea drinking. Having a ceramic mouse looking at you from the depths of your tea or a mug handle in the shape of an ear is simply annoying. Not only that, but these embellishments collect limescale and grime. Sometimes the dishwasher will do you a favour and smash it up. Either that or it will spontaneously fracture or topple over, thereby bringing its sad existence to an end.

Pint glass. There is always somebody who insists on drinking their tea out of a pint glass. As a general rule, it simply isn't worth engaging these people in conversation.

Rude. Something fairly crude and usually belonging to one of the girls in telesales. This mug is very successful at keeping mug thieves at bay. Most people don't have the bottle to be seen drinking out of something that says 'World's Greatest Lover' or is shaped like a part of the body.

Tall, thin mugs. People who use these like to imagine that really they are drinking from fine bone china. Well, they're not.

Obviously yours. Something with your name, your face, your children or your pet on it.

Dull. A promotional mug given to you by one of your suppliers, like 'Dreary and Wett, suppliers of long bits of wire with little lumps at the end'. Typically there will be a very dull logo which looks just like a square, or possibly a circle.

Tragic. The promotional mug for the last company that you worked for, which you still use even though they made you redundant.

Wifey says

That's all very well, Nicey, but why do we insist on keeping all our old promotional work mugs from years ago at the back of the cupboard? All they do is collect dust, and no matter how many people turn up for tea we would never be bold enough to get them out. It's ridiculous! Let's get our house mug situation sorted out before we start insulting people's work mugs!

Filthy Mugs

As we have seen, most personal mugs are designed to repel others. However, this will not always be enough of a deterrent on its own.

Some people resort to using filth in the war against mug crime. By giving their mugs little more than a cursory rinse under the cold tap, a thick laminated crust of brown muck can be created inside the mug. Those who prey on unattached clean mugs are naturally put off by this, as is virtually any creature higher up the food chain than a woodlouse. The people who have been driven to plumb such depths of mug hygiene – generally men – actually seem to enjoy drinking tea from these filthy vessels. The long-term health consequences are unknown but their chances of starting an office romance are almost zero.

Dark Mugs

In the headlong rush to create ever more varieties of mug, there is one problem that occurs time and time again: dark mugs. Anything finished with navy-blue, bottle-green or even black glazes simply doesn't make good tea. The contents of the mug will always appear weak and pallid, as if deficient in tea and milk, even when they are not. Nevertheless, the bewildered tea drinker will keep dunking their tea bag and adding milk until their brew takes on the appearance of tea. By now they have completely ruined their cuppa, unless they like very strong, very milky tea, of course.

Even if the tea drinker finds the mental strength to ignore the evil dark mug mind games, their tea will still look weak and wishy-washy, causing them background levels of anguish.

Some
Biscuits

Biscuits

It is important to celebrate all that biscuits have achieved throughout the course of history and certainly since the 1970s. We should also look forward to a time when advanced, satisfying and tasty biscuits are being routinely eaten by pioneering tea drinkers in space, or in colonies on the distant moons of the great gas giant planets, or possibly even in France.

How to Taste Biscuits

At times the sheer number and variety of biscuits in the world can seem overwhelming and daunting. Even the small selection that we have assembled for this book may contain some that are new or unfamiliar to you.

Be not afraid.

Tasting biscuits at a professional level, you might think, requires great discipline and skill. Perhaps a point system that assesses crunch, taste, size, dunking suitability, pack design, fruit content, chocolate quality and so on could be devised. But would this really tell us anything? No, not really.

The best approach I have found is to eat the first one quite slowly, then just steam into the rest, washing them down with lots of tea. You'll soon get the measure of them and, as you can imagine, this technique requires virtually no skill and a complete lack of discipline. You can also tell yourself that you are using a holistic approach, even if you didn't really have any sort of approach in mind.

For the sake of thoroughness, you might want to see off a whole packet to yourself. Through this you'll learn exactly how filling an entire pack is and be better able to make important quantitative buying decisions should you decide to share the next pack with family and friends. You'll run the risk of being seen as a fairly tight and selfish individual but that's a small price to pay for disciplined rigour.

Let's face it, if you look at wine tasting as a comparable sort of thing then there isn't much to fear. I've lost count of the amount of times I've heard a wine critic describe a red wine as being full of 'lots of red fruits'. Well, yes, that's how they make it. Perhaps they might want to follow that up with 'It's a liquid at room temperature' and some other obvious statement like 'Gravity stops it coming out of the top of the bottle by itself'. Or how about 'It goes great with a meal or can be enjoyed by itself'? Well, yes, that's because it's a drink. That's what they're for.

How to Buy Biscuits

Supermarkets, corner shops, petrol stations and newsagents' are all good places to view and buy biscuits. Of course, none of these establishments offer tasting, or as the French call it '*degustation*', so you have to buy before you can try. Sometimes you will encounter biscuits in 'touristy' type shops that you'll naturally view with a healthy scepticism, and you'd be right to. Many probably have more in common with 'olde-worlde' surroundings than just the quaint pictures of cottages on the box. Always check the best-before dates to see if they were baked in living memory. If the box is covered in Olde English writing make sure it wasn't baked in Olde England.

If you are in one of those 'buy anything for a pound' shops then you'll find the biscuits between the giant ceramic Dalmatians and the commemorative disbanded boy band full-length mirrors. This might be a good place to buy a novelty biscuit tin, in the shape of a large frog or teddy bear, if that's the bag you're into.

When buying biscuits, by all means pick up the packets to examine them. The most obvious thing you can learn from this are the actual dimensions of the biscuits, which often bear little correlation with the picture on the pack. You might even go as far as measuring them with a little tape measure to see if the unopened packs will fit in your tins. (A tip for married men: it's best not to have your wife present if you decide to measure biscuits in public.)

You may wish to read the product description and then tally this up against the ingredients, to see if these 'lemony' biscuits have ever seen a real lemon. Another useful guide is that ingredients are listed in descending order of mass. So any ingredients listed after the salt and raising agents are present only in trace element amounts. For example, this is not where you want to find the raisins.

Carry your biscuits carefully to the checkout to avoid damaging them. If using a basket or trolley, place your biscuits safely in the bottom. If you are also buying frozen poultry, try not to drop this on your biscuits from a great height. Don't attempt to fold any boxes or packs in half, and don't use long packs to act out any of the light-sabre scenes from *Star Wars*.

It's also a good idea to form a strategy for dealing with BOGOF (buy one get one free) and multi-buy savers. These are designed to strip away any free will you thought you had and get you to buy something else. A good strategy is to simply give in to their mind games and buy a big bunch of whatever it is they think you should have. You'll be all right, providing you eat them sensibly and not all in one go in the car park.

Wifey says

Here's the formula I use when Nicey lets me near the biscuit aisle (which is not very often):

🫖 **Buying for the children** – buy the cheap ones. Avoid chocolate at all costs, as it causes too much staining.

🫖 **Buying for the family** – Assortments are good, though make sure you keep the good ones for after the children go to bed, or are at school. Remember that hiding in the kitchen, eating biscuits very quietly so the children don't catch you is very demeaning. And it often doesn't work due to their acute hearing.

🫖 **Buying for work** – If work is paying, get the top of the range ones. If you're buying them yourself, go for the cheap option. Who cares if they think you're a cheapskate? Oh, and go for the ones with a nice packet that fit in with the decor in the kitchen.

How to Store Biscuits

Why should you want to store your biscuits? If you have managed to breach their packaging and not eaten them all then the proper storage of your biscuits is a good idea. Not only will it stop them going stale and limp but it may protect against casual and opportunistic theft. Many people take an open biscuit packet as an invitation to help themselves to whichever biscuit treat you may currently be enjoying. Also, eating biscuits straight from the pack makes it all too obvious to the biscuit thief when you have something new and glamorous in your possession.

In the office, some individuals may be labouring under the illusion that there is a feudal system at work in which biscuits are paid as some form of tithe, to directors and various upper management. Those with a shred of conscience will tend to buy on an annual basis an inappropriate, if well-intentioned pack of biscuits. The biscuits produced will either be too small, too fancy or just too few in number to be a credible offering. The pack or packs will be offered to all and sundry in a flamboyant and public and fashion, while the giver warmly reminds everyone of the last packet of biscuits that they dispensed. The intention is to flood your consciousness with images of you receiving biscuits from them. Absolutely nobody is taken in by this, with the possible exception of the new starter.

Another common misconception is that people who are 'working late' are entitled to lay siege to any biscuits that they can locate on company property. This is wrong for so many reasons it's almost beneath us to go into them. Apologetic yellow notes stuck to your computer screen saying 'Sorry for eating all your biscuits' don't cut it, but a pay rise might go some way to assuaging the pain.

There are two main schools of thought when it comes to biscuit storage. One simply advocates placing the open packs still intact inside the storage vessel. This has the advantage of keeping the documentation that accompanies your biscuits (the pack) close at hand should it become necessary to refer to it. It also allows you to keep a tight hold on your stock levels without having to turf through random piles of biscuits. The second approach is simply to empty the packs straight into your storage vessel. This seemingly haphazard approach is actually a subtle and complex art, which has parallels in such pastimes as flower arranging, the construction of drystone walls and making a really good tossed salad. In fact all those Japanese Zen Buddhist rock gardeners should try arranging Custard Creams, Fruit Shortcakes and Digestives in an old Rover selection tin for an alternative path to enlightenment.

Like it or not, other people will always judge you on the contents of your biscuit tin, and if they are polite they may not even tell you that they are doing so. You'll have nothing to fear from this if your tin is up to scratch. In fact, it might provide the opportunity for a little light-hearted recreational disagreement on the merits of various biscuits.

A really accomplished mixed tin should be pleasing to the eye as well as the palate. Each species of biscuit should contribute to the harmonious whole, and no one type should dominate the others. The overall effect should not be ostentatious nor should it appear austere. If you do feel the need to favour each extreme then you should seriously consider setting aside a second tin for the purpose. That way you can indulge your need for self-denial by having a spartan tin of Thin Arrowroots and Rich Teas, while your friends can enjoy a decent selection of biscuits from your second, public-facing tin. Alternatively you may like to wallow in a sea of thick chocolate-covered excess, leaving your guests to look for the simple pleasures of Fruit Shortcake. Then again, you may simply be a bit stingy, and prefer to hide all your chocolate biscuits.

Strong flavours should be stored separately as the other milder shortcake or Digestive-based biscuits will absorb ginger, fruity, spicy or even coconut flavours, to their detriment. New and radical biscuits such as maple syrup and toffee apple flavour should be quarantined until such times as they are proven safe to mix with other biscuits, though this is seldom the case.

A great many of nature's bounties require a little work before we can reap the rewards. Nature provides fruits, shellfish and nuts with skins and shells that force us to work a little before we feast upon what's inside. Biscuits echo this age-old struggle of hunter-gatherer pitted against nature's harvest. The tough and durable outer wrappers of biscuit packs have evolved to protect their sweet and tasty contents from humidity, sunlight, pests, other biscuits and, of course, us, the consumer. At times it appears that the strongest substance yet devised by mankind isn't titanium or stainless steel but cellophane.

Just as those three little dark holes at the top of a coconut appear to offer some means of access, which actually rarely helps, so the little red strip round a biscuit pack is purely there to mock us. At home there are plenty of ways of cracking open a stubborn pack of biscuits, from a full set of steak knives to that circular saw in the shed. However, in the office environment the hungry biscuit eater may have to improvise when faced with a particularly intractable pack. Some resort to the logical reversal of the packing process, deliberately undoing each seam in succession until access is finally gained. The biscuit packers are expecting just this sort of attack and will have fused both pack ends into laminated shields, in a process licensed to or from the manufacturers of tank armour, I expect.

Typically there follows a short but vicious biting attack on the pack, mostly involving the canine teeth. This is only appropriate for those situations where the biscuits are solely for personal consumption, as there is nothing nastier than being offered biscuits from a pack covered in dribble. The pack can usually defeat such an obvious attack through two simple means: a specially hardened pack seam and high-tension wrapping. This results in the cellophane being pulled so tightly over the biscuits that it proves impossible to nip any part of it between the teeth.

When faced with such an impervious pack most office workers will take the only sensible course of action: seeking out the holder of the office Swiss Army knife. Most often this is the guy who insists on dismantling his computer, window blind and gas-pump chair for no apparent reason. He is also uncharacteristically popular at the Christmas party when all those bottles of Australian Shiraz languishing in drawer bottoms need opening.

Of course, if you really do need to break in to some biscuits then simply straighten out a thin paper clip and push the end into the pack between two biscuits, then move it round in a lateral fashion. Depending on the cellophane, this will often produce an attractive frilly cut in the pack, which is an added bonus. A note of caution: always take care with straightened-out paper clips or you'll have somebody's eye out.

Grrrr, we hate wrappers – especially when things are wrapped about six times for no reason. What a waste of money, time and resources. If you're out there, Mr Big Biscuit Manufacturer, take note. We don't like it. So there.

It goes without saying, but let's say it: don't keep your biscuit storage vessel in direct sunlight or on top of a radiator, especially if it contains chocolate biscuits. If you insist on doing this then you might want to keep a spoon, barbecue tongs, some straws, a kitchen roll and a pack of wet wipes handy.

Try to layer your biscuits in such a way that all varieties are easily accessible without the need to struggle down to the bottom of the tin, causing unnecessary and unsightly breakages. It may be tempting to arrange your biscuits in stacks: however, this will simply cause you anxiety and upset as eager hands lay waste to your neatly regimented biscuits.

Watch out for hidden biscuits that behave like little man traps, crushing the ends of your fingers in their powerful vice-like grip. Luckily I can't think of any that are like that. Still, no harm in staying alert.

Anybody who routinely kills pot plants will probably not have realised that you need to water them or, alternatively, that they don't need watering three times a day. Biscuits are also extraordinarily sensitive to moisture, and the microclimate of your biscuit tin will need careful attention. Moist biscuits such as the Fig Roll dry out while the other biscuits around them will absorb their moisture. This effectively turns both types of biscuit stale despite using a sealed container. The danger can be lessened by choosing a variety of Fig Roll that has been cut before baking, such as a Jacob's or Crawford's, as the moist fig is less exposed. You should also avoid mixing biscuits and cakes in the same tin for the same reasons.

Finally, don't bury your biscuit tin in the garden, then dig it up twenty-nine years later and expect everything to be fine. They tried that on *Blue Peter* in 1971. When they dug it up in 2000, all the stuff in the tin was badly messed up, having turned into a sort of inky black soup. It wasn't even biscuits in the tin but a copy of the *Radio Times*, a *Blue Peter Annual*, pictures and tapes.

Some Storage Options

A Biscuit Barrel

Designed for the job, a biscuit barrel is the expert's choice: it provides portability and tight seals and maintains confidentiality until such times as it is opened. Most are fitted with a silica-gel insert in the lid, designed to draw the moisture from the air and keep your biscuits crisp and crunchy. A little gold-coloured knob on the top is best, and some of the finest examples are decorated, confusingly, with pictures of fruit.

If you really want to do your biscuit barrel proud then decorate your kitchen with that wallpaper that has little pictures of teapots and coffee pots on it. Or just strip away seven or eight layers of paper and find that somebody already did it for you.

A Tin

A good alternative, especially for those on a budget, or who dislike the effects of the silica-gel thingy. The most important aspect is a sensible lid which fits snugly, yet may easily be removed. The older the tin, the better, as it will have an air of authority to it.

A Plastic Container

This is not an elegant solution, and can trap strong flavours long after the biscuits have been eaten. Given that it can create the impression that you are on some kind of picnic, maybe you can complete the image by drinking your tea from an enamel mug and sitting on your coat on the floor.

A Drawer

Handy if you work in an office but hardly airtight. Take care not to get items of stationery such as staples and paper clips mixed up in your biscuits. It does have the frequent advantage of being lockable.

A Cookie Jar

Placing your biscuits inside something that is meant for cookies or, worse still, has 'Cookies' written on the outside is too traumatic for many. Most right-thinking biscuit eaters will be more than a little irritated by the sheer cultural imperialism of the word 'cookie'. Overall, the British response to cookies is much the same as that of a parent being enlightened by their child on popular music. It's not that we don't like it; we just don't want them to think they invented it.

Glass cookie jars are a particularly bad idea, in much the same way as those ludicrous transparent vinyl bags, briefly popular in the 1980s, which showed pickpockets all they needed to know, as well as letting the whole world view your hairbrush. If your biscuit selection is a bit lacklustre then it will be on show for all to see and may cause you embarrassment which might otherwise have been avoided. The really big ones are also far from portable, limiting their usefulness: you may be forced to abandon your nice sit down to traipse over to where the cookie jar is holding court.

Classification

The Class Struggle

There are broadly speaking three bands into which biscuits fall: entry level, mid-range and luxury. It's useful to be aware of the bands as each is more expensive than the one before, and it might help you to spot a bargain. Another way of viewing it is as a sort of class structure for biscuits, moving from dead common, through middle class to terribly posh.

Here are some approximate guidelines for determining a biscuit's grouping. Exercise these with caution as sometimes you can find mutton dressed as lamb, or equally something swish that has fallen on hard times.

 Entry-Level Biscuits: homogeneous and simple biscuits often in clear cellophane wrappers. They don't mind shacking up and sometimes you can find up to three different types of biscuit sharing the same outer wrapper. Expect nothing more glamorous than a bit of cream filling or some sugar on top. You are likely to find such biscuits at convenience shops, petrol stations and dreary town-centre supermarkets run by companies you thought went to the wall years ago. Unless you are ravenously hungry it's unlikely that you'll eat a whole pack of these in one sitting.

Mid-Range Biscuits: perhaps best understood by what it is that lifts them above the entry-level biscuits. Primarily this is some form of seduction, such as some fruit, jam or maybe a revealing picture of the biscuit printed on thick glossy cellophane. Mid-range biscuits might even have their own strapline as footnote to their full-frontal picture, such as, 'I've got lovely crunchy oats', or 'Flat yet fruity'. Occasionally you'll find mid-range biscuits in corner shops and convenience stores: they are there to raise the tone. Beware of treating a mid-range biscuit with the same sort of off-hand disregard as entry-level biscuits: you may find yourself unwittingly eating the entire pack.

 Luxury Biscuits: it would be a gross oversimplification to say luxury biscuits simply have chocolate on them and come in a box. However, that is their typical image. Most mid-range biscuits aspire to be luxury biscuits, and some think that simply by slapping on some chocolate and popping on a few extra wrappers everyone will be taken in. But it takes breeding to be a luxury biscuit, an established name in biscuit society and a really terrific box. Expect to see imperial or royal colours like purple and gold, and 'Since 1800 and something' written on the pack. Specifically look out for shortbread which has mad delusions of grandeur and often likes to pass itself off as 'luxury', despite simply being a bit of flour, sugar and butter. I don't know why it keeps on insisting that it's something special; it's embarrassing really.

The Science Bit

One striking thing is how the shape of a biscuit-centric universe bears an uncanny resemblance to the Mandelbrot Set often referred to as the most complicated object in mathematics. Benoit Mandelbrot is a French mathematician whose work has led to a branch of mathematics called fractals, or fractal geometry. Mandelbrot Sets were hugely popular a few years ago as it used to take the average desktop computer all day to make the calculations needed to draw a picture of one. Now it takes only a few seconds, so their popularity has waned in favour of rudimentary animations of dancing kittens.

Fractal shapes like the Mandelbrot Set are often compared to forms of nature such as coastlines, tree bark and other gnarly stuff. It should not be left unsaid that some of the curly swirly bits around the edge of the Mandelbrot Set look just like the patterns on top of a Custard Cream. Of course, this could just be another coincidence, but they are starting to form a trend.

Venn Diagram

Even experienced biscuit eaters are sometimes bewildered about what exactly a biscuit is and what it isn't. They can easily be thrown into self-doubt by a simple Rusk or Flapjack. When does the combination of biscuit and chocolate cross from the realm of biscuits to the realm of confectionery? If there were easy answers to these questions people wouldn't be confused in the first place, and I wouldn't need to draw the Venn diagram of biscuits.

The Venn diagram was a very popular thing when I was at school. I remember for a week or two they were all the rage. The teacher would draw two large overlapping circles on the blackboard and then write our names in them according to which of us had dogs, how many had cats, and who had dogs and cats. Of course, the kids with hamsters, rabbits and goldfish felt they had been glossed over, but that's life sometimes.

Venn diagrams were thought up by a chap called John Venn, who lived in the olden days. For the younger members of staff this is anything that predates *The Fimbles* and *Balamory*. He obviously enjoyed putting things into sets and thought that drawing circles around them was the way forward. He also had quite a large beard, and so probably predated the invention of the triple-blade razor.

Now a diagram like this is always going to raise more questions than it answers, so if you are expecting ultimate biscuit enlightenment be warned.

Biscuits form the centre, with crackers above and cake below. Running from left to right we move from bread into biscuits, then on to chocolate-covered biscuits until we reach confectionery in the shape of chocolate bars. The first thing to notice is that you can put very little store in the

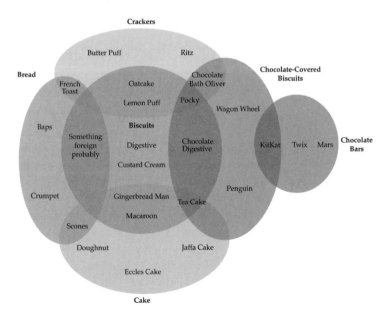

Crackers

Butter Puff · Ritz

Bread

Chocolate-Covered
Biscuits

French
Toast · Oatcake · Chocolate
Bath Oliver

Lemon Puff · Pocky

Wagon Wheel

Baps

Biscuits

Something
foreign
probably

Digestive · Chocolate
Digestive · KitKat · Twix · Mars

**Chocolate
Bars**

Custard Cream

Penguin

Crumpet

Gingerbread Man

Tea Cake

Macaroon

Scones

Doughnut · Jaffa Cake

Eccles Cake

Cake

names of things. Just look at oatcakes. Clearly they are somewhere between biscuits and crackers, being an unsweetened oat biscuit, and so are not really a cake at all.

Gingerbread men cause more than their fair share of trouble, roaming across our Venn diagram. By no stretch of the imagination are they some form of bread, so they are swiftly moved along. They freely associate themselves with cakes, frequenting, as they are known to do, cake shops. It's no secret that underneath that icing and attached confectionery they are really a large man-shaped biscuit, so it's here in the union of cakes and biscuits that we'll allow them to go about their business. Occasionally at Easter or Christmas they are inclined to turn into rabbits or trees but they are not fooling anyone.

From Japan the exceedingly odd Pocky, a long straight pretzel 80 per cent dipped in chocolate, sits in the triple union of crackers, chocolate-covered biscuits and biscuits. That dark horse the KitKat sits in the union of chocolate bars and chocolate-covered biscuits, refusing to align itself with either side, enjoying as it does the best of both worlds.

The Jaffa Cake is drawn to the union of cake and chocolate-covered biscuits occupied by the Teacake. However, it must remain with its cake brethren by virtue of its sponge base. Meanwhile, the dreadful old Lemon Puff loiters close to its cousin next door in the crackers, the equally dubious Butter Puff.

Ideally the diagram should be drawn on the surface of a sphere, allowing crackers and cake to join, although I can't think what with. Rice cakes, possibly.

I'm sure by now that I've probably either confused or annoyed you. Either way, try drawing your own biscuit Venn diagram down the pub, over a cup of tea or maybe slipping it in to your next Powerpoint presentation if you are in the habit of making such things.

🫖 Plain Dunkers

There is a lot of glamour in the biscuit world: enticing jam, seductive chocolate, tempting cream and abrasive sugar crusts. Alluring fruits such as the cranberry and guava are also adding exotic appeal to large soft-baked biscuit temptresses. It's all packaged in immodest boxes with cut-away cellophane panels or cartons with provocative and frilly lines. Oh yes, and they put the really good stuff on the top shelf in the supermarket, so that younger shoppers can't get their hands on them.

Then there are the plain old biscuits. A humble bunch, they are happy to be semi-submerged in a hot cuppa, their features swollen and barely legible, soaking up the scalding brew while we scarcely give them a second thought. Without them a great many cups of tea would be solitary affairs, devoid of biscuit companionship. They may not be glamorous, but they will still be around long after the appeal of the latest chocolate-clad bombshell or aspiring jam tart has ebbed away.

Rich Tea

Where would we be without the Rich Tea? It provides the ground floor on which the rest of the biscuit tower block rests. Without it we would be directionless. With it we have a marker that says, 'Above me it just gets better and better, while below are animal feeds, Spanish holiday biscuits and special medical biscuits from chemists'.'

The Rich Tea presents us straight away with a paradox. If these are 'Rich' Tea, where are 'Poor' Tea biscuits and what on earth do they taste like? Well, they would have to be fairly ropey old affairs because the Rich Tea itself is not exactly a self-contained one-biscuit flavour festival. We can only presume that 'Poor Tea' or even just 'Tea' was not the runaway success that Rich Tea has become.

What flavour it does manage to achieve comes from the various sugars in its recipe – sucrose, maltose and some glucose – plus a little bit of salt. So what are they good for? Dunking, of course. The Rich Tea can drive even the staunchest anti-dunker to dunk. It then comes into its own, convincing you that you have done the right thing by giving the eater the reward of sloppy, hot Rich Tea, which is actually better than what you started with.

So suitable for dunking is the Rich Tea that there are those who demand it as their biscuit of preference. Many builders, for example, seem to be chemically dependent on them, washed down with mugs of tea, two sugars please. If you are having substantial building work carried out it may be worth getting a case of Rich Tea in.

Most Rich Tea aficionados prefer the classic round Rich Tea, which is generally available in broad gauge and narrow gauge, depending on the brand. Whilst smaller-sized Rich Teas are easier to dunk than their larger brethren, many people seem to enjoy the challenge and skill needed to handle the big stuff. This explains the lesser popularity of the Rich Tea finger. However, those new to dunking will find the finger configuration much more predictable, being to dunking what rear-wheel stabilisers are to cycling. Nevertheless it should not be overlooked that the finger often seems to have the edge over its round sibling taste-wise, possibly due to its smaller build giving it a slightly higher bake.

There are attempts at turning the Rich Tea into something more enticing by covering them in chocolate or sticking some sort of cream up the middle, but it's all a bit akin to sticking a spoiler on the boot of your family car. There are a small band of people who seem to want a chunkier set version of the Rich Tea. Rather than be seen as purely aberrant they are occasionally catered for by some manufacturers, and therefore shouldn't cause a problem to the rest of us, other than harking on about it from time to time.

Marie

In the UK we have the Rich Tea. The rest of the world has the Marie. The Marie biscuit really isn't much to get worked up about. In fact, I'm struggling to think of anything to say about it. It's like a fluffy Rich Tea with a hint of vanilla. There. Oh, and it has some quite intricate patterns and writing. And some people use it as a vehicle for making a sandwich using soft butter. It is an essential part of the proceedings that little buttery worms can be extruded through the holes in the biscuit by pressing the two halves together.

India, Australia, South Africa and many other countries think of the Marie biscuit as part of their cuisine. How has this biscuit secured a position of global importance? No, that wasn't a rhetorical question: I really don't know. It must simply occupy the same ecological biscuit niche as the Rich Tea does in our biscuit environment. Just as in Australia where the large grassland grazers are not the northern hemisphere antelopes but kangaroos, so they have Marie biscuits rather than Rich Tea. The same goes for South Africa, but of course they actually do have antelopes. I think they are doing fine for deer in India, too.

Actually, I remember a splendid TV documentary about Indian wildlife where the stags of a type of wetland deer make a small scrape in the ground in which they urinate and then roll around in. After they are fairly well covered in that, they scrape up filthy bits of old moss and grass which they drape over their antlers. This apparently makes them irresistible to all the lady deer. I'm fairly sure I tried that in my student days too, but I don't recall it ever being successful.

Thin Arrowroot

Often found lurking among the other biscuits but never presenting more than one public-facing pack on the supermarket shelves is the Thin Arrowroot. But why are they thin, and what on earth is Arrowroot? Well, the answer to the first lies in the second. Arrowroot is a starchy powder obtained from the rhizomes of the plant of the same name, grown in places like the West Indies. Typical uses for Arrowroot are to make a sort of gloopy fruit slop for desserts and the like, as it works a bit like corn flour. Adding arrowroot to biscuits seems to work a bit like adding sulphur to rubber to vulcanise it. Thin Arrowroots contain 2 per cent arrowroot and this appears to be enough to make them a bit like a really hard, dry and generally hostile Rich Tea.

I am more impressed with the structural properties of the biscuit than what it tastes like. For instance, the resonant frequencies possessed by the biscuit produced a higher note when dropped in comparison to a similar-sized Rich Tea. It therefore seems likely that such a thing as a 'Thick Arrowroot', while technically feasible, would be too much for the average consumer's dental facilities (although they would probably make terrific load-bearing walls). As result of this high level of structural integrity, the writing on top of the biscuits is fantastically detailed, as if engraved onto metal.

Older biscuit eaters remember when pubs used to have a jar of large Thin Arrowroots on the bar. Apparently these were given to children along with a glass of lemonade, or sometimes as a treat for dogs. Given that there was a war on, it would be unfair to suggest that these weren't genuine treats. However, it's easy to see why crisps, peanuts and Scampi fries caught on in the face of such competition.

There are also those who eat Thin Arrowroot biscuits as some sort of digestive aid, as its starch is easily digested. At only 2 per cent arrowroot you would have to eat an awful lot of biscuits before you gained much nutrition from that ingredient. The fresh mashed rhizomes of arrowroot are believed to be good for wounds from poisoned arrows, scorpion stings and spider bites. The biscuits, on the other hand, would probably be moderately deadly if you chucked them hard at spiders, scorpions and those aiming bows and arrows at you.

Morning Coffee

Back in the 1970s we used to watch a lot of *Kung Fu* on the telly. I was always impressed how he carried a small bag of dirt around with him, and used to add a pinch to a glass of water for a refreshing drink. As part of his training as a young apprentice monk, he had to walk down a long sheet of rice paper. His slow and presumably sweaty footsteps tore holes in the paper and he knew that he would be at monk school for some years to come. The answer may have been to substitute lino or a nice bit of carpet for rice paper, especially in high traffic areas like halls and kitchens. In fact, I would just stick to those flying-saucer sweets with sherbert inside as the predominant use for rice paper. No, the lesson was to go off and learn the whole 'being a monk' thing properly from the old fellow with the funny eyes.

As Wifey just said, 'What's this got to do with Morning Coffee?' Well, the Morning Coffee, like *Kung Fu*, first came to my attention during the 1970s. Having been raised in a household of keen biscuit eaters with progressive, liberal attitudes towards the baked snacks, it came as a shock that some people chose to eat such bland biscuits. In fact, I remember the first Morning Coffee I had while visiting my Aunty Sheila for 'morning coffee'. I was immediately struck by its intricate graphics. The Morning Coffee held out the promise of sophistication, of hidden depths in order to fulfil its stated mission as a pre-lunch coffee biscuit. Unlike *Kung Fu*, the Morning Coffee didn't have an associated hit record ('Everybody Was Morning Coffee Eating'), however, I was still keen to taste this 'now' biscuit. It was a bitter blow to find that essentially it was a turncoat Rich Tea. Those intricate pictures of coffee pots and wisps of steam were the only noteworthy point to the biscuit. The rewards to be had from nibbling out the coffee pot from the biscuit compared to, say, a 'cow-ectomy' performed on a Malted Milk were scant. A simple mental note to avoid the Morning Coffee for the rest of my life appeared to be the answer.

Now, some thirty years later, fate has conspired to confront me with that knobbly rectangle of biscuit under-achievement once again. The local branch of the Macmillan Cancer Relief charity run an annual event called 'The World's Biggest Coffee Morning' and they got in touch to see which biscuit I would recommend for such an occasion. I explained to the nice Canadian organising lady on the phone, 'You'll need some Morning Coffees then.' 'Good and what cookies do you recommend?' she replied, never having heard of the Morning Coffee biscuit and assuming I was being evasive and odd. 'Who makes them?' she continued. I admitted I had no idea, as I couldn't think of a branded Morning Coffee, but replied that all the big supermarkets have them.

I thought I had better get some in case I had to answer any tricky questions. So here I am staring into a biscuit tin of Morning Coffees, reaping what I have sown. Well, I couldn't recommend them and not try them again. We grabbed a pack from two different supermarkets: the biscuits appear to be identical; no doubt they are. I'm sure past Morning Coffees had pictures of coffee pots on them but these have resorted to a simple cup and saucer image. Maybe it's because the coffee pot itself has been relegated to such niches as the hotel breakfast, and certainly isn't used regularly in the domestic setting.

A little while ago I backed myself into a corner, resulting in my taste testing seven types of Rich Tea side by side. Some may have been scarred for life with the memory of such a trial. In fact, some raw recruits to Nicey's biscuit-tasting boot camp were. However, I vowed to become a better biscuit reviewer through the experience. And now finally we get to the point: *the Morning Coffee, when compared to most types of Rich Tea, is ever so slightly tastier!* I was, of course, shocked to my very core, my whole belief system threatening to crumble before me. How could this be? Well, ingredient number four is malt extract. This, it seems, has given the Morning Coffee a very faint malty sweetness, earning a small measure of individuality other than its pictures of cups and steam.

His Rich Tea lesson learnt, Nicey notes the slight difference in taste and skips over the tricky rice paper of bland biscuit sampling leaving not a single footmark.

⑨ Shortcake

It's very difficult to pin down what is exactly meant by shortcake. The 'short' part refers to the fat in the recipe that has the effect of making the baked biscuit soft and crumbly. One explanation offered is that the fat serves to 'shorten' the gluten molecules from the wheat, which makes for a less rigid molecular structure. The biscuits in this section either completely or loosely fall into the shortcake biscuit category. Of course, you may aggressively disagree with my choices, in which case you might want to consider some sort of anger-management counselling. After all, we are only trying to sort out a few biscuits.

Shorties

Ah, the simple shortcake biscuit or 'Shortie': always there to bulk out the biscuit tin or make up the numbers in a family biscuit assortment. A steady performer, the Shortie is often overlooked but is always a welcome sight on the biscuit plate. It comes into its own in those little packs of biscuits you get in hotel rooms, which the biscuit eater will greet like a long-lost friend.

However, the shortcake has a surprising history which we can trace back to the pagan winter solstice festivals. In Scotland, large round oat-cake Bannocks were baked with the edges decorated with sun rays, as people looked forward to the return of the summer sun. At Hogmanay the 'First Footers' (the first to set foot in the house after midnight) would be required to bring with them a bottle of whisky and a Bannock at the very least. Providing they were dark haired (a good sign of not being a Viking), and not a minister, doctor or gravedigger, then they could expect a kiss from the ladies of the house. The intermingling of Christian and pagan elements sees us buying Yuletide tins of Scottish shortbread complete with their sun-ray design to give away as Christmas presents.

Traditionally, any small, round shortcake biscuit will emulate its ances-tors with the sun's rays scalloping around its rim, and a pattern of marks on its centre. As we move to the workaday rectangular Shortie, the edge pattern and prick marks are retained, telling us that this is a mini-shortbread. Perhaps small self-contained 'First Footer' kits could be made using a three-pack of shortbread fingers and a whisky miniature.

Lincoln

Technically, the Lincoln is a short-dough biscuit, and belongs to the larger family of shortcake biscuits. It's a very serviceable biscuit, not so nice that you would want to eat a truckload, but not so bland that you can't cheerfully tuck several away in a session.

What is really exciting about the Lincoln is the pattern of dots on the top.

Now it appears that the pattern of dots can take two forms: concentric circles as shown on the McVitie's one here, or a tightly packed pattern a bit like that formed by the ends of pipes which have been stacked up. So what are the dots for? I like to think that they give the Lincoln superior traction, affording the eater a great non-slip grip. As is their custom, McVitie's have also tried to emboss the word 'Lincoln' on to the biscuit, which shouldn't be necessary, given the distinctive dots.

Our good friend and fellow biscuit enthusiast Mandy often recounts the tale of her mother's experimental Lincoln biscuit trifle. I'm assured by Mandy that anybody contemplating pushing the envelope of trifle technology in a similar direction really shouldn't bother.

Abernethy (vs Bath Oliver)

I have to admit to being a very recent convert to the Abernethy biscuit. The best-known examples are made in Edinburgh by Simmers and have a distinctive red and yellow pack; so much so that I was possibly slightly and fairly irrationally intimidated by them. When I finally did pluck up the courage to buy a pack, it was all very easy. The anticipated probing look from the checkout girl never happened. And the biscuit itself? Well, they are very nice actually, a bit like a cross between an All Butter and a shortcake. The biscuit mix is raised with ammonium bicarbonate. Apparently this means they smell a bit odd prior to baking.

Abernethy biscuits are named after their Scottish inventor, Dr John Abernethy, who in turn was probably named after the Scottish town. The town takes its name from the Gaelic word '*aber*', which doesn't mean platform-heeled Viking singing group but 'mouth of', and 'Nethy' which is the name of a river. In the past biscuit inventing seems to have been a very popular activity for doctors, and it's a shame that they don't do it today. Information like 'Dr D. Taylor MB, BS, MRCGP with a special interest in orthopaedics and making a new sort of jam ring' would be of use when registering with a medical practice.

The other famous biscuit-inventing doctor was Dr William Oliver, who invented the Bath Oliver in the mid-eighteenth century. The Bath Oliver is a cracker gravitating naturally towards the cheese board, but its rare chocolate-covered version is best described as a biscuit. Bath Olivers are so named because Dr Oliver invented them in Bath, while serving as the physician to those visiting the famous spa for its restorative waters. Just as eating salted nuts or crisps is going to have you gasping for a drink, drinking pints of Bath water would probably have you craving something dry and moistureless. Not only was Dr Oliver's cracker suitably non-wet, it contained a very small amount of hops, which were presumably in there for their active properties. Just to make sure everybody knew who invented them, Bath Olivers are stamped with a picture of the late Dr Oliver and the words 'Dr Oliver Inventor'.

It is said that upon his death, Dr Oliver bequeathed the recipe to his coachman, Atkins, along with four bags of flour and a sizeable amount of cash. Most people would have retired to the country with the cash to live on pancakes, but Atkins chose to open a shop selling the crackers and became a rich man. Apparently the shop is now a pub in Green Street, not far from the Roman Baths. Huntley & Palmer's took over baking of the Bath Oliver and today they are made by Jacob's under licence from Fortts, who acquired the recipe in the 1950s.

We'll never know who would have won a head-to-head biscuit inventing competition between Dr Abernethy and Dr Oliver. I think Dr Oliver certainly appears to be the madder of the two, and as such would have been a fairly unpredictable adversary. Dr Abernethy, on the other hand, would be drawing on an extensive cultural background of Scottish biscuit making and so would probably come up with much more sensible and plausible designs. So my money would be on him.

All About Hydrogenated Fat

Fat molecules have long chains of carbon atoms with a couple of hydrogen atoms to each one of carbon. Oils from plants tend to have a double bond in the chain between two of the carbons and can only join to one hydrogen. These are called **unsaturated fats** as not all the carbons are saturated with hydrogen atoms. Now, one double bond in the chain and you have a monosaturate. More than one double bond and you have a **polyunsaturated fat**. Hoorah for organic chemistry and margarine. Unsaturated fats have a lower melting point than the saturated fats from animals, which is why the fat from plants forms liquid oils, and that from animals forms solids like butter and lard. Eating a diet that has unsaturated fat is considered to be healthy, and it also provides so-called essential 'fatty acids', which are ones our bodies can't make for themselves.

Hydrogenation, by contrast, is an industrial process which stuffs extra hydrogen into the molecules, removing the double bonds as it does so. The resulting **hydrogenated vegetable fat** will tend to be a solid at room temperature rather than a liquid. This is basically the way in which margarine is made. Yes, I know, nothing funny here yet.

Partial hydrogenation doesn't quite finish the job and produces some fairly exotic compounds called **trans-fats** that wouldn't normally occur in our diet. Current advice from the UK Food Standards Agency and the US FDA associates trans-fats with raised blood cholesterol levels, via a lowering of LDL and a raising of HDL cholesterol. Yes, nothing funny here either, but now you know.

So, like many things in modern life, there are upsides and downsides to all of this, and the old adage 'all things in moderation' coupled with a well-balanced diet and regular exercise seems to be the advice from all quarters.

All Butter

The first thing that you notice about an All Butter biscuit is that it's not all butter. If it were, it would indeed be butter, and therefore be suitable for spreading on toast. Judging from the lack of warnings to this effect on the packet, it appears that people don't routinely make this mistake.

The All Butter biscuit gets its name from the fact that its fat content is derived from butter alone. That's got to be good: butter is fine, wholesome stuff. Typically biscuits use something called hydrogenated vegetable oil, which has physical characteristics that make it suited to biscuit manufacture: it produces biscuits with the desired sort of texture; it's also cheaper than butter and produces a biscuit with a longer shelf life, which helps keep the cost to consumers low.

If you are concerned about hydrogenated fats stick to All Butter biscuits: they cost a bit more but they do taste superb. One can easily imagine that these were baked specially for you by your aunty or some skilled biscuit-making acquaintance.

Malted Milk

I get so carried away talking about this utterly fantastic biscuit that sometimes I sense people becoming slightly tense and uneasy, as if concerned for their personal safety. Still, it is easy to get overexcited about a biscuit that has dairy cattle embossed on to it. Known to many simply as 'Cow biscuits', they have perhaps the finest artwork of any biscuit ever.

Malted Milks are the Elgin Marbles of the biscuit world, except without any of the accompanying controversy. Just look at the picture: it's got a standing-up cow and another one sitting down. The second cow is the cause of some confusion among biscuit eaters, often being mistaken for a calf due to its smaller size. In fact, it's another heifer placed further away in the scene: that's perspective, a drawing technique refined by Renaissance artists. The first cow grazes and the second ruminates while sitting down, no doubt relaxing after some hectic grazing. The skilled 'Cow biscuit' eater will be able to nibble off the outer bits of the biscuit to leave just the cows, which surely are the most delicious bits. If I were some kind of sultan bloke I would no doubt have my harem busily nibbling the cows out of Malted Milks for me.

One thing that does trouble me about this aspect of the Malted Milk is that there are no mirror-image Malted Milks. If such things existed then it would be possible to place two nibbled-out cows back-to-back to create a whole three-dimensional biscuit cow. This would be an event much like an alignment of the planets, or the deciphering of the Rosetta Stone. If they were the excellent half chocolate-coated sub-species then no doubt both halves could be coaxed to adhere to each other with some gentle melting of the chocolate. It's hard to face the bitter truth that we will never see this.

If all of that weren't enough excitement for one biscuit, there's also the fact that they taste fantastic due to the malt used in their recipe. It's the interplay between this and the intense sweetness of sucrose that gives the Malted Milk its wonderful and rich flavour.

How Malt is Made

Malt is made by allowing barley grains to begin to germinate, spraying them with warm water and gently turning them. Enzymes in the seed begin the work of converting the stored starch into useful sugar that can be used by the growing seed. An enzyme called maltase breaks down the long chains of glucose molecules that form the starch into the simple disaccharide of two joined glucose molecules, maltose. At this point the whole lot is brought abruptly to a halt by a good swift roasting, the length of which determines if any of the sugars caramelise to give an even more complex sweetness. A bit more processing and the sticky foodstuff malt is produced, which can be used as the raw ingredient of beer or, just as nobly, find itself in the biscuit factory.

Sports Biscuit

There was a point when I thought the Sports biscuit had gone to the big biscuit tin in the sky. Another shortcake biscuit, its recipe seems to have drifted from Malted Milk to Lincoln over the years. Its real claim on biscuit fame is the relief pictures of stickmen playing various sports.

Back in the 1970s they used to confine their sporting activities mainly to proper Olympic sports, and a smattering of football and tennis. Even with their fairly limited sporting prowess not all of the sports were easy to probably the hardest sport to recognise from all the little lines and circles. Given their stick-like design, there wasn't much scope for nibbling out the figures, so once the sport was identified the biscuit could be munched down without ceremony.

After a quest a couple of years ago to find the Sports biscuit, it turned up safe and sound in a Welsh Kwik Save. After a bit more searching we found that Fox's Biscuits, who make a great deal of the biscuits for Marks and Spencer, now supply the Sports biscuit to most major supermarkets. Today stickmen can be seen skateboarding, but the basic intention remain the same: a cheerful little shortcake-style biscuit.

Trying to get a handle on the vast quantities of biscuits produced by factories is obviously fraught with drawbacks which is why we have developed the standard measurement of 'How long to reach the moon'. This is the amount of biscuit production measured in years, months and days to reach the moon when the biscuits are laid end to end. Ideally we would have thought up a really snappy name for this unit of measurement, like the light year or the parsec, but we haven't. Perhaps this is something you could worry about on our behalf, maybe on your way to work or while waiting in a long queue of traffic.

If we were to use Tunnock's Wafers, it would take nineteen years and ten months to reach the moon. As for interstellar travel, it would take 514 million years to make enough of them to stretch for one light year. If we go back in time 514 million years that puts us in the late Cambrian period at the start of the Palaeozoic era: at this time most creatures looked like the sort of creepy-crawly stuff that lives in your compost heap, only bigger, and fish hadn't even been invented.

Switching to the Penguin as a means of space travel, we find that we can get to the moon and back twice in one year. That's enough to build a sort of square tube thing, which would no doubt be especially handy in space. As for interstellar travel, the Penguin is going to take about 6.5 million years to travel a light year, which is fairly brisk. That's about how long it took for mankind to evolve from those proto-human guys who looked like nightclub bouncers.

Digestives

The undisputed king of the large-diameter biscuits, this is truly an iconic biscuit. It was originally conceived as an aid to digestion, due to the amount of baking soda (sodium bicarbonate) used in its recipe. This explanation seems a little contrived to me: the baking soda would decompose under the heat of baking to release carbon dioxide, thereby raising the biscuit and making itself ineffectual as a digestive aid, other than via its accompanying payload of roughage.

Unfortunately, poor-quality Digestives tend to taste like damp cardboard, and can easily pull the whole genre into disrepute. On the other hand, a good one is a thing of wonder and sustenance. As I found out on a walking holiday in Wales many years ago, sheep seem to feel the same way about Digestives. While sat atop a lonely Welsh peak in the mist and drizzling rain, brewing a cuppa on my camping stove and munching on Digestives, ovine faces began appearing in the gloom. Eventually we were surrounded by a small flock who quickly breached our defences and made off with five or six biscuits before we managed to regroup and fend them off by quickly improvising gruff sheep-scaring noises.

The Digestive

Found in two main varieties, sweetmeal and wholemeal, the Digestive sets a standard for the whole biscuit world. Its satisfying nature and large size make the biscuit eater pause to consider how many to take at a time: one, two or maybe three. As biscuits go, the Digestive has quite a lot of salt in it, which can lead it into trouble with cheese and other acquaintances. The unwary Digestive can often be found covered in strange toppings, which

I always think is demeaning to its nature. It's a bit like when rugby players appear in drag, or elderly dogs are forced to wear hats, sunglasses and dresses by little girls because they are too lethargic to make a run for it. Having said that, there is one Digestive that positively seeks out this sort of attention, and that's the one shaped like a little loaf of Hovis bread. It happily associates itself with all sorts of undesirable characters such as the Butter Puff and the High Baked Water Biscuit to form a selection of crackers and biscuits for cheese. It's not uncommon to see it tottering around with a slice of Edam and mandarin orange segment stuck on top of it. Mind you, it does tend to do this at Christmas and it's easy to go a little off the rails and make a spectacle of oneself at Yuletide.

The Digestive is no stranger to the ways of dunking and would bid against many other old-school biscuits, such as the Rich Tea or Gingernut, to claim the crown of archetypal dunker. However, its large diameter can create awkward social situations when paired with a mug or cup of a smaller diameter. Dunk, nibble, rotate is the usual way out of this dilemma. That said, it's quite common for the Digestive to break obligingly in two. This fills the biscuit eater with mixed emotions as they come to terms with the disintegration of their previously pristine Digestive. The upside is they now can quickly and humanely dispatch the little fella in three or four swift dunks.

As a young man at university I often saw girls slip a sheet of kitchen roll in the bottom of their biscuit tins when opening a new packet of Digestives. I imagine this was to catch the crumbs. Although completely unnecessary, I always found it somewhat alluring. I was used to eating them straight from the pack, which also did a good job of catching the crumbs (they could then be polished off in much the same way as the bits at the bottom of crisp bags). I'm not aware if this more direct approach to crumb containment was ever considered to be alluring by girls. I've probably just answered my own question there.

Milk Chocolate Digestive

There can be few biscuits which garner such respect as the McVitie's Chocolate Digestive. Referred to by most as simply 'chocolate biscuits', they provide a figurehead for the entire chocolate biscuit world. They were created in 1925 by McVitie's in Edinburgh, and are made today at Europe's biggest biscuit factory in Harlesden in London, which produces 4,860,000 or thereabouts of them every day.

Due in no small part to the quality of its chocolate-less brother the Digestive, upon which it is based, McVitie's simply outclass all other contenders. Mind you, they did invent the Digestive, or rather an ambitious young Scottish baker called Alexander Grant did. He came up with it about five years after beginning work for Robert McVitie in Edinburgh at the end of the nineteenth century. Some thirty years later and they popped some milk chocolate on top to create this classic.

The distinctive horizontal and vertical patterning in the chocolate serves to distinguish the McVitie's instantly from other, lesser biscuits. The quantity of chocolate used shows thoughtful restraint, resulting in a harmonious balance of biscuit and topping. This is good to see in these times when an almost vulgar overuse of chocolate seems to be the norm. We sometimes seem to be in danger of drowning in a sea of mediocre chocolate excess, at the expense of the biscuit buried below. The Chocolate Digestive shows us that 29 per cent milk chocolate brings just enough sweet indulgence to tell our taste buds that we are being spoilt, while still allowing the satisfying biscuit taste plenty of space.

People of my generation carry round with them a chocolate biscuit-related trauma thanks to the legendary 1970s British animated series, *Bagpuss*. Bagpuss was a saggy old cloth cat, who belonged to Emily. Due to special magic, he would awaken and as he came to life so too would the other toys and objects around him, such as Professor Yaffle, the carved wooden woodpecker bookend, and the carved mice on the front of the mouse organ. Part of the brilliance of any of the works of Oliver Postgate and Peter Firmin, the show's creators, was the emotional range in their little films, which made all their characters and the worlds they inhabited completely real. It was this which contributed to my issue with chocolate biscuits.

In the episode 'The Mouse Mill' Emily produces a box containing the Marvellous Mechanical Mouse Mill. The mice open it up and begin using it as a biscuit factory, manufacturing chocolate biscuits from breadcrumbs and butter beans. As a ten-year-old I quite happily accepted this, although I remember wondering where they were getting the chocolate from. However, magic was often at work in the world of Bagpuss, so I made allowances and was happy to accept that this was a possible means by which chocolate biscuits could be made. I still remember clearly the bitter disappointment when Professor Yaffle revealed that the mice simply had one ready-made chocolate biscuit which they kept producing from round the back. If nothing else, I learnt never to take a reanimated carved wooden mouse at its word, and always to look behind Mechanical Mouse Mills, marvellous or not. To this day I check the ingredients on the back of a packet of Chocolate Digestives from time to time to see if butter beans are in there. If they ever do turn up, I won't be in the least bit surprised.

Apparently McVitie's arrive at the output figure of fifty-two biscuits a second by dividing down the annual metric tonnage of biscuits baked. Right now McVitie's estimate that they produce some seventy-one million packs of Chocolate Digestives a year, which surely is a big number. However, a while back, an amusing slip, which was promptly corrected, on their website had managed to change the word 'year' for 'day'. This had us eating sixty-five million packs a day, which I calculated as 1.12 packs for every man, woman and child in the country. Put another way, it meant that the Nice Cup Of Tea And A Sit Down weekly provisions should include thirty-one packs of chocolate digestives. Some of our plucky correspondents suggested ways of accounting for the 23.6 billion extra packets of Chocolate Digestives McVitie's should really be selling each year. One chap helpfully suggested that cash and carries do buy a 'hell of a lot of biscuits all at once'.

Dark Chocolate Digestive

Something that has always impressed me is the fierce loyalty shown by those who prefer the dark chocolate variant of the Chocolate Digestive. Despite being in the minority, they behave in a somewhat superior way, believing that only they, the elite, can appreciate the true chocolate biscuit, a dark chocolate biscuit. The usual implication is that dark chocolate is for the grown-ups. This dark chocolate superiority complex is not confined to the Digestive and extends to other chocolate biscuits.

If that were as far as it went that would be fine. However, all too often the dark chocolate faction can't help but pass off their opinions as facts. Where a harmless 'I prefer the dark chocolate ones' would suffice, they have to push it with provocative statements such as 'The dark chocolate ones are best'. This is tantamount to spoiling for a fight. However, most people will let it go, as the votes have been counted and the dark chocolate guys lost so it's not worth coming to blows.

If you've ever tried constructing any sort of large building out of biscuits then you'll know that it has its fair share of drawbacks. That's not to say it can't be done, but you may have to cheat a bit and maybe mix up a biscuit cement by crushing some up and adding melted butter or margarine. Then simply pop the whole lot into your fridge for about thirty minutes and your new property will be ready to use. Of course, you're going to need a huge fridge for this, so a handy tip is to make prefabricated sections that just about fit. These can simply be slotted together and fastened using some extra jam, butter, chocolate spread, peanut butter or something.

Your biscuit house is obviously going to attract enormous numbers of ants, wasps, maggots and rats, which is going to be embarrassing as you show friends and family around. This could also be offputting to a potential buyer, should you wish to sell. Your estate agent, who is earning a month's salary for approximately two hours' work, may suggest that you describe this as 'rustic charm' or a 'haven for wildlife'. I would expect starlings are going to find it very easy to nest in your roof as well. Let's face it, starlings can get into anything – wood, slate, UPVC soffits and facia boards – so chocolate biscuits are going to be no problem.

Should you happen to be the witch out of Hansel and Gretel, then you'll know that children can be a particular source of problems to a biscuit dwelling. Apparently boys are likely to eat your roof, while girls will munch their way through your clear sugar windows. You can lessen the risk to your residence by choosing a site that's well away from places frequented by the under twelves. A clearing in the deepest, darkest part of the forest is a very popular choice for many witches. This is obviously going to make access to your property less than straightforward, and services such as mains sewerage are probably not going to be available. Still, if you plan on commuting by broomstick and you don't mind having a septic tank then this shouldn't present a problem.

It's almost inevitable that from time to time a couple of little lost children are somehow going to make it through to your isolated clearing. Typically they'll be leaving a trail of breadcrumbs behind themselves as a means of retracing their steps and subsequently finding their way back home. Unfortunately for you and for them the local birds seem to have acquired a taste for baked offerings. Any that are still capable of flight after gorging themselves on your roofing will simply swoop down and polish off the breadcrumb trail as well. After they have polished them off they'll be back over to your gaff to see off your skirting boards.

As a witch, you'll be wanting to roast or boil any children that come your way. Obviously in this day and age that just simply isn't acceptable. So why not try microwaving them on full power for no more than twenty minutes: this will leave your evening free for coven meetings and the like.

Wifey says

Oh dear. Time for Nicey to take a holiday, I think.

Chocolate Caramel

The chocolate and Digestive innovation has continued apace and a mere seventy years after the introduction of the original Chocolate Digestive along came the Chocolate Caramel from McVitie's. This is basically like a narrow-gauge Chocolate Digestive, with a layer of caramel slipped in between the biscuit and the chocolate. It takes even the prepared eater a little by surprise as the biscuit has a little more fight in it than your average chocolate biscuit, ensuring that you don't eat them all in one go. The caramel acts almost like a layer of tasty glue. If they weren't so tasty, I would constantly be put in mind of vinyl floor tiles stuck to MDF with lashings of brown tile adhesive. However, that image very rarely comes to mind, unless I think about it, as I'm doing now.

Gingernuts

There are few biscuits I can think of that are so emphatically of their genre and yet vary so much from manufacturer to manufacturer as the Gingernut. Perhaps the closest analogy lies in the world of single-malt whiskeys (yes, that's right, I meant to put the 'e' in denoting Irish whiskey as that's Wifey's favourite tipple). Whiskey is all made from the same stuff: water, malted barley and yeast. This is fermented, distilled and put into oak casks. After some years it's bottled, we buy it and Wifey drinks it with an ice-cube. Simple. Well, evidently not given all the different brands and prices that there are to choose from (and to be perfectly fair the different flavours and tastes). As with whiskey, so with the Gingernut: from a few simple ingredients comes a surprising and delightful variety.

The Gingernut is the spiciest biscuit in the tin and can range from a rich warm mellowness to a fiery tongue tingler. All Gingernuts should be crisp and crunchy; if they are not then they are either stale or not Gingernuts. It is thought the 'nut' in the name comes purely from their physicality and from the Middle English 'nute' or Olde English 'hnutu', which used to be the appellation for all sorts of small, hard things. So Gingernut conveys not only the flavour but also the texture.

Actually, talking of Olde English, it has always puzzled me that the refreshment trolley on the 8.15 to King's Cross always has two cans of cider on it. Who exactly starts the day with two cans of cider? Well, so far nobody, as they are inexorably there. This reminds me of the sign in the window of the lounge bar of the Britannia Inn in Pencoed, South Wales, which from about 1972 until 1981 said, 'Always something hot to eat'. The sign was a daily feature of village life to anybody who had ever waited outside the 'Brit' for the level-crossing gates on the main London to Swansea line to open. We would often wonder exactly what the hot edible thing could be. My friend Clust, a budding Welsh hippy, asked the landlord, Dilwyn, what exactly it was they had hot to eat. He replied, 'Well, we've got a pasty.' Clust took up the offer of the pasty, anointed it with brown sauce and pepper, and washed it down with two pints of Welsh bitter. A few days later the sign was permanently removed.

Similarly, I'm often tempted to buy the two cans of cider on the 8.15 to King's Cross to see if they ever return. Maybe, like the mystery of the pasty, the world would be forever altered from that point on. I look at the other passengers, trying to work out if any of them have noticed that the two cans of cider in the bottom of the trolley could be a potential cusp for humanity. If we cross that threshold we might enter a new age of cider-less early morning commuter trains.

So why are Gingernuts capable of such diversity? From where I'm sitting, it's down to two things: sugar and ginger. The sugar, depending on the recipe, may be refined white sugar or less refined brown and demerara sugars. It is also present as golden syrup, molasses or black treacle, all of which have their own balance of component sugars: sucrose, glucose and fructose. The ginger, meanwhile, is usually added in the form of ground ginger, which is the dried and powdered rhizome of the ginger plant *Zingiber officinale*. The roots are scraped of their smooth outer skin, dried in the sun and then ground to produce powdered ginger. The best ginger in the world comes from Jamaica, and when combined with Caribbean sugar from sugar cane it seems that the Gingernut is really a West Indian treat.

With any biscuit the baking is crucial to its final taste and appearance, and never more so than the Gingernut: the deep brown colour is caused by the caramelising of the sugar to form a sweet brittle toffee which gets puffed up by the raising agent. Gingernuts start life as little flattened balls of mix and the heat of the oven makes the mix runny so it sinks down and flattens out. It also causes bubbles of carbon dioxide to be produced from the raising agent which puffs up the biscuit, filling it with little air pockets. The interplay of these three processes leads to such subtleties as where the cracks are formed on the surface, how brittle the biscuit is, and – crucially – how much tea it soaks up.

Anybody who has munched Gingernuts while looking at a computer monitor across a room may have noticed odd visual disturbances which occur as the illusion of persistence of vision is interrupted by the clatter inside your mouth. Momentary black flashes appear on the monitor. In these days of LCD monitors and high refresh rates it's becoming a rarer phenomenon, but it's still worth trying out if you can.

Oh dear. I'm giving myself quite an unnatural Gingernut craving writing this, which isn't going to be made better as we take a look at some wonderful examples of the genre.

Types of Gingernut

Perhaps the most famous Gingernut in the UK is made by McVitie's. A very dark biscuit that uses molasses in its recipe, it has a little calm zone in the middle of the biscuit where the cracks and fissures don't venture. McVitie's have also added a little lemon oil which provides a subtle zesty note against the rich warm sweetness. Overall, the McVitie's has a rich sweetness with spicy fragrant notes from the ginger. If it were a whiskey then it would be a blend of spirits aged in sherry and rum casks, I expect.

On the other side of the planet, from New Zealand, comes the Griffin's Gingernut. It has a wonderful elegance and simplicity, which allows its ginger flavour to burst out with a peppery exuberance. The cracks on its surface have a homogeneous distribution, and its recipe uses brown sugar. But the really impressive thing about the Griffin's Gingernut is how hard it is. While the McVitie's offers a nice hard biscuit which soon yields to give a pleasant munchy mouthful, the Griffin's presents much more of a challenge. In fact, if these were indeed nuts I would rate the McVitie's as a pecan with the Griffin's as a Brazil and a control Digestive as, say, a peanut shell. To use our whiskey analogy, I would have to say that the Griffin's is a fine single malt aged in bourbon casks (the spirit not the biscuit).

Another UK favourite is the Marks and Spencer Gingernut, which has a lovely golden colour and a light, open texture. Again there is a good distribution of cracks on its surface. A syrupy sweetness with bright but restrained ginger notes makes this a very vulnerable biscuit pack, which can easily sustain heavy losses from even the most casual biscuit eater. As a whiskey I would see it as one of those broadly appealing blends that slips down without a second thought.

As if to justify my stance on the Gingernut, the Australian biscuit-making legend Arnott's produce four different types using Queensland ginger. At one time Arnott's had four bakeries serving the various states, each baking its Gingernuts in its own way. In Queensland Gingernuts are thin and sweet, with a dark colour. In New South Wales they are small, thick and hard, with a light colour. In Victoria and Tasmania they are bigger, softer and sweeter. And in South and Western Australia, the biscuits look similar to their Victorian cousins, but taste sweeter. When Arnott's experimented with a unified pan-Australian Gingernut, their taste tests told them that people preferred their own local variety. So to this day Arnott's still produce four regional variations. Go on, it's your turn to think of a whiskey analogy.

Oats

Oats have long been a valuable source of sustenance for both mankind and the Scottish. For generations the humble oatcake has been made from oats and water baked on a hot stone. While no doubt nutritious and full of slow-release carbohydrate and dietary fibre, they still make a Rich Tea seem like an extravagantly sweet and fanciful treat. Then along came oats' soulmate, golden syrup, in 1881, courtesy of Lyles. Oats and golden syrup complement each other superbly well, and are the basis for Flapjacks, Anzac biscuits and the biscuits in this section. From time to time you'll see golden syrup listed in ingredients as 'partially invert refiner's sugar', but it's just being coy.

Lyles' distinctive and odd logo is a dead lion with bees swarming around it, apparently choosing to make a nest inside the carcass. Underneath is written, 'Out of the strong came forth sweetness'. We have Samson of the long hair and temple-knocking-down fame to thank for that line. As an adult, Nanny Nicey was very disappointed to find out that her firmly held childhood belief that dead lions are an integral part of the production of golden syrup wasn't so. If bees really were routinely keen on using dead animals as nesting sites then Winnie the Pooh might have been a much more macabre book.

Abbey Crunch

The 'original oat biscuit' was how the sadly missed Abbey Crunch described itself. The last production run was made in September 2003, and closed the book on what was for me an inspirational biscuit. When I started my website, the very first biscuit I chose to review was the Abbey Crunch.

I remember my first encounter with it in the 1970s in my nan's house in Essex, which is where the Abbey Crunch claims its heritage (Essex, not my nan's house). In the 1970s most biscuits were in clear cellophane wrap with some overprinting. The dark blue packaging with the golden biscuit standing out vividly was like nothing else I had ever seen.

Perhaps it was the name that let my nan feel comfortable experimenting with such dazzling packaging. Apparently based on a recipe used by the monks of the Abbey of St John the Baptist, Colchester, the Abbey Crunch was baked by McVitie's, who put a picture of the abbey on the packs. A more convincing bloodline is given via the prewar Colchester baker Priory Biscuits, who produced a crunchy oat biscuit based on a recipe given to its owner Frank Curtis by his mother. I'm inclined to believe this, as the main ingredient in an Abbey Crunch is sugar, something which would have been unknown to eleventh-century monks.

There has always been an affinity between oats and sugar, which is played out in many biscuits and cakes. The pairing evokes images of wholesome homemade biscuits and Flapjacks with nutty savoury notes. I was thus astounded by the brittle toffee sweetness of the Abbey Crunch when my nan first produced them. I think she quickly realised that the packs of Petit Beurre biscuits that she used to buy in the Hadleigh branch of Safeway would no longer be an option. Actually, the Petit Beurre were never really an option, and I started to suspect my biscuit leanings came from my paternal lineage. (Although I have yet to display my dad's liking for eating a big stack of High Baked Water Biscuits, or three or four Cream Crackers unaccompanied by any form or topping or spread. Mind you, a cup of tea was usually required fairly soon after.)

I personally believe that without the Abbey Crunch we could never have had its descendant, the wildly popular HobNob. Indeed, as McVitie's try to console those who miss the Abbey Crunch, they often point them towards the HobNob.

HobNob

McVitie's rolled out the HobNob in the mid-1980s, capturing the biscuit-buying public's attention with this oat biscuit and creating an overnight classic. The HobNob was simply a *tour de force*, ticking all the boxes for a successful new biscuit. Most important was the taste, and by turning to the oat once again McVitie's were able to achieve that tasty and slightly irregular charm. The oaty knobbles made the HobNob seem less manufactured than its contemporaries and no doubt contributed to its name. A relatively large diameter and suitable thickness made it both satisfying and a great dunker.

The HobNob achieved one of those rare feats for new products by being simultaneously new and yet familiar, as if we were merely being reintroduced after an unexplained absence. Could this have been an echo of the Abbey Crunch in the biscuit-eating public's mind, or was it simply the disarming and approachable oat at work? The cheerful orange pack, the strap line 'One nibble and you're nobbled' and, of course, the name all helped to place the biscuit comfortably on the stage of UK biscuits. The name begged not to be taken seriously, and told us that this was a biscuit for the honest masses, at the time of the rise of the yuppie in Britain under Margaret Thatcher.

After two years the HobNob was firmly cemented into the biscuit landscape of the nation and ready to don its ennobling covering of milk chocolate. This was closely followed by a plain chocolate variety. I can remember exactly where I was standing when I first heard of the plain chocolate version, much in the way people remember where they were when they heard of the assassination of Kennedy. Obviously, it wasn't quite that dramatic; it just oddly located itself near the front of my mind rather than at the back. What's even stranger is that the plain chocolate ones are my least favourite.

The Chocolate HobNob is also a fairly sure bet when looking for a romantic biscuit with which to woo the opposite sex. I have had couples tell me of crucial tea and sit downs where love has taken root and blossomed over a pack of HobNobs. This is important because whipping out your HobNobs for just anybody could be misinterpreted as coming on a bit strong. If you are not after forming a relationship with whoever you are flashing your biscuits at, it's best to come right out with it, rather than cause an unpleasant scene later.

The HobNob quickly rose to become one of McVitie's' most important lines, and has found itself on the cutting edge of new developments. The tube, a small self-contained cardboard biscuit barrel with polythene lid, was pioneered by the Chocolate HobNob and stablemate the Milk Chocolate Digestive. Hobnobs are also now available in mini-packs, as the core of chocolate biscuit bars, and, turning full circle, smashed up and added as an ingredient to Flapjacks. Perhaps the success of the HobNob played its part in the waning popularity of the Abbey Crunch. If that is true then perhaps the HobNob should have a little ceremony each year when it observes a minute's silence, remembering the biscuits that went before so that it might enjoy the freedom and liberty of the oats section on supermarket shelves.

ⓩ Sandwich Biscuits

Take two biscuits, place them back to back with a blob of something in between and you have a sandwich biscuit. This basic sandwich design has a lot of things going for it: most importantly, you are effectively eating two biscuits at once, and in any social situation where you don't want to be seen as a selfish biscuit glutton, a few well-chosen sandwich biscuits are going to maximise your handful. Additionally, the laminated construction results in a composite material that allows them to stand up to stresses and strains quite well. This can be important for extended dunking experiments or when building little piles of them on plates.

Bourbon

I fear I am going to create controversy here. My views on the Bourbon biscuit are somewhat similar to my feelings towards Jennifer Lopez. When described to the uninitiated, both sound lovely and each is greatly admired. I, however, find myself somewhat underwhelmed. I often feel that I'm missing the point with the Bourbon biscuit, and by rights I should like it a lot more than I do. Though it frequents a great number of biscuit assortments, I often find that I will pass it over, often in favour of biscuits with apparently lesser charms.

I can quite imagine that some people think that a Bourbon is about as good as it gets. I'm just not one of them. Nevertheless, I still have a great deal of respect for it, being as it is one of the elder statesmen of the biscuit tin, and it can certainly show the Johnny-come-lately biscuits a thing or two about classic biscuit design.

Why it should be named after a sixteenth-century French–Italian royal dynasty is anybody's guess. When faced with such historical conundrums there is really only one way forward for the semi-diligent biscuit critic, and that is to fabricate some weak theory. Let's say that Charles II of Bourbon

liked a plate of chocolate sandwich creams as he conquered the crowns of Naples and Sicily and restored them to a united and independent kingdom.

The one shown here is a Crawford's Bourbon, also well known for their Custard Creams. As you can see, these Bourbons have excellent embossing and the regulation ten holes, and you can clearly make out the little sugar crystals embedded in it. There is good sport to be had in breaking Bourbons apart to get at their chocolate cream filling, with points being scored for precision and full marks going to complete removal of the cream as a single entity.

Bourbons are also reassuringly uniform in size, regardless of the manufacturer: 61mm by 31mm being the accepted standard. Given their regular dimensions, perhaps Bourbon biscuits could form the basis of an SI unit of measurement, with biscuits being measured in Bourbons: for example, the digestive has a diameter of 1.13 bourbons, or that ocean liner over there is 7.6 kilobourbons long, or the wavelength of light emitted by that Krypton laser is approximately 46.1 nanobourbons. I'm sure you see what I'm getting at.

Custard Cream

When Hollywood wanted a time machine to carry Michael J. Fox around, not only did they decide to make it out of a sports car, but they plumped for plutonium, lightning and nuclear fusion as its power sources. If the British ever build a time machine then not only would it resemble some form of comfy chair but my betting is that it will have at its core a twin pack of Custard Creams. This biscuit, perhaps more than any other, has the ability to warp the fabric of space–time and transport us effortlessly back to days gone by. This is particularly impressive as a recent TV programme I saw about time machines said that it's the ones that go backwards in time that are the trickiest to build.

The Custard Cream was actually the first true adult biscuit that I tackled, back in the mid–1960s, as a small baby. Actually, I wasn't small, I was huge: about the size of a Mini, judging from Nanny Nicey's old photos. Before then I had been developing nascent biscuit-munching skills on Bickiepegs, a specially designed teething biscuit for babies. Bickiepegs, which are still available today, are possibly the hardest substance for ingestion that can be bought over a chemist's counter. When I tried one recently, it was a bit like gnawing on an everlasting wholemeal super-strength bread stick. It took twenty-five minutes just to blunt one end. After going up against a Bickiepeg, you simply have to view teething babies with a great deal of respect and caution.

Stepping up from the Bickiepeg to the Custard Cream made quite an impression on me. Having been told by several of Nanny Nicey's cohorts what an objectionable little chap I used to be, it was a very rare occasion indeed when somebody would actually find themselves in the unenviable position of babysitting me. On one such occasion my Aunty Edna quickly established that feeding me the filling from Custard Creams had a calming effect upon me: this no doubt contributed to my life-

long interest in the subject of biscuits. Even today, I find it difficult not to resist prising open the two halves and scoffing the filling. In general, the cream always adheres more strongly to one biscuit than the other, and it's this one which often bears the tell-tale twin furrows, where it has been de-creamed using the front two upper incisors.

With its baroque detailing, the Custard Cream defies us to pin it down to any particular period of history. It is tempting to think that it was knocking around in the sixteenth century, its ornate swirls providing the muse for such great artists as Rubens or Caravaggio, as they nibbled on one over a late morning cuppa. It is equally at home in any decade of the twentieth century and now through into the twenty-first.

Perhaps Custard Creams habitually transport themselves through time and we are simply unaware of it. The ones in your biscuit tin could be exchanging themselves with a pack from some time during the 1950s and you'd never know. But what would a time machine based on the Custard Cream look like? Taking our design cues from the biscuit, then it looks like it is going to need a set of ornate wrought-iron gates, front and back. It also needs a large diamond shape on the front with the words 'Time Machine' written in the middle. However, the filling or passenger area must not resemble custard in any discernible way, apart from being opaque and quite sweet. There would probably need to be a small travel kettle in there as well, a bit like the ones you get in hotel rooms.

Actually, talking of hotel rooms, the Custard Cream, in the form of a three-pack, can often be found next to the complementary tea and coffee and should be consumed within five to ten minutes of first entering the room, even prior to figuring out how the TV remote works. I have always thought that hotels should make it very clear which type and how many complementary biscuits they provide. Maybe on their signs, underneath their various stars and ratings, they could have a small weatherproof facsimile of the biscuit selection on offer. I for one would find that helpful.

Jam

Just looking at the word 'jam' tells us how important it is. All the really fundamental words have three or four letters: 'man', 'cat', 'pot' and 'car'. Why the Americans persist on calling cars 'automobiles' is beyond me. Are they making a rod for their own back? Of course, you can only really effectively rhyme 'wheel' with 'automobile' in song lyrics which is why songs about cars were in danger of stalling at the works of Chuck Berry. After that, American writers were forced to start using brand names like 'Cadillac' in their songs. By contrast, the British were able enjoy the Beatles' 'Drive my Car', Madness's 'Driving in my Car' and Gary Numan's 'Cars'.

Now jam is pretty terrific stuff all by itself. In fact, younger readers would cheerfully eat it with a spoon if allowed. In the world of biscuits, cakes and puddings, jam has always been available to bring a bit of fruit-based interest and often plays an important structural role, acting as an all-purpose adhesive. Pectin from the fruit sets the jam and determines how stiff it is. When heated and cooled, it forms a big tangled mass which holds the jam together, but still allows it some movement: if it weren't for pectin, jam would be either a drink or a boiled sweet.

Jammie Dodger

A modern-day jam classic, the Jammie Dodger is made by Burton's Biscuits, producers of a wide range of biscuits but best known for their highly individual brands like Toffypops, Wagon Wheels and Viscount, all iconic brands in their own rights.

Like myself, Jammie Dodgers are a child of the sixties and have been made in Burton's Llantarnam factory in South Wales ever since they were introduced. Output runs at twelve biscuits a second, which is quite brisk, but we are still looking at around seventy years before achieving lunar orbit. However, if Burton's used some of their jam to stick the biscuits together then it might not be the fastest biscuit to the moon, but it could well be the best constructed.

Conceptually simple, a Jammie Dodger is a sandwich of jam and two shortcake biscuits with a heart-shaped hole in the upper biscuit to reveal the jam. The jam is billed as raspberry flavour but is in fact made from plums and a few other things, presumably because actual raspberry jam wasn't up to the biscuit-engineering task of adhering the two biscuits together. The biscuit itself has undergone some changes over the years. It has become somewhat paler in colour, and with this slightly softer. Also, the original heart-shaped embossing has been replaced by 'jammie' splashes so as to emphasise to the eater that jam plays a pivotal role in this biscuit.

Despite its relative youth, the reason why a Jammie Dodger is so called have mostly been forgotten. I think the explanation is to be found in a nursery rhyme:

> The Queen of Hearts,
> She baked some tarts,
> All on a summer's day.
> The Knave of Hearts,
> He stole the tarts,
> And took them clean away.

Jammie Dodger packs used to feature the Knave of Hearts, and to this day the heart-shaped jam hole echoes the past. I assume the Knave had to do some dodging, in the manner of Dickens' Artful Dodger, in order to carry out the theft. (By the way, tart baking seems like a very domestic pastime for royalty to be involved in. And baking during the heat of a summer's day is possibly going to lead to personal hygiene issues for Her Majesty, especially if she is wearing her full Queen outfit.)

A recent innovation has been the Mini-Jammie Dodger, which sees yet another old faithful following a trend seen across both biscuits and confectionery. Making smaller versions of something has long equated with 'fun', as pioneered by Mars. Of course, it has its place, but I think I'll always prefer seriously big, rather than little and fun. Perhaps it is because I remember my first encounter with the Jammie Dodger at the school tuck shop in 1971, where one of these substantial biscuits could be bought for two pence.

Jam Cream Sandwich

A common mistake is to call a Jam Cream Sandwich biscuit a Jammie Dodger. This is akin to calling all vacuum cleaners 'Hoovers', and it's perfectly fine to pour scorn upon anybody who makes this mistake. No, honestly, go ahead: people have to learn. For many, the Jam Cream Sandwich is the pinnacle of jam biscuitry. Normally such biscuits are to be found in assortment tins with their numbers strictly regulated to single figures, making them highly prized. However, most supermarkets now sell their own-label packs of fifteen, so you can go mad and potentially get your hands on quantities running into the hundreds.

The first thing that strikes you about these biscuits is their relatively small diameter. Straight away, you know that you'll need at least three just to get the measure of them. Sticking both halves of the biscuit together is a team effort between the jam and cream, with the jam occupying the bit below the hole. Separating the two halves is easy as the jam is quite pliable, typically being made using actual raspberries. Pulling the biscuits gently apart creates a small well in the jam, a bit like one of those visualisations of the gravity field around a black hole. If you don't know what I mean just imagine a small well. Yes, with a bucket if you like. A traditional dusting of granulated sugar on top of the sticky jam completes the picture.

Osmosis

Jam has been made throughout the ages by boiling fruit, a little water and, when it became available, sugar. The sugar in the fruit acts as a natural preservative once it becomes concentrated enough, and acts through a process called osmosis.

Osmosis is one of those words that people tend to bandy around without knowing what it actually means. It's specifically the diffusion of water molecules from an area of high concentration to one of low concentration. This is made possible if the solutes, the stuff dissolved in the water, are prevented from moving by some sort of barrier. This is exactly how jam works at the molecular level and means that water molecules that are free to move from anything landing on the jam will do so. Bacteria and fungi cells that land on jam have all of their life-giving water sucked from them, causing the naughty little unicells to implode. This helps stop the jam from going bad and gives rise to its alternative name of 'Preserve'.

So when you hear people say something flowery like, 'Oh, he learnt to play the guitar by osmosis really', what they are actually saying is that water diffused into him despite his skin having evolved since the time of the first reptiles to prevent this. Not only that, but the water conferred upon him musical ability. Of course, if the guitar was in a solution that he swallowed then the water could have been taken up by the lining of the gut. It's all fairly unlikely, and at best a very poor metaphor.

Happy Face

Jacob's Happy Face is a shining example of a jam and cream sandwich biscuit. A very good sign is that the pack has little pictures of raspberries all over it and, yes, it is real raspberry jam, no apples and plums in disguise. You can certainly taste the difference. The effect of the filling being viewed through the eyes and mouth of the face creates teeth and eyelids. The picture on the front of the pack is a little off in this regard as the faces have top teeth rather than bottom teeth. The biscuits themselves, 45mm in diameter, are simple smooth shortcake type of affairs, which hold their face graphics well enough. Altogether we have observed five types of face, which is very good going for a pack of ten biscuits.

A little while ago while waiting to do a spot of TV I found myself sitting next to a wine 'expert' from the US, who was of the opinion that it was a lot of hoo-ha that wine should be drunk at the correct temperature, allowed to breathe, and so on. I have to say that being surrounded by a studio of food and drink lovers, this chap's theories were met with some very stony faces. When it comes to biscuits, ask any Aussie and they will tell you that Tim Tams are best eaten fresh from the fridge. As for the Happy Face, it would seem to suit a fairly warm environment as its jam is liable to become a bit glassy at low temperatures, even snapping in two when bitten. It can also break away from the biscuits completely, leaving you with just a lump of jam to chew, which admittedly is no bad thing. When the jam is pliable, however, the whole biscuit works in concert, and is very good indeed.

15 Marshmallow Sort of Things

Biscuit bakers have lots of construction materials available to them which they can use to create new and interesting designs. One of the most whimsical of these is marshmallow, which can be used to add colour, texture and precise amounts of 'squidginess' to biscuits. The small band of biscuits that have opted for marshmallow fixtures have formed an elite group, both widely revered and often misunderstood. Having a marshmallow is often seen as a sign of immaturity in a biscuit, and marshmallow biscuits often find themselves on duty at children's parties or occasionally at a family picnic. This is a great shame as they have so much more to offer than that.

I would like to see a new dinner course invented that brings these noble and fluffy treats in from the cold, taking their rightful place alongside cheese and crackers or after-dinner mints. Actually, I think the Scottish may have already done this with their high tea, a hybrid of afternoon tea and a conventional high tea. A Scottish high tea has a course for scones, cakes, biscuits and teacakes in which our marshmallow-based biscuits are afforded the proper deference.

Marshmallow manifests itself in two distinct forms: the most common of these contains gelatin. Gelatin, a protein, is the stuff which sets jellies, and it is an animal product. Various people, such as vegetarians, avoid gelatin: for those who choose to consume it, this can be a handy way of warding such people off your biscuits. In fact, you can pretend that even stuff that doesn't have gelatin is loaded with it. Conversely, fairly dire biscuits that people have brought back from Spanish holidays can be palmed off on mildly desperate vegetarians as being totally free of gelatin (mind you, they might be full of whale oil and veal, so if you have a shred of conscience you might want to check for that with your Spanish-to-English dictionary).

Marshmallows with gelatin can be thought of as a foamed-up jelly or, put another way, a stiff jelly full of air. The other form of marshmallow is essentially an uncooked meringue, in which egg white or albumen is beaten with sugar, again to trap air. Such 'mallow' is very sticky indeed and has properties somewhere between bath sealant and shaving foam. I'm in constant awe of the factories that manage to handle this stuff in a directed and deliberate way for the purposes of biscuit production. Given just a tiny amount, the younger members of staff are able to lay waste to entire dining tables and sets of clothes.

I often wonder what would happen if we were required to handle marshmallow on an industrial scale, say for an experimental run of biscuits. I'm sure it would quickly lead to a bakery equivalent of the Chernobyl disaster: one vast gungy white mess with bits of bakery stuck in it. Enormous and heroic helicopters would be needed to drop tons of concrete on the site, risking almost certain adhesion in the process. Vast sheets of thin aluminium foil with attractive little patterns on them would also be required to wrap it up to protect future generations.

Wagon Wheel

The Wagon Wheel is another biscuit-based wonder from that iconic biscuit maker, Burton's. If biscuits were music then Burton's would have a big foothold in the Glam Rock section, with such wonderful and individual biscuits as the Jammie Dodger, Toffypop and the Wagon Wheel. Loved by kids and adults alike, Wagon Wheels create an instant sense of nostalgia. Perhaps more than any other biscuit, it has a rich and intriguing history, so much so that some of it has passed into the realms of urban myth.

The Wagon Wheel traces its origins back to the 1950s and a biscuit baron called Garfield Weston. An entrepreneurial Canadian, he made a fortune out of supplying biscuits to the forces during the war and had a facility in Slough. Mr Weston had three sons. One inherited the UK business, one had the Canadian, and the third got Australia. To this day, the Wagon Wheel can be found in these three locations. The brainchild of Garry Weston, the UK son, they were originally sold in the UK as Weston's Wagon Wheels.

If we look at today's UK Wagon Wheel then we find ourselves on familiar ground. Originally they were supplied in boxes of four as two stacks of two with a brown plastic tray keeping them in order. Individually wrapped since the 1980s, today the wrapped versions are again arranged in stacks of two to make eight-and six-packs. The individual wrap also allowed Wagon Wheels to venture into new territories such as canteens and cafés, not to mention the all-important lunchbox, rubbing shoulders with such experienced practitioners as the Penguin and Club.

The original packaging featured cowboys and gingham cloth, and this endured for many years. The designs then changed quite a bit, at one point even having American footballers on them, but Burton's eventually returned to their roots. Today's pack features a wagon train image with the strapline 'A Taste for Adventure', which becomes progressively less clear the more you think about it.

The Wagon Wheel has always been a bit of a conundrum, because if we consider its components in turn, it's puzzling why we like them at all. Its unique chocolate-flavoured coating, apparently called 'Blackpool coating', gives the Wagon Wheel a strange grey vinyl silk sheen, reminiscent of the bloom on ripe wild fruits. It forms a tortured mass of ripply bumps on the surface, almost as if it's not meant to be there at all and has managed to adhere to the surface despite the odds. As for what it tastes like compared to chocolate, who knows? The largest deposits are to be found in the gully formed where the two biscuits meet. You might just be able to pick out a big enough bit of it to tell what it tastes like in isolation.

Now on to the marshmallow centre. Its main role is to provide an interesting structural layer, allowing both biscuit layers a degree of independent horizontal movement once the flimsy chocolate seal has been compromised. As for what it tastes like in isolation, again, I doubt if anybody knows for sure. Finally, there are the two biscuit layers themselves. Your guess is as good as mine as to what is happening there. They seem to be a bit like a vaguely pliable thin shortcake biscuit. Research leads me to believe that they are a type of Marie biscuit, but I find it hard to believe.

However, put all of these unique things together, as Burton's have, and something magic happens: you get the compelling whole that is the Wagon Wheel. In some form of biscuit synergy the whole is far greater than the sum of its parts.

Other taste variants have come and gone, including a malted milk-based version called 'Big Country', which may have been all the reason the late Stuart Adamson needed to leave Scottish punk rockers the Skids and form the bagpipe-guitar-sound band with the same name. Later, 'Big Country' would be replaced by an excellent Toffee Wagon Wheel, which had a reservoir of runny toffee engineered into it. Regrettably this too is now just a memory but the jam version is still going strong and in fact is the default version in both Australia and Canada.

A few years ago Wifey and I enjoyed a Wagon Wheel bonanza when our friend Emma provided us with two forty-eight-packs of Toffee and Jam Wagon Wheels. Her dad ran an intermittent sandwich round and the Wagon Wheels were languishing in his lock-up, looking for a good home. I can honestly say that I was sorry to finish them and hadn't grown the least bit sick of them. I'm unsure if this is a plus for the Wagon Wheel or a minus for myself. It's also said that when the Soviet Union broke up at the end of the Cold War, lots of Wagon Wheels were discovered in the KGB's headquarters. If you ever have Mr Putin round for tea you know what to whip out after the trifle.

HAS THE WAGON WHEEL GOT SMALLER?

No discussion of the Wagon Wheel can be complete without reference to the perennial 'Has it got smaller?' question. Burton's are quick to dismiss this with the plausible explanation that the reduction in size of the Wagon Wheel is due to our childhood memories recalling a biscuit that was relatively larger compared to us. If you ever visit your old junior school you will experience much the same thing as you tower over your old tables and chairs. It should be noted that this phenomenon doesn't appear to occur with other large-diameter biscuits such as the Digestive, but then they probably didn't have such an impact on our impressionable young minds.

It does seem logical that if each successive generation of biscuit eaters since the 1950s had witnessed a real and substantiated shrinking then by now the Wagon Wheel would be so small that we would need special equipment just to see it, let alone remove the wrapper. Burton's by association would have pioneered the now emerging field of nanotechnology, and we could all enjoy Wagon Wheels as some form of molecular spray applied to the back of the hand. There has, however, been one very minor and reported shrinkage some twenty years ago when production was moved from the original factory in Slough to a new site at Llantarnam. At this time a new and more efficient biscuit-cutting roller was introduced and this did away with the old scalloped edge. In doing so, it shaved a couple of millimetres off the biscuit.

Interestingly, the Australian Wagon Wheel still has the scalloped edge, like some living fossil, an echo of a distant age of giant biscuits. I recently ate a pack which was sent to me purely for research purposes. As I gazed upon it I felt like Doug McClure in *The Land that Time Forgot* when the pterodactyl is going for him. The Australian biscuit had a diameter which measured 88mm: that's a whole 14mm bigger than our version. However, the British version comes right back at its colonial cousin with a depth of approximately 15mm compared to 11mm. In fact, the Aussie Wagon Wheel has some of the thinnest mallow I've ever witnessed. I'm sure if NASA had to produce some sort of super-thin mallow-based biscuit for use in space, say as a solar sail, then they would be down to Australia like a shot.

Teacakes

The overlord of the Teacakes is the Tunnock's, which registers a Victoria plum, possibly a clementine, on the fruit and nut scale of measurement, intimidating its walnut-sized competitors. While on the subject of its competitors, they all seem to need intricate plastic trays to protect their puny chocolate shells, while the Scottish Tunnock's makes do with a bit of thin tin foil and a cardboard box.

The Tunnock is a classic example of the egg-based marshmallow Teacake. Yet again I'm still left wondering how exactly the famous Tunnock's factory in Uddingston, Glasgow, is still standing, working with such tricky materials. I'm sure if I asked Mr Boyd Tunnock nicely enough he would come and let me have a peep, but I think I actually prefer not to know. I'd rather construct vast Heath-Robinson Teacake-baking machines in my imagination. Nevertheless, somehow a biscuit base gets a generous dollop of sticky marshmallow, and then is entirely coated in chocolate. Finally we must note that the Tunnock's contains no jam, which I assume is a level of extra gunge that would push their machine into the realms of fantasy.

The other sort of Teacake is the generally smaller gelatin marshmallow-based variety. Brands to look out for here are Burton's and, from Scotland again, Lee's. Here the marshmallow offers enough structural integrity to fashion a small jam reservoir, and runny jam at that. This slightly smaller Teacake is seldom individually wrapped and prefers a custom-moulded tray insert as its packing.

With such an elaborate construction, there are many ways to deconstruct a Teacake during its eating. The first and most prized is the complete removal of the upper chocolate dome as a single intact entity. This exposes the marshmallow, which can be peeled off the base and then eaten. Finally the base itself may be consumed. Sometimes the chocolate shell needs to be cracked and removed in sections, which is obviously more time-consuming.

In circumstances where numbers of Teacakes per person are strictly rationed, this can prolong one's eating pleasure.

Kimberley

The marshmallow genre contains some of the most divisive biscuits. Like olives, you either love them or hate them. Half the world claim some sort of Irish lineage: if they really were then they would possess the genes that enable them to enjoy the Kimberley biscuit. As Irish as rain, followed by a big downpour and then some showers, the Kimberley is a keystone of Irish tea and sits downs, as much as Barry's tea is. Indeed, the importance of the Kimberley to Irish culture and the affection in which it is held have been impressed upon me by most Irish people wishing to educate me further. Irish folks travelling from their native land are genuinely shocked that the rest of the world doesn't have the Kimberley. The truth is that most of the world has never even heard of them.

When I heard of its faintly gingery biscuits enclosing a marshmallow centre encrusted with sugar, I thought, Yes, this is a biscuit I would like to track down and sample. So it came as somewhat of a shock to find that it tasted a bit like damp MDF with a squirt of bath sealant. I paused, shocked and alarmed, and gathered my taste buds. What could be going on here? Maybe they were more reminiscent of a pack of errant Digestives that had been carelessly left in the garden for a week? Still reeling, I checked to see if the packet was out of date, but found that it was good for another six months. The locals informed me that it is the nature of the Kimberley to be variable in its texture and that I had probably got a particularly soft batch. I think they were just trying to make me feel better, knowing full well that I lacked the correct complement of DNA to get the most out of them.

Undaunted I set out to find another packet, and soon happened across the rarer (and slightly frowned upon by the purists) chocolate-covered variety. The crust of sugar granules over the edge of the marsh-mallow centre had been completely replaced by a coat of real milk chocolate. Although not apparent from the outer box, each biscuit was individually wrapped, and upon eating I was delighted to find these extra layers of protection had given rise to a Kimberley that had a slight crumble to it. In all respects it was excellent, worthy of a place on the greater world stage of biscuits. In fact, they are really worth tracking down.

Jacob's Mikado

For many people the marshmallow biscuit that springs to mind at the head of the queue is the Mikado or Mallow. Jacob's is the leading baker of this style of biscuit, although there are many smaller bakeries which make their own versions, with different names and variations of colour.

The Mikado is classically associated with children's birthday parties, where it provides a staple source of marshmallow and jam. I always have reservations about the use of coconut in biscuits, which seems more of a nod towards dietary fibre content than flavour. In the Mikado, however, the tartness of the simulated raspberry jam (it's actually apple) keeps the coconut at bay. The biscuit base is quite soft, with a crunch nowhere to be found. But it manages to sport some grid-like biscuit graphics, so it does appear to have some sort of mechanical properties. The pink marshmallow is arranged in two rows, five blobs in each. So what is the overall effect of this teatime treat technology? Well, it's possibly the closest thing in the biscuit world to a salad. Having said that, younger members of staff destroy their ration at an impressive rate and even ask nicely for more, so it appears that the Mikado has lost none of its party time magic.

It must be mentioned that there is another form of Mikado, which is a strange international affair, being a German-style snack developed in Japan and baked in France (see p.130). We acquire them for UK consumption on sorties to the continent. This is the level of international collaboration usually seen with the development of a fighter aircraft or space stations, so it's nice to see it in the world of biscuits.

Fruity

Fruit. You can put it in a bowl and paint its picture, you can make it into salads or batter it flat, dry it out and stick it in biscuits. Could this crude explanation be the reason why melons aren't a familiar biscuit ingredient?

Fig Rolls

A lot of people tend to think of the Fig Roll as quite an outdated biscuit. I'm not actually sure why as they are just as relevant now as they have always been. Today we have many wonders: superglue, the interweb, Teflon, geo-synchronous communications satellites, extra-absorbent kitchen towels that stay strong even when wet, and the Fig Roll, which combines all the goodness of figs with the convenience of conventional biscuits.

I've often thought that the Fig Roll is as close to spaceman food as the biscuit world has ever got. I've never subscribed to that old science-fiction chestnut that in the future we'll all simply swallow a couple of nutrient pills and a glass of water instead of eating proper food. I, for one, find pills difficult to swallow, and it takes between three and four attempts for me to deal with a paracetamol, much to Wifey's disgust. In space, I would happily make do with just a couple of sandwiches, a cup of tea and five or six biscuits, insisting that all the little pills were saved for those who were really hungry.

After a hard morning working in space (realigning, say, your errant AE45 module) you're going to be fairly ravenous. You'll be wanting a decent biscuit and a cuppa, not some simulated little mid-morning snack-pill thing. Of course, what constitutes a morning's work will be subject to 'time dilation' as predicted by Einstein's laws of spacial relativity and caused by the immense interstellar velocities at which you'll no doubt be travelling. What seems like a morning's work for you could be a mere ten minutes. Actually, come to think of it, I'm sure I've seen the same thing occur in conventional terrestrial offices.

In space, Fig Rolls would be the perfect snack. I'm sure you could live on them for months and that their high-density and non-crumbly nature would lend itself to use in the space programme. Their sticky figgy filling makes them ideally suited to zero or micro gravity operating environments, as it helps stop stray bits of crust detaching and getting lodged in any sensitive or safety-critical systems. They are also high in fibre and complex carbohydrates, and would probably help with those all-important and tricky zero-gravity bathroom visits. No doubt if we ran into other space-faring alien races they'd have crates of alien Fig Rolls stashed away in the backs of their spaceships. Although it might take months or even years of effort by our best linguists before we work out enough of their alien tongue to ask them where they keep their Fig Rolls, or even if they have biscuits as we understand them.

Mind you, I also like to imagine that the Fig Roll was well known to the ancients, who were no strangers to the fig. Let's face it, back then puddings were a bit basic to say the least, the Black Forest Gateau or banoffee pie were unknown, so a few figs would probably have been about the size of it. I expect that the Egyptians built massive plantations all along the River Nile to satisfy their fig appetites. The Greeks, on the other hand, probably captured Phoenician fig ships in mad Jason and the Argonauts-style vessels, taking all the figs home for enormous fig parties. The historical evidence relating to the Roman Empire, meanwhile, is clear. Emperor Augustus, as played by Brian Blessed in the BBC production of *I Claudius*, loved a good fig, so no need to consult the history texts there.

I have heard it said that the Fig Roll is one of the oldest forms of sweet biscuit made in Britain. I don't know who said it, but it is entirely plausible. The Americans are under the impression that they created the whole genre in 1891, when baker James Henry Mitchell invented a machine for stuffing one lot of squidgy stuff inside something else equally pastry-like. They settled on fig jam as the middle bit, and named them Newtons after a nearby suburb of Boston.

There are two forms of Fig Roll – 'bake then cut' and 'cut then bake' and each has its merits. The Jacob's Fig Roll is perhaps the best-known example of cut then bake. They used to have ridges on the top, which was no good as it appeared to alter the fig-to-crust ratio, and these have now been sensibly removed. The cutting and baking process also gives them a distinctive slight curvature, which makes them less than straightforward to package. Various arrangements of plastic trays with no more than about three or four biscuits per compartment are used. Cut then bake Fig Rolls typically will have the pastry crimped at each end, which goes some way to sealing in the moist fig contents. As well as making them better citizens of the biscuit tin, this means that the nature of the fig filling cannot be easily assessed through a casual glance. Such Fig Rolls have an air of mystery due to their concealed innards, and upon first encountering them it is a little like unwrapping a surprise present.

Bake then cut Fig Rolls, on the other hand, are much more candid. As the continuous strip of biscuit leaves the oven it is cut to length. Each biscuit end is a cross-sectional study of the finished product. Nothing is left to the imagination and fig and crust may be compared in a single glance. The Fig Rolls also have a regular linear shape, which lets them stack neatly, and very impressive packing densities are possible. Such Fig Rolls come into their own when space is at a premium, such as Wifey's little rucksack which we use for picnics. Most of the own-label Fig Rolls in the UK are bake then cut, and are made by Burton's Foods.

One of the interesting aspects for the keen Fig Roll buyer is the variance in fig content from own-label to own-label, which can vary from a minimum of 20 per cent to a maximum of 30 per cent. In a perfect world there would simply be a dial on the side of the Fig Roll production line by which the desired fig content could be selected. I can't help but picture imaginary designs for the workings of Fig Roll extruding machines in my head. I also like to imagine high-powered biscuit executives thrashing out business deals relating to fig percentages, hopefully while wearing enormous *Dallas*-esque Stetsons.

Garibaldi

There can be few biscuits as unique as the Garibaldi. Technically it's a semi-sweet hard fruit biscuit, but that description really doesn't do justice to this unparalleled teatime treat. They are often affectionately known as 'dead fly' or 'squashed fly' biscuits due to their payload of little flattened raisins. This name is sometimes also used for the Fruit Shortcake, which has a cargo of currants, but personally I don't hold with that.

With Garibaldi, a layer of raisins is squashed between an upper and lower sheet of biscuit dough, and here and there the odd raisin pokes through. The biscuits are finished with a shiny but non-sticky glaze (egg, I presume) which gives them a high specular index (important to know for anybody wishing to make a three-dimensional computer model of a Garibaldi). The biscuits are cut into rectangular slabs, each of which consists typically of five biscuits. Scoring made before baking leaves the biscuit equivalent of perforations in a sheet of raffle tickets.

I can't think of another biscuit that ships in this partially completed kit form. Conceivably you could just pick up one enormous slab and start gnawing on the corner but this would surely be the height of poor etiquette, and not as much fun. The skill in breaking up the Garibaldi slab is to achieve nice rectangular biscuits. Success depends on the subcutaneous raisin distribution, but even if you end up with some hopelessly odd shapes it doesn't matter. Where Garibaldis are concerned it's the taking part that matters, rather than the taking apart. As with any biscuit that has suffered some form of disfigurement, the kindest thing to do is to put the

little chaps out of their misery, quickly and painlessly, using hot tea.

The most famous Garibaldi in history, apart from the bald bloke in *Babylon Five*, was undoubtedly the Italian revolutionary, Giuseppe. He spent a large part of the nine-

teenth century up to all sorts of warfare but is best known for trying to unify the various states, city states and kingdoms of Italy. People often ask if the biscuit was named after this Garibaldi, and I say, 'Yes, sure, why not.' It's claimed that to sustain his fighting force of Redshirts, Garibaldi's cooks came up with the compact and energy-rich biscuit. Having tucked away a few Garibaldis, they were all set up to invade Naples. Personally, I think I would need at least half a packet for a job of that size, as I can quite easily see off five or six after mowing the lawn. I suppose it's lucky that the biscuit wasn't called a 'Redshirt'.

During the 1970s a chocolate-covered variant of the Garibaldi could be found in some supermarkets, and those who recall this biscuit are still vainly searching the aisles a quarter of a century later. I encountered the chocolate-covered Garibaldi only once, but I remember it clearly. It was at a village fête that we visited, late one summer's afternoon. A tea and cake stall was selling them, and my dad knew we could not pass up this particular opportunity. Due to my limited exposure to the biscuits, I couldn't say if they were manufactured that way or if they had been created by the lady running the stall from biscuits and her own melted chocolate. Looking back, I assume it was the latter but either way they were utterly fantastic.

Fruit Shortcake

Pure class in a biscuit, the Fruit Shortcake delivers a great deal of punch for a mid-range biscuit, which is often even seen as a low-end biscuit. The clever distribution of fruit and a topping of sugar granules ramps up the sugar content to make this quite unlike any of its shortcake-based cousins: the unwary biscuit eater may easily work their way through half a packet of these beguiling little biscuits before they realise it. The edge detail and the patterning on the back also serve to give this biscuit an almost frilly, harmless look that is very disarming, and again can lead to very high numbers of biscuits being consumed.

Of course, any biscuit that is crusted with sugar in this way will tend to condition us to find such things appealing. I have big problems at our local builders' merchants with the sheets of forty-grit sandpaper, which produce a sort of Pavlov's dog response, my mind turning to large sugary baking-sheet-sized biscuits. It's a good job they don't print a raisin pattern on the paper or I don't think I would be able to resist a nibble.

Icing

Icing is a gloriously lo-tech way of making biscuits sweeter. Simply mix sugar with water to make a paste and spread it on top. Sometimes icing has some baking soda and acetic acid added to it that fizzes away to create little bubbles of carbon dioxide, making for a light and crispy, if slightly vinegary, shell. Children especially understand the value of icing as it is a crude form of 'sweets', and will set about picking it off the underlying biscuit, no matter how impractical this is.

Iced Gems

It is 1850 and in the town of Reading, Berkshire, emerging biscuit giant Huntley and Palmer is experimenting with some new biscuit technology. However, the new biscuits emerge from the oven having actually shrunk. But Thomas Huntley likes the resulting mini-biscuits, which are christened Gems, and they sell well. Sixty years later the company added icing and from hereon children's birthday parties would be incomplete without them. Now made in Liverpool, there are very few biscuits that can trace their origins back 150 years, and which everybody can remember from their childhood, even if they have just had their telegram from the Queen.

I have to say that it was with a certain amount of trepidation that I recently decided to revisit the Iced Gem after a thirty-year gap. I've always pictured them as a sort of sweetened gravel. There have been some changes to the Iced Gem since I last had them: however, these seem to be mainly confined to the icing, which is no bad thing. Today's Iced Gems come in five main colours and flavours – white, yellow, orange, red and purple – and a chocolate version is also now available.

I also recall that the icing originally tasted of sugar and artificial blancmange-type flavours, and that there were some fairly lethal sharp points on the icing that could inflict minor havoc on the roof of one's mouth. So I don't know if I was happy or sad to see that the points have largely gone and that the icing actually has discernible flavours, slightly fruity ones at that. In fact, I really was put in mind of various berries, red-currants and blackberries. Anyway, a ten-point piping nozzle places the icing somewhere on the base and the vertical orientation of the biscuit is pot luck. The chances of getting a bag of entirely intact iced gems are remote, so there are lots of lumps of icing that can be eaten directly.

Just in case I was getting carried away, the biscuit base is still as dry and uninspiring as ever. Back in the late 1850s, things must have been pretty rough if just straight non-Iced Gems were a big hit. If we hopped in our time machine and went back to the mid-nineteenth century armed with a pack of Chocolate HobNobs or even just a simple Fruit Shortcake, no doubt we could produce sensory overload and stupefaction in the populace.

After my long absence, I did find myself mildly enjoying these little old biscuits, but I also strangely missed the puncture wounds in the top of my mouth. Needless to say, the younger members of staff devoured them with relish.

Party Rings

The primary mission of ring-shaped food is that it be briefly worn as a ring before being eaten. This in itself raises the potential to amuse, and when a shiny, hard icing topping is added you have something so enthralling that it graces events such as birthday parties and Sunday teas at your aunty's house. The Iced Ring was once a common sight: however, it suffered with its habitat being given over to the all-pervasive chocolate biscuit and now has been beaten back to its final stronghold as the Fox's Party Ring. Luckily the Party Ring is a splendid example of the genre, having brightly coloured icing with feathered details.

There is an advert on telly right now where a lady has strange food-related hallucinations. The cushions next to her on the settee turn into big slices of sponge cake and the rug becomes a large puddle of chocolate in which she starts to sink in the manner of someone drowning in quicksand. As a portent against bad interior design the patterns on her wallpaper turn into a flock of Iced Rings which fly across the room, just missing her head. You would have thought that she would be well advised to find out who has been spiking her hot chocolate with mescaline. But no, it appears that she merely needs to eat a small portion of a specific type of chicken korma ready meal to banish these disturbing visions. I would probably stay clear of cheese at bedtime as well, just to be on the safe side.

Wafers

The wafer is one of the many varied techniques whereby the food industry persuades us to buy and consume air. Prawn crackers are another, but at least the prawn cracker alerts the casual consumer to stay vigilant by bearing little relation to an actual prawn. In fact, if a prawn cracker ever encountered a prawn alive, dead or stir-fried, the prawn's surface moisture would inflict terrible soggy lesions upon the cracker, causing it to release tiny and harmless quantities of air. In an all-out fight between even a medium-sized prawn and a prawn cracker, my money would be on the prawn every time.

Pink Wafer

I like to think that I'm a fairly even-handed sort of chap when it comes to biscuit appraisal. After all, there is no need for spiteful comments or cheap jibes aimed at biscuits plying an honest trade, asking only of you that you eat them. One person's poison is another's pleasure, and the very reasons we might cite for detesting something may be the very reasons why somebody else adores it. However, when it comes to pink wafers, that all goes out the window.

Mostly, with such dreadful old biscuits, a simple mutual understanding is all that is needed: I won't bother you if you don't bother me. I had come to just such an arrangement with the Lemon Puff, whose tangy lemon cream, while stimulating, could never compensate for its cracker-box-reject taste. Still, I had a certain respect for its position. A sticky caramelised sugar glaze on the biscuit was futile and messy but it was at least individual. The scalloping around the edges of the rectangular biscuit also failed to add any real value, but merely provided more detritus to dislodge and get gummed under one's fingernails thanks to that sticky glaze. Yes, I may not have liked it, even thought it misguided and pompous, but after our initial falling out we steered clear of one another.

The Pink Wafer has never known such good grace, and takes every opportunity to parade its loathsome pink carcass. It doesn't even have the manners to keep itself to itself, frequently soiling nearby biscuits with tatty flakes shed from its miserable husk. It's not unknown for its corners to drop off, as if afflicted by some fearsome tropical disease. What could be less appetising than the biscuit version of the Singing Detective? I would prefer not to mention its cream filling, but for the sake of rigour let's quickly consider it. It really is nothing more than wafer adhesive, usually present in mere trace amounts. One enterprising manufacturer has stoked theirs full of vitamins and minerals, so you can get 10 per cent of the recommended daily intake of zinc from eating one. This is no doubt aimed at children, and concerned parents. Well,

that's fine, if you intend relying on Pink Wafers as an integral part of your daily diet. I think I might just stick to eating lots of fresh vegetables.

By rights, the Pink Wafer should have been left to disintegrate safely inside its own packet. Alas, it appears that it has friends in high places, or at least in the places that decide on the contents of biscuit selection packs. Perhaps it is its ability to add air which is prized here. It can't be its appeal because the Pink Wafers are always the last to go. Perhaps that is because the Pink Wafer seems to be the most manufactured of all biscuits. There is simply no way that you are ever going to be able to knock up a tray of them using your gas cooker, or to capture that artificial flavour.

The final damning piece of evidence is the appearance from time to time of packs in 'pound' shops alongside the imitation cookware and gingham tea towels. I have seen an even more troubling sight in one such shop: *Green* Wafers. I can tell you no more than that due to the very wide berth I afforded them.

Baking your own biscuits is not a difficult thing to do. The recipes tend to be very simple, the ingredients relatively straightforward and most can be baked in under thirty minutes with results that are, as often as not, sublime. The aroma of a rack of biscuits hot from the oven is beyond compare.

At this point you might think that we are about to regale you with at least seven or eight of our favourite recipes. Well, no. The trouble is most of us simply can't be bothered. Let's face it, biscuits are for relaxing with. Who wants to spend an hour or more fussing around in the kitchen with weighing scales and a wooden spoon?

The answer is Americans, who like to bake their cookies. Given that most American kitchens seem to be the size of the average UK leisure centre, perhaps it's just a means of passing the time while they try to recall the route out of the rest of the house. However, they often resort to shop-bought ready-made cookie dough which just needs baking. This is an operation of about equal complexity to popping some deep-frozen sausage rolls in the oven. Mind you, if we were faced with supermarket shelves filled with Oreos we would feel compelled to bake our own biscuits, too.

Does Somebody Live There?

There is a wonderfully lazy way of getting hold of homemade biscuits without suffering the washing-up fallout from actually making them in your own home. Simply buy 'homemade' biscuits. I've often wondered how 'homemade' biscuits are made commercially. Even if Wifey and I spent eight hours a day baking biscuits in our

1960s Cannon gas oven (now converted to North Sea gas) I doubt whether we could produce enough to supply and support a national distribution chain. This is to say nothing of the amount of trips we would need to make to the supermarket to buy flour and so forth, or the strain it would place on our already ageing food mixer. So how do they do it? There are two possible answers.

🫖 **The manufacturers subcontract out the baking to a community of biscuit-baking homes.** This would probably work best if all the houses were on the same street or estate. Production could be scaled up by enrolling more streets into the production line, and could be streamlined by delivering all the raw ingredients as they pick up the finished homemade biscuits.

🫖 **The manufacturers get somebody to live permanently in their biscuit factory, thereby turning it into a home, and rendering anything made there 'homemade'.** For good measure they should also decorate, get some new curtains, a cat or dog and a real log fire, as these are often the things that turn a house into a home, and should work on an industrial unit or factory, too.

The most troubling moniker for biscuits is 'hand-baked', implying that individuals with incredibly hot hands cook the biscuits one at a time by cupping them in their hands. Alternatively they might just be grabbing a handful of biscuit mix and shoving it in the oven. Either way, it has to be a dangerous and probably unhygienic practice.

Tunnock's Wafer

On their own, wafers are pretty woeful specimens. They need to seek the help of other foodstuffs whenever possible to cover up the fact that they taste like mildly sweetened cardboard. Most gleefully accept their destiny as a glorified handle to a scoop of ice cream. The really lucky ones are reprieved, rehabilitated and end up inside a 'Tunnock's Real Milk Chocolate Caramel Wafer Biscuit'.

The Scottish have more experience of biscuit baking and the skilled deployment of sugar in biscuits and cakes than perhaps any other nation on earth. T. Tunnock Ltd of Uddingston, Glasgow, a family-run company that dates back to the 1890s, are a Scottish national treasure. The basic design of the Tunnock's Wafer consists of four layers of caramel sandwiched between five wafers. This is wrapped in a thin shell of actual milk chocolate. Each biscuit is clad in its own rectangle of foil and paper, adorned with distinctive red and gold stripes. Poet Laureate Ted Hughes was fond of scribbling short verses on the backs of Tunnock's wrappers, some of which he donated to the Tunnock's Caramel Wafer Appreciation Society of St Andrew's University. Apparently some in the society thought that he had committed a sacrilegious act and defiled the great wafer's wrapper, and as such weren't as impressed as no doubt they were supposed to be.

The wrapper bears the legendary and proud boast that 'More than 4,000,000 of these biscuits are made and sold each week'. Who eats this unrelenting tide of biscuits? That's the question that regularly crosses the mind of the casual Tunnock's eater. It was once assumed that the answer to this paradox lay with the Scots themselves. There are over 5 million of them. They should be able to take care of them all, even if they ate only one each a week. It has also been pointed out that the Scottish apparently enjoy a higher standard of healthcare than the rest of the UK. Maybe this helps certain individuals cope with massive intakes of Tunnock's wafers while strapped into advanced medical devices. I don't know for sure as this is pure speculation.

I was very happy to see the review eight-pack of wafers bearing the informative message 'Still original size'. It's wonderful to see a biscuit manufacturer taking such direct steps to address the issues that often trouble biscuit eaters.

Chocolate Covered

Chocolate-covered biscuits and their adversaries, the chocolate bars, size each other up across the Venn diagram as they jostle to provide that most keenly contested of moments, the mid-morning treat. Pat Benatar was fond of saying back in the 1980s, 'Love is a battlefield'. Well, Pat, it's a walk in the park compared to the titanic struggles for supremacy in the chocolate-covered snack arena. Let's take a look at a few classics.

Mint Viscount

When growing up, there were certain biscuits that enjoyed a status above the proletariats in the biscuit tin. Such biscuits typically descended from their special shelf in the larder at Sunday teatime after the ham sandwiches and celery sticks had given it their best shot. Such 'second cup of tea' biscuits tended to put in alternate weeks with their peers from the cake world, such as Ginger Cake and Battenberg. Given their high status, a single biscuit was considered a fair portion, two was definitely a treat and three completely out of the question.

The Mint Viscount was such a biscuit. Anything covered in chocolate and robed in finest coloured foil was obviously from the same plane of existence as Easter eggs and Christmas selection tins. The name Viscount conveyed the status and opulent splendour of the little mint-cream-filled biscuits. Indeed, had that famous advert contained the line 'Ambassador, with this third offer of a Mint Viscount you are really spoiling us', then it would have portrayed a much more convincing representation of Ambassadorial hospitality.

Burton's Viscount biscuit has never strayed from its chosen path of two flavours, mint and orange, shunning all others for reasons we can only guess at. The mint flavour seems to have been the more popular, possibly due to its end of teatime appearances making appropriate allusions to after-dinner mints. The Viscount design consists of a circular, crunchy, slightly gritty biscuit base, with a small disc-shaped blob of cream on top, all covered in a fairly useful milk chocolate. Each biscuit is then wrapped in a square of colour-coded foil, green for mint and orange for . . . orange. The skilled Viscount eater will flatten out the foil and use it to make a small model, trinket or some form of projectile.

The image of luxury is further enhanced by the Viscount's unwavering insistence on travelling in a reclined position, thirty-two degrees above the horizontal by my protractor. Like transatlantic passengers flying business class, Viscounts would arrive at the tea-table well rested and seated comfortably in their specially moulded insert tray.

Club

I find it hard, even painful, to talk about Jacob's Club biscuit. For many, myself included, the Club biscuit at its height represented the pinnacle of chocolate-covered biscuit bars. It was widely admired both by consumers and by those in the industry. Nanny Nicey, who worked in a canteen during the early 1970s, remembers how the Club biscuits always sold out first, way ahead of some of the other biscuits that grace these pages.

The Club had it all: useful, well-executed flavours such as fruit, orange and mint, each delivered in a generous and crispy biscuit. It was entirely covered in a hard dark milk chocolate, so thick that in strategic places you could bite it off in lumps. Its wrappers were elegant and instantly recognisable, so much so that spotting a lesser-known variety was an event, of equal magnitude to seeing a Ford Escort in a colour other than pale blue. (Actually, at the height of the Club's powers, cars were painted in various sorts of metallic-effect brown, occasionally reminiscent of wooden fence panelling or fake tan, and this would be considered bad taste even in 1970s Britain.)

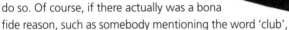

TV advertising featured a jingle so catchy that people would sing and hum it, for no good reason other than they liked to do so. Of course, if there actually was a bona fide reason, such as somebody mentioning the word 'club', then everybody would chime up in unison, 'If you like a lot of chocolate on your biscuit, join our Club'. The adverts featured various groups or clubs of individuals all singing the jingle, such as pensioners playing bowls and American footballers (I could well be making this up).

Unwrapping a Club was a series of personal preferences. First, slip off the outer paper tube, leaving it intact, or tug at its seam, opening it to form a small rectangular sheet. Then unwrap the foil-backed paper inner, either peeling the foil away from the paper or reforming the wrapper back into the shape of the biscuit. Personally, I liked to make two small origami dogs from the wrappers. Others rolled them into tubes or folded them over and over to make a minute and rather poor mirror.

Club biscuits are still available today but they have been entirely redesigned. This is the reason for my anguish, and I would appreciate it now if I could have a little time to myself. Thanks, I'll be all right in a minute or two.

Penguin

Take two cocoa-flavoured biscuits, sandwich some chocolate-cream icing between them, then coat lightly in chocolate. Finally, think of a name for your creation. In 1932, William McDonald, a biscuit manufacturer in Glasgow, did just that and decided that he should call his new creation 'Penguin'. This became a McVitie's brand when McDonald joined with McVitie's and Price, MacFarlane Lang and Crawford's to form United Biscuits in 1946. So if you think that you can't remember a time before Penguins you are probably right. Unless you are older than seventy, or you have lousy memory. Or perhaps you've never heard of them in which case I expect you're American and somebody British is forcing you to read this.

The Penguin is the flagship chocolate-covered biscuit bar of the mighty McVitie's, and has been the yardstick by which other chocolate-covered biscuits bars are measured. It pretty much created the now familiar 'chocolate count line' genre, whereby individually wrapped biscuits are sold by number rather than by weight. As we will see, it has been the inspiration for other biscuits which have gone on to become icons in their own right. It also had its imitators which had to be dealt with.

There are many people to whom it has occurred that the Penguin is nothing more than a chocolate-covered Bourbon biscuit. It's not. The texture of the biscuits is altogether different, being crisper and less dense. The chocolate-cream filling is also much paler. The covering of milk chocolate is quite thin and yet registers as the main ingredient. In the Penguin we see once again a biscuit that must be enjoyed as a whole, as analysis of its components does not convey its charm.

When I was little, Penguins were wrapped simply in three different-coloured wrappers: green, blue and red. Each had the minimal Penguin logo and they were identical save for the colour. Green ones were usually left to last as it was common knowledge to children that all green sweets or confectionery are in some way derived from washing-up liquid. Today's Penguin eaters are treated to lolly-stick-style jokes on the back of the wrapper, and pictures of penguins in a variety of amusing situations. I think the old foil wraps were better, much in the way that radio is better than TV, and books are better than radio, right back to no cave painting was better than cave painting. Anyway, with their seventy-fifth anniversary fast approaching, maybe United Biscuits could knock out a big batch of retro Penguins in the old wrappers. That would be the biscuit equivalent of driving a beautifully restored classic car. Or, even better, pick eight wrappers from the past and put them in the pack in chronological order, to form a little history lesson.

Penguin was one of the first biscuits to be advertised by name rather than company, so much so that the Penguin brand now forms an umbrella in its own right under which a recent slew of new products has been created. The Penguin itself is sometimes available in mint and orange flavours, but has kept its dignity thus far and resisted the urge to go mini or giant. Other products include cake bars, dipping pots, Chuckas (which are little pots of biscuit, chocolate and caramel pellets) and Splatz and Mini-Splatz (which appear to be re-engineered BN biscuits). I think there is enough continuity with the original Penguin to make a valid link but they stay far enough away from it so as not to erode its integrity. So, despite all this activity, Penguins have lost none of their self-esteem, which is no mean feat. Still, there is always the ice cream or breakfast cereal option available.

Perhaps one of the reasons for Penguin's appeal is its association with the emperor penguin. Penguins are one of nature's premium comedy birds, which is a bit of a coup, seeing as Guinness had already bagged the Toucan and the Ostrich. The famous 'P . . P . . Pick up a . . . Penguin' strapline is now confined to the packs; however, in the golden days of Penguin TV advertising a few shots of some penguins waddling around and the uttering of the catchphrase were all that was needed to deliver a memorable advert.

Penguin has had to defend its honour against those who would seek to pass themselves off as one. In 1997 Mr Justice Walker found in favour of United Biscuits (McVitie's), who were more than a little upset by UK supermarket chain Asda's Puffin biscuit. Asda had chosen to sail as close to the wind as they could with their packaging, so that consumers would know that they were offering a Penguin-like product. However, they went too far, and the combination of seabirds beginning with the letter P, its cartoon picture and the pack design landed them in court. As the learned judge so ably put it, 'Had the Asda product been called, for example, "Bison", to take another name from the original list, with a cartoon picture of a brown woolly bison on the packaging, these proceedings could not possibly succeed.' The case proved to be something of a landmark ruling for UK supermarkets, who have subsequently all backed off with their 'me-too' type products.

Foreign

Travel broadens the mind. It also teaches us that the rest of the world doesn't really have a clue about making decent biscuits, but why should they when they don't drink proper tea either? Occasionally there are glimmers of hope, but it's all a bit fleeting as they don't really understand why one biscuit might be better than another when it comes to teaming it up with a nice cuppa. Still, they muddle on in their own well-meaning way, so let's take a look at a few handpicked examples that offer some hope.

Tim Tam

In 1958 an Australian called Ian Norris, director of biscuit technology for Australian biscuit maker Arnott's, was on a world tour hunting for ideas. While in the UK he encountered the Penguin and as legend has it thought, That's not a bad idea for a biscuit . . . but we'll make a better one. On return to Australia he began work and five years later Arnott's launched the Tim Tam. The name was taken from the winner of the 1958 Kentucky Derby, attended by Ross Arnott, who thought the name perfect for their new biscuit. Of course, he may have had to think again if the outcome of the race had been different. Biscuit history could have been changed for ever if the third-placed 'Noureddin' or unplaced 'Red Hot Pistol' had triumphed.

The average Australian is a modest type, not in the habit of making overblown or exaggerated claims. However, they all seem confident in two things: that the Tim Tam is a work of perfection; and not to have eaten one is not to have truly lived. The UK and Australia have a common cultural heritage and are forever engaging in friendly rivalry in such areas as sport, music, low-budget TV soaps and blokes that annoy crocodiles (I'm sure we could find some lads who would do that: Bez from the Happy Mondays, for instance). So how does the Tim Tam stack up against its forbear, the Penguin; was Ian Norris right in thinking he had made a better biscuit?

First, the Tim Tam is quite a bit smaller and lighter than the Penguin, and its biscuit layers are seemingly closer to meringue or honeycomb than an ancestral Bourbon. It's this highly porous biscuit that enables the execution of the Tim Tam Slam, a messy pastime that I'll discuss in the following chapter on 'Dunking'. The tone of the two biscuits is also somewhat different: the Tim Tam is a warm bronze to the Penguin's almost slate-grey chocolate and biscuit. The more expensive Tim Tam has a buttery richness to both its chocolate and its chocolate cream. Arnott's actually describe their chocolate as having a caramel flavour. This all begins to make more sense when we consider that Arnott's markets the Tim Tam primarily to females between twenty and thirty-five, whereas the Penguin is aimed at the broader target of the family shopping basket. This is also reflected in their packaging: the individually wrapped Penguin can find its way into lunchboxes and sit alongside tills in cafés and shops, whereas the Tim Tam simply rests with its cohorts in a little plastic tray inside its outer wrapper. The Tim Tam has a rolling list of varieties, of which eight are available at any one time, with Original, Double Coat and Caramel forming the unchanging core. All the obvious bases are covered, such as Mocha, Dark Chocolate, White Chocolate, and Hazelnut, which seems to be a favourite Arnott's ingredient.

In an ironic twist, Tim Tams, like its mentor the Penguin, have had their own problems with 'me-tooism'. When the American food giant Campbell's added Arnott's to its portfolio, many Australians saw this as a threat to their much-loved biscuit heritage. No doubt as some form of protest, Australian entrepreneur Dick Smith saw this as a perfect opportunity to launch a virtually identical biscuit called the 'Tem-*p*-tin'. I got my hands on a pack and found the flavour to be not quite up to Tim Tam levels. Nevertheless Arnott's acted to protect its brand. They settled out of court and forced Dick Smith to make some changes. The troublesome, italicised '*p*' was Romanised, and the hyphens vanished altogether: the Tem-*p*-tin became Temptin. Maybe if he had called it 'Bison' he wouldn't have got into any trouble in the first place.

I see the Tim Tam and Penguin as two quite different biscuits in most respects. The Tim Tam is a classy little product, tastes great and its insubstantial nature affords the sucking of tea and coffee through it by Tim Tam Slammers such as Natalie Imbruglia. However, the mighty Penguin offers a more satisfying mouthful with a taste that has stood the test of time. There is something to learn from both biscuits and if you haven't tried one or the other then seek it out.

Euro-choc

Every year during the summer our music charts are invaded by saccharine and repetitive tunes from Spain, Germany and even, on occasion, Belgium. It's our own fault, of course: we hear them while on holiday with our guards lowered by sun and sangria. Once home a kind of withdrawal sets in and we look to prolong the suffering by demanding them from our local record shop. In this way another pan-European pop phenomenon is created. Then, at the end of September they become casualties of the first frosts of autumn, much like my French beans. So, does the same thing occur with biscuits? Not really, because by and large continental biscuits are pretty grim and misguided affairs.

There has been a long-running dispute between Britain and the rest of the EU concerning chocolate that dates back to 1973. An opt-out from European law allowed the UK (along with Ireland and Denmark) to continue to call our favourite brands 'chocolate', even though they contained milk or vegetable oil. The purists led by Belgium and France insisted that chocolate may only be called chocolate if it is made using solely cocoa butter for its fat content. In March 2000, it was decided that the simple addition of the word 'family' to describe UK products abroad as 'family milk chocolate' would do the trick. Before then, several UK governments had had to fend off Brussels' attempts to rename our chocolate 'vegelate' and even calling for an outright ban. So, with our blood boiling, let's look at Euro-choc, whatever that turns out to be.

Petit Beurre and Petit Écolier

The French Petit Beurre biscuit is one of those things that makes you question if you've grasped the rudiments of the French language. Does it mean 'little butter biscuit' in a cute sort of way? I incline to the other possibility – that they are made with a little butter – which would explain why they don't taste very buttery. If you want a buttery French biscuit, then get yourself a pack of Galettes Breton. They don't even mention butter in their name, but are really one of the best French biscuits I've encountered, with melt-in-the-mouth buttery tenderness. Perhaps there is some strange Gallic inverted biscuit nomenclature. I must look out for '*sans absolutement les poissions et canards*' biscuits next time in the hypermarket.

It is an exceedingly French thing to combine bread and chocolate. There are numerous examples such as the 'pain au chocolat' and huge jars of chocolate spread for French bread. It was only a matter of time before somebody took a Petit Beurre and slapped a big old lump of chocolate on it. Leading French biscuit manufacturer LU did just that and called it, rather dubiously, a 'small schoolboy'.

On first encountering the Petit Écolier it appears bizarre, having embossed onto its slab of chocolate an odd-looking child carrying a basket. I think I ate my way through about four packs before I worked out that's what it was. You may also infer from that statement that no matter how much of a ribbing I'm about to deliver, they are actually quite tasty. On further investigation it turns out that the lad in question is called Jacques, son of poster artist Firmin Bouisset and painted by him in 1897. The baker and biscuit-maker LU adopted the image of the small schoolboy, originally pictured eating a straightforward Petit Beurre, over the even stranger image of a flying, trumpeting, laurel-distributing angel. Back in the nineteenth century, Jacques must have thought Petit Beurres were cutting-edge biscuit heaven. Nowadays they are ranked just below balsa wood, charcoal briquettes and airline food in the league table of appetising things to eat.

But back to the Petit Écolier. There is something decidedly disjointed about it: the chocolate and biscuit are very obviously created separately, then quickly fused together to create the finished item. While the edge of the slab is firmly attached, underneath gaps abound. I can appreciate the technical imperatives for this, but the result is a bit like eating a packet of Rich Teas while stealing bites off a block of milk chocolate. The overall effect is unsettling as it seems that the Petit Beurre has acquired the chocolate out of desperation, and indeed the slab may choose to up and leave if it gets a better offer, which seems likely.

Choco Leibniz

German bakers Bahlsen are perhaps best known in the UK for their Choco Leibniz, a refined chocolate slab with a biscuit stuck in it. Bahlsen, who were founded in Hannover in 1891, have biscuit bakeries in several European countries but none in the UK. As such the whole Bahlsen range is distinctively continental, which is to say it makes perhaps the most sense when viewed from over the brim of a coffee cup rather than a mug of tea.

The Choco Leibniz is a cult biscuit that enjoys a fiercely loyal following. This ensures that there is always a place for it in your supermarket. The base biscuit is essentially a German version of the Petit Beurre, renamed the Leibniz. I actually found it to be quite a pleasant little biscuit, with the butter flavour clearly present. These are available without chocolate or formed into animal-shaped biscuits to make Leibniz Zoo, which boast a particularly amusing penguin.

The Choco Leibniz prides itself on its unique construction, which involves filling moulds with melted chocolate. Just as the chocolate starts to set in goes the Leibniz biscuit, interesting side up. German engineering ensures that there is excellent chocolate-to-biscuit bonding here, and no whimsical holes or gaps. The result is a biscuit that has an outer frill of chocolate and very fine detail in its chocolate relief. The first thing to do when eating one is to remove the chocolate frill with your incisors. Having done so, you can hold the biscuit securely without getting chocolatey fingers.

So rich is a Choco Leibniz that it can almost get caught around one's tonsils. I find it requires hot drinks to wash it down, or having experience of eating full-strength EU-sanctioned chocolate. Bahlsen tell me that people are most loyal to the plain chocolate version; however, when the product is in any sort of promotion the milk chocolate one takes the lion's share of sales. Once again we see the semi-fanatical plain chocolate crowd making their voice heard.

Oreo

Oh dear, oh dear. It's the biggest-selling biscuit on the planet and it doesn't even know it is a biscuit. The Oreo is baked across the world by Nabisco, the name being a contraction of 'The National Biscuit Company' of the USA. Like so many biscuits, the Oreo displays that innate quality

The word 'cookie' is derived from the Dutch word 'koekje' meaning 'little cake'. Clearly these aren't little cakes so that's slightly annoying. The word 'biscuit', by contrast, comes from the French words 'bis' and 'cuir', meaning literally twice-cooked. This refers to how biscuits used to be made back in the sixteenth century, for ship's rations. The simple dough was baked once to form the biscuit, and then received a long slow baking that dried it out as a form of preservation. The resulting 'hard tack' was then eaten with meals or ground up to make a fairly nasty sort of porridge. These biscuits were so hard that it was common for sailors to break their teeth on them.

The French settlers in the southern states of the USA were also fond of a few 'twice cookeds'. However, these biscuits were a sort of dumpling or cobbler, which were served with stews and gravy. When I say gravy I use the term in its loosest possible sense, as the 'gravy' most popular with biscuits is made from lumps of sausage, flour and sausage fat and is a glutinous, white, pasty-looking affair. Anyone who has spent time with a large family dog suffering from a weak stomach would have a powerful sense of déjà-vu if they asked for a plate of biscuits in the USA.

We can therefore at least sympathise with the imperative not to order the wrong sort of biscuits, which must have led to the adoption of the Dutch word over the French for the same thing. So, before we wade into the Americans for annoyingly calling their biscuits cookies, let's pause for a moment and blame the French instead. We might want to tick off the Dutch but I seriously doubt they would even notice.

that you have to be raised on them to like them. Outside of the US, I suspect it's sold mainly to Americans abroad or eccentrics, yet within its homeland it apparently enjoys sales of eleven billion a year (or four billion, it's hard to be sure).

The main ingredient in Oreos is our old friend sugar, which is used to fashion two dark cocoa biscuits decorated with the Oreo's logo. Sandwiched between is a layer of white stuff which is euphemistically called cream, but is probably best thought of as soft icing. Variations in the cream's depth and coatings of fudge also help shoehorn in extra quantities of sugar. In fact, the minty ones would probably put up a good fight against a slab of Kendal Mint Cake in terms of sheer carbohydrate loading potential.

Oreos seem to be supplied in cardboard boxes bearing eating instructions on their sides. To non-American eyes, the idea of putting instructions on how to eat a biscuit on the box might seem ridiculous. Little diagrams and captions tell you to disassemble your Oreo and then scrape out the white stuff, which, rather than discard, you're supposed to eat first. You are also advised to drink milk while doing this. Any Americans whom I've approached about this whole area become a bit prickly, saying it's all part of the ritual of the product, but it appears that the absurdity isn't entirely lost on them.

Still, it is a testament to the success of the Oreo and the strength of the brand that they are imitated around the world. Some time ago I got my hands on a pack of Hi-Ro from the Philippines, an Oreo-alike which a little misguidedly claimed to be of 'English Quality'.

Pocky

You are going to have to allow me a little leeway here, as we are about to visit a unique spot on the mighty biscuit Venn diagram: the triple union of biscuits, crackers and chocolate-covered biscuits. What do we find here? None other than the exceedingly odd Mikado, also known as Pocky, and not to be confused with Jacob's Mikado (see p.99).

Essentially a long, straight, salt-less pretzel 80 per cent dipped in chocolate, the Mikado is made by French biscuit manufacturer LU under licence from the Japanese snack firm Glico. LU make two varieties: the traditional plain chocolate one and a more recent milk chocolate version. In Japan one can find Pocky in strawberry, green tea, rainbow and even lime and watermelon flavours. I've been told that it offends Japanese sensibilities to touch the chocolate directly, hence the little lolly-stick uncovered bit. It also offends some people to hear Beatles songs being publicly murdered so Tokyo karaoke bars have bowls of Pocky on the tables to help ease the suffering. At least, I think that's why they're there.

As everybody no doubt knows, pretzels were invented by a seventh-century Italian monk, who was trying to come up with something that could be eaten during Lent. Given the restrictions on what could be consumed, he didn't have much to work with, namely flour, water and salt. Believe it or not, the first pretzels were soft, which is remarkable, given their ingredients: I would have thought they would have come out like bricks. It is believed that in order to remind the eater that Lent was a time of prayer, our baking monk formed the familiar pretzel shape as an echo of the folded arms of somebody at prayer. It's also thought that a possible derivation for 'pretzel' is the Latin word '*pretiola*' which means 'little reward'.

The kind monks gave pretzels to the poor, who, being poor, were grateful for them (though no doubt once the poor had sorted themselves out and got back on their feet, pretzels wouldn't be top of their shopping list). They were also given to children as a reward for reciting their prayers correctly. It appears that back in the seventh century children had a much lower threshold for bribery. The younger members of staff can't be persuaded to tidy their room for anything less than half a pack of Jaffa Cakes.

Eventually a baking accident led to pretzels becoming even harder, and with it smaller, I expect. This was seen as a bonus as they lasted longer and could be distributed to the poor with greater ease. By now the poor must have had quite a serious thirst on them, and were no doubt gasping for a pint or maybe a gin and tonic. Presumably at some point the Germans, who had a keen interest in drinking beer, must have noticed the crowds of poor beating a path from the monastery to their pubs after eating too many salty snacks. As a result, Germany took over the mantle of leading pretzel-making nation.

No doubt dry-roasted peanuts have a very similar story to tell.

㉑ Dunking

Dunking is probably as old as the first hot meal cooked by mankind. Whenever we look for the originators of stuff that is really old (but not cave man old) it always seems to be the ancient civilisations that grew up around the Tigris and Euphrates rivers in what is modern day Iraq, about 8,000 years ago. Sometimes it's the ancient Egyptians but that is so predictable. The ancient Sumerians don't seem to have so many TV documentaries as the rest so we'll give them a break and pretend they came up with it. Now of course I have no idea if this was actually the case but it sounds good doesn't it? Anyhow the Iraqis like a good pot of strong tea and a biscuit or cake if there is one going, so that is good circumstantial evidence.

Things probably didn't change much until the reign of Queen Victoria, who had just had a jam and cream sponge named after her. Not content with leaving her mark on the cake world, Victoria set her sights on the world of biscuits by inventing the Butter Osborne, after her much-loved holiday home on the Isle of Wight. And butter. Being a queen, and as it was her first go at biscuit invention, the results were a fairly grim, thick, chalky Rich Tea sort of biscuit. Insisting that her subjects eat at least one packet each on her birthday, it quickly became the fashion to dunk them, in order to successfully complete one's patriotic duty. No doubt the colonies decided they would take up dunking as well, just to be on the safe side.

Right, that's history rewritten. Let's take a look at some dunking techniques and issues.

How To Do It

To the casual observer, dunking is purely the act of submerging part of your biscuit in your tea, pulling it out and eating the wet bit. Anybody who has tried dunking or is a full-time dunking enthusiast will know that there is much, much more to it than that. Let's explore some of the things that can go wrong and strategies that you can use for successful dunking.

The Biscuit Is Too Big For The Cup

There are a few simple things that you can try here. First, simply try to find a larger cup. Second, choose smaller biscuits or those that lend themselves to dunking, such as finger-shaped or rectangular ones.

If you are hell bent on a particular combination of biscuit and cup despite the problems, then the first thing you can try is to break the biscuit in two, and dunking the two halves. This is of course a crude and unsightly technique but it's always there as an option. Its main drawbacks are the unnecessary creation of crumbs leading to 'bottom sludge' (see below), and the disfiguring of perfectly good biscuits. You could try taking a bite or two out of the biscuit, but this too is prone to creating crumbs. Try to minimise this with a mouth-hoovering action over the broken edges.

The experienced approach is called 'dunk nibble rotate'. This requires a fairly full cup or mug of tea to begin with, and it should be piping hot. In the case of round biscuits, even something as large as a Digestive will be able to dip a small portion of its edge into the cup to meet the hot tea. This creates a geometric line called a 'chord' whose endpoints lie on the circumference and whose perpendicular bisector passes through the centre of the circle. The angle theta subtended by joining the ends of the chord to the centre of the circle is crucial. The higher the value of theta, the quicker you'll be able to eat your biscuit. All fairly straightforward so far?

The dunked bit can then be nibbled off to create a slight corner. The biscuit should then be rotated so that a perpendicular line passes through the centre of the biscuit and the end of the chord. Either end will do: you don't have to be too scientific about it. This time much more of the biscuit will 'dip' into the hot tea and you'll be able to nibble off a bigger bit. Repeat the process until the biscuit is narrowed enough to fit into the mug when rotated through ninety degrees. Typically you should reach complete immersion potential in one to four dunk-nibble-rotate cycles. As the tea is absorbed or drunk the degree of difficulty increases until you reach the limit at which point the tea is too low to be reached by the biscuit edge. At this point simply revert back to the inferior crumb-prone techniques.

Don't worry if that sounded complex: it's really quite easy once you get used to it. It can also become quite an addictive pastime, with proponents getting a buzz by deliberately seeking out challenging large-diameter biscuits, although still avoiding small cups and mugs.

Bottom Sludge

The facets of dunking are interrelated so we have touched on sludge already. Bottom sludge is caused by crumbs falling to the bottom of the cup and creating a biscuity porridge. As you near the end of your tea, this sludge rushes down the edge of the cup or mug to meet you, like a small mud slide. While it is no doubt nutritious and maybe even tasty, being formed from biscuits and tea, the vast majority of people don't care for it, preferring to drink pure tea.

So what can be done to avoid sludge issues? The first and most obvious is to prevent the build-up of sludge in the first place, limiting the amount of biscuit crumbs. Here are some other simple tips:

- Always tap your biscuit a couple of times on the side of the biscuit tin to eliminate excess crumbs.
- Avoid broken or damaged biscuits for dunking, and if you do use them, dunk the unbroken side.
- Avoid very crumbly biscuits or those with loosely attached frilly bits.

Breakage

It should always be remembered that dunking times will vary depending on tea temperature. Very hot tea will penetrate biscuits much faster than warm tea. Failure to compensate for tea temperature is one of the most common reasons for breakage, which is when the bottom of your biscuit fails to re-emerge from your tea, or drops off and falls back into your tea as you lift out the biscuit.

As a dunked biscuit absorbs tea, it begins to swell. Sugars in the biscuit begin to dissolve, fats melt, starch grains swell and unravel and the whole structure becomes soft and pliable. In addition, it becomes substantially heavier. If the tea has penetrated right to the biscuit's core, then there is a very high chance that breakage will occur. To lessen the risk, the biscuit should always be lifted vertically from the tea. Deviating from ninety degrees will cause the now heavier and flexible dunked portion to swing down to the vertical position like a plumb line, and this could cause a tear near to the dunking boundary, quickly leading to breakage.

When moving close to breakage, you should avoid rapid acceleration and deceleration. Overcoming the inertial mass of the damp biscuit can again lead to unscheduled breakage. This applies even if you are in a micro-gravity environment such as a plane in a parabolic freefall trajectory or lift that has become detached from its supporting cables. It's only going to make a bad situation worse if you drop half a soggy Rich Tea in your lap.

Differential Uptake

Sometimes biscuits can display a 'differential uptake' in tea across their structure. This is especially common in composite sandwich structures: outer surfaces may be baked harder than the inner, which may itself be porous. This can lead the tea to permeate at different rates across the biscuit. It's not really a problem; I just thought you might like to know, that's all. Once again, use a good hot cuppa and you'll be fine.

The Tim Tam Slam

The Tim Tam Slam goes by many names but the basic principle is very simple to grasp: it's simply a matter of using the biscuit as a straw. Due to the lightness of the biscuit, its airtight seal of chocolate, and its sprightly dimensions, the Tim Tam is eminently suited to this procedure. To perform the Tim Tam Slam, bite off diagonally opposed corners, pop one corner in your tea, the other in your mouth, and suck. The hot tea will off course wreak havoc on the little Antipodean biscuit's innards, leading to a complete and often catastrophic failure of structural integrity. For this reason you are advised to pop the whole thing into your mouth before it disintegrates. I would certainly recommend not doing this sort of thing in front of impressionable youngsters, unless you particularly enjoy frequent redecorating.

Although this might sound like a grubby old business, I have been told that in Australia the Tim Tam Slam is a perfectly acceptable activity whatever the social situation or occasion. As an alternative, the smaller Cadbury's Chocolate Finger is also very good for slamming.

A Little Bit
of Cake

Cake

Biscuits don't always have the attention of the teapot all to themselves. Often they have to share the table with small sandwiches and, more worryingly, with that other rival for our sweet-toothed affection, cake.

Cake has always taken itself much more seriously than the humble biscuit, which it considers merely as a supporting actor upon its own glittering stage. Biscuits are always ready for action, there at a moment's notice. Cake, on the other hand, likes to make a bit of an entrance by being nicely cut up and arranged on plates. It also likes to frequent exclusive little boutiques, called cake shops, where it can compare its fillings and diameters with other cakes. Cake loves being seen in the window, displaying its various toppings and fruits, both fresh and dried. Often such places have a little back room where cake, with the help of a pot of tea and maybe even a trolley, can entertain eager visitors.

Homemade cakes demand complete attention even when in the oven, and often take hours getting themselves made and decorated. They like to have nice things bought for them from the cake-making section in the supermarket, such as their own special bars of chocolate, which nobody else is allowed to touch.

Cake likes to trot out its part in history, like the time it got burnt by King Alfred. And who can forget its Gothic moment as Miss Havisham's decaying wedding cake in *Great Expectations*? It also insists that it gets invited to parties, which it often brings to a complete standstill, demanding that the music is turned off and the lights dimmed as it gets to do its little bit.

Cake manifests itself in a variety of ways, from the lowly tart to the grandest gateau, from a simple sticky bun to a candle-topped birthday cake. Plainly cake is a big subject and would like to have a whole book to itself, or a series of books, or a section in the library. However, we are going to look at just a few examples simply because they make me laugh.

Jaffa Cakes

The Eternal Debate

Throughout the course of human history there have been a few really big philosophical questions that have occupied the world's great minds. Does God exist? Is there a theory that can unify general relativity and quantum mechanics? However, 'Are Jaffa Cakes biscuits or cakes?' shouldn't be one of them, as they are plainly cakes. That's why they are called Jaffa *Cakes*, not Jaffa Biscuits. Simple. Let's move on. But this is a question that doesn't seem to want to go away. Who is the main culprit still insisting that the Jaffa Cake is a biscuit? None other than the civil service in the guise of the Inland Revenue. They have a vested interest, and would love the Jaffa Cake to be a biscuit. It all comes down to tax: when VAT was created, it was decided not to tax the staple things in life that we simply cannot do without, this fine book being one of them, of course. Cake is another. Biscuits, however, have to tread very carefully: it all comes down to where you put your chocolate. If it is discreetly hidden away in chunks or between two halves of biscuit, as in a chocolate Viennese finger, then the VAT man won't spot it. Slap it ostentatiously all over the top of your biscuit and he'll instantly tell you that your 'luxury' product is now liable for VAT.

ORANGES

When everything else is letting you down, there is one fruit above all others that you can rely on: the orange. Oranges have a special role in the universe by providing one of the key reference points in our perception of reality, and the bonus is that they grow on trees. Not only do oranges taste of orange, but they smell of orange. Their masterstroke, though, was to get a whole colour named after them. Not some dodgy made-up paint-chart colour like 'watermelon'. No, a proper colour that appears in the rainbow. To make sure that orange continues in its unassailable position it has even ensured that no new words have entered the English language that might properly rhyme with it. That's why there is no such thing as a 'boringe' or a 'morange', when plainly these are perfectly good words that deserve a chance.

This is the essential problem. If the Jaffa Cake were to be a biscuit, it would swiftly be taxed, where as a cake it gets away with it. Unsurprisingly, the Inland Revenue thought that the Jaffa Cake was really a biscuit while McVitie's knew it was a cake. The VAT Act of 1983 was a bit woolly about what constituted a cake, so in 1991 it fell to a tribunal to decide. First of all they thought about the sponge base, and accepted that it really was sponge cake, containing fat, sugar, eggs and flour, like sponge cake should. They worked out that it starts off moist and goes hard when stale, like a cake. Biscuits on the other hand start crisp and hard and go soft when stale. It was all looking rosy in the garden for McVitie's. But the tribunal then went on to consider that Jaffa Cakes were sold in packs of three up to twenty-four, and that they associated themselves with the biscuits in retail outlets. It looked like the tribunal was going to find in favour of the Inland Revenue, when McVitie's played their trump card in the form of a twelve inch-wide Jaffa Cake. The tribunal decided it needed a pot of tea to consider the evidence. One giant Jaffa Cake later, the tribunal concluded that, while the product had some of the characteristics of biscuits or confectionery, it had sufficient cake characteristics to be a cake for the purposes of zero-rating. (The Irish Inland Revenue, meanwhile, simply noted that 'moisture content >12% = cake'. Very sensible, though if they had made a scene maybe they too would have been able to have a crack at a few foot-wide Jaffa Cakes.)

Confusion still reigns, though, as people try to decide the nature of the 'smashing orangey bit in the middle'. Is it jelly or jam? In the UK we think of jelly as a colloidal state of the protein called gelatin. The smashing orangey bit, however, is set using pectin, a complex polysaccharide. Not only is this terrific news for vegetarians, but it means that we are dealing with jam. In fact, according to McVitie's, it's a form of industrial jam, which everybody knows is one level up from domestic jam, but not as impressive or possibly dangerous as military-strength jam.

There is one last important question about the Jaffa Cake that I feel remains as yet unanswered. With its domed sponge underside and its raised inner jammy bit, why doesn't anybody ever mention the fact that it looks like a little flying saucer? Is this so obvious that it doesn't require mentioning, or is it a giant conspiracy?

The combination of plain chocolate and tangy orange jam complement each other very well, but the Jaffa Cake also has some more exotic cousins, mostly in continental Europe. There is a dark cherry jam version with a white chocolate top, decorated with dark chocolate detailing, called Pims. They were last spotted in the UK in the 1980s. Today, in France, Pims are made with a moulded chocolate top and filled with orange, pear and lemon jam.

The Polish have many Jaffa Cake-alikes, with strawberry being used to good effect in their flavours. Reading Polish biscuit packets isn't much use if you don't speak Polish, though I found it very thought-provoking. For instance, the letter Z seems to enjoy immense popularity in Poland and is probably on a par with the letter N or maybe even F in this country. In fact, if it wasn't for the Polish I dare say we could have phased out the letter Z altogether a long time ago. That would have got the alphabet down to 25 letters that could be arranged in nice, neat five-by-five squares. Lovely. Most Polish people seem to have a few Zs in their names, thereby personally ensuring that the letter is still with us, and potentially they could help out by keeping the poor old Zebra company on the last page of any children's alphabet book.

All that is very well, but we all know deep down that the Jaffa Cake is really a biscuit. It lives beside the biscuits in my local supermarket, and when I tell people that my favourite biscuit is a Jaffa Cake they don't look at me in horror saying, 'But it can't be, it's a cake!' They just shrug, and even sometimes agree with me. I imagine the manufacturers also know it's really a biscuit but went to all the trouble of calling it a cake so that it would be zero-rated, therefore making it cheaper for us to buy.

I don't blame them for doing this. I blame our VAT system for being so complicated that such things become a problem. Hundreds of millions of pounds must be spent every year by the government employing people to decide if new products are cake or not, or if a biscuit has that little bit of extra chocolate that makes it a 'luxury'. My solution? Well, it's easy. The government should just admit that all biscuits are part of our staple diet. They would save a fortune and we could go back to admitting that the Jaffa Cake is really a biscuit. The biscuit manufacturers, meanwhile, could get back to the important task of making bigger, better, more chocolatey biscuits without fear of the tax man, who in turn could spend more time chasing proper tax-evading criminals. Simple.

Wedding Cake

Out of all the many cakes in the world, there is one more than any other which demands 'A'-list celebrity treatment: the prima donna of the baked goods world, the wedding cake. The ego of the wedding cake knows no bounds and often gets so completely overboard that it seems that the whole event has been contrived just so that it could come into existence.

THE HISTORY OF THE WEDDING CAKE

If wedding cake is feeling sorry for itself, it would do well to remember that the original wedding cakes, baked by the Romans, were simply thrown directly at the bride's head. Originally, handfuls of wheat were thrown, apparently as a sign of wealth, fertility and prosperity. Then, after a while, Roman bakers decided that it would be nice to make the wheat into little sweetened cakes; and the congregations simply started throwing these instead. It can't have been much fun being caught full in the face by what was essentially a crude Iron Age bun, and so it became good etiquette at least to crumble them up and sprinkle them over the bride's head. This was known as *confarreatio* or 'eating together', from which our word 'confetti' is derived.

In Britain, it became the custom to arrange the little cakes into enormous piles, the higher the better, to demonstrate that you obviously had loads of impressive wheat at your disposal. But these were forever falling over, which led a French chef – on a visit to London – to invent the tiered wedding cake.

Of course, the truth is that most wedding cakes are simply Christmas cake recipes that have been given the chance to play to a bigger crowd.

From the beginning, the wedding cake throws its weight around, demanding that it works with only the best. This is preferably a team of really experienced aunts plus their friend from over the road who does the icing. Special baking tins are commissioned and ovens have their diaries emptied to make way for some extra-long, six-hour cake jobs. It's quite usual in these early stages for a cake to hype up its forthcoming debut by circulating outrageous stories of its dried fruit consumption, coupled with its appetite for eggs. This is designed to intimidate the couple who will be taking to the stage alongside the cake when the big day comes. The electric mixer is pushed way beyond its theoretical design limits, as the mixing bowl becomes a culinary black hole, dragging in every last currant and glacé cherry in the neighbourhood. As the mix grows ever larger, even exotic stuff like dried pineapple isn't safe. Even tea itself cannot escape, spiralling into the churning vortex.

It is at this formative stage in its career that the wedding cake, flushed no doubt with its successful removal of every last pack of chopped almonds from the local supermarket, reaches for the bottle. It all begins innocently enough: a couple of glasses of sherry, and maybe the odd tot of brandy. However, after a few days out of the oven, the cake starts complaining that it might be 'drying out a little' in its tin. The answer could be to splash a little more brandy over it. The cake likes this, and is soon demanding more and more brandy sessions on a regular basis. With only a few days left to go before it's due to be smeared with apricot jam and fitted with its marzipan under-layer, the cake embarrassingly sees off a whole bottle of Three Barrels brandy. For good measure, it then demands that it is doused with the last of a bottle of Johnny Walker Red Label. By now the cake has imbibed so much spirit that its underside has become distinctly mushy. It would be prudent not to smoke in its presence.

Any really impressive cake will need to be arranged in tiers, although how it is planning on remaining upright after all that booze is anybody's guess. Luckily, the experienced team of aunts swings into action and, having dealt with many a dipsomaniac cake in the past, know that a cake board and a good strong supporting coat of royal icing will do the trick. Finally, after donning its sugar flowers and ribbons, the wedding cake is ready for its big day.

To meet its public properly, the wedding cake gets its own table to sit on. The lucky bride and groom have their picture taken with it. Eventually the cake's big moment arrives and a special silver knife is called for, which has no other purpose than the glorious ceremonial doing-in of cakes. The happy couple pretends at some length to cut the cake with the ceremonial silver cake knife. The cake breathes a palpable sigh of relief as these amateurs are quickly led away and it is handed over to a dedicated team of skilled cake-cutters. Of course, the cutters have to deal with the cake's all-too-obvious drink problem, which can lead to lumps of it falling to pieces under the slightest pressure.

The wedding cake now faces its first big challenge: will anybody actually like it? This isn't going to be an easy gig as the audience has already eaten their fill of starter, main course and dessert. In addition, quite a few are drunk and there are also those who don't like marzipan, others who don't like icing and even those who admit to not even liking cake itself, any cake. There follows the probing and personal questions that are fielded by the cake's crack team of aunts. Just what is in it? Straight away, those with nut, wheat, dairy and egg allergies rule themselves out. In fact, anyone who is allergic to, or in some way has a problem with, any given substance should stay well clear of any wedding cake, as no doubt it contains at least four ounces of it. Still, the cake makes the best of it, aided by some very helpful pots of tea and even some coffee. Before long the compliments start to flow, and the cake can be proud that it is 'lovely and moist' (there is apparently nothing worse than a 'dry' cake). Though how many of the wedding party have been rendered unfit for driving by a portion of cake is another matter.

If anybody thought they could sneak off without a piece of cake then they didn't reckon on its final wish, that it be carved up and distributed to all and sundry wrapped in serviettes. The bitter truth, however, is that most of these pieces of cake are given to children who, after picking off the icing, abandon the rest of the alcohol-pickled remains. These are then unceremoniously consigned to the pedal bin, still conveniently shrouded in their serviette.

I would just like to add that Nicey and I were very sneaky and only gave the aunties (i.e., my mother) and the 'friend over the road' (i.e., Norma from next door) six weeks' notice of our impending wedding. Nonetheless, we had a wonderful wedding cake that managed to hold its own, despite being ignored for quite some time while we all had a barbecue in our back garden.

Lovely.

Fairy Cakes

A few years ago Wifey and I were in France doing a spot of wine tasting with a view to buying a few cases of 'deep strike' wine to bring back to Blighty. Flushed with the success of selling us two cases of the Cuvée St George, the chap at the cave (though this one was in fact a large shed) insisted that we try the local speciality wine, called 'Gris'. This was a pale pink, thin, stalky affair. I think our stifled grimaces told the chap that he needed to hit the hard sell, so he ventured that (literally excuse my French), *'C'est bien avec les petits gateaux dans l'apres-midi.'* For any of you whose French is even worse than mine, he was advocating drinking it in the afternoon while eating small cakes.

It's funny how so such a small phrase can convey such big cultural differences. I don't know what sort of country the French are running over there, but sitting around drinking wine and eating cakes all afternoon isn't going to get the bills paid. Mind you, this could explain why the rural French lunch hour seems to extend from midday on the dot to about 3 p.m. It takes an hour or two to sleep off all that cake and booze.

So, I've managed to mention small cakes there, but not fairy cakes specifically, only now I have. For many people, the fairy cake is 'the' small cake. For some, it's the rock cake; and for others, if it doesn't have cream in it then it's not even worth talking about. Despite its small size, the fairy

GLACÉ CHERRIES

There is one very simple way to make a small cake happy, and that is to put a glacé cherry on top of it, or even just half a glacé cherry. A properly specified slice of Genoa fruit cake should ideally have at least two cross-sectional glacé cherries clearly visible, and any proper full-spectrum fruit cake needs its helping of glacé cherries.

But just what are glacé cherries and where do they come from? Surprisingly, glacé cherries are actually made using fairly conventional cherries that grow on trees. This is startling stuff because, apart from their size, glacé cherries are almost nothing like their straight-off-the-tree counterparts. So what is this dramatic transformational process that can render a normally opaque cherry into a semi-transparent entity, and is it called 'glacé-ing'? The sad truth is it's not called 'glacé-ing', but 'candying', which is a dangerously transatlantic type of word. A firm-fleshed white cherry, after being washed with a yeast-killing solution containing E220 (sulphur dioxide), is bathed in increasingly concentrated syrup solutions. Then some E127 (erythrosine) or maybe E120 (see 'Pink Icing' on p.150), and some E202 (potassium sorbate) are added to colour it red and to stop it going off. A great deal of glacé cherries are produced in France, but, not really having much use for them, the French send most of them to Britain.

I'm surprised that there hasn't been a super-villain who has used glacé-ing in some form of world domination, or at the very least a big gun capable of glacé-ing things. I wonder what glacéd dogs, cars or postboxes would be like, and if they would be suitable for baking.

cake is really a party animal and doesn't mind mixing it with the big boys, such as birthday cakes, even if they are decked out in ribbons with rock and roll flames on their tops. The fairy cake's secret is to travel around by the plateload, which can be quite impressive. If birthday cakes don't want to risk being upstaged by their warm-up act they should up the ante by getting some dry ice, lightning flashes and a laser show.

The exact specification of a fairy cake seems to be a little vague, but what is universally agreed upon is that it's a small sponge cake baked in its own paper case. As the cake bakes, a small domed peak is formed. Some designs, which probably gave rise to the name, call for this peak to be sliced off, cut in two and placed back on top, stuck down with some form of butter-cream or icing. This gives the impression of two small wings. However, I always thought that they were called angel or butterfly cakes. Most fairy cakes simply make do with a coating of water icing, and a glacé cherry half or a couple of pieces of angelica.

Packet Cakes

Not all cakes give themselves such airs and graces as the likes of the celebration wedding, birthday and Christmas cakes. Some cakes are quite humble and approachable: they still like being sliced up and put on a plate, but they are happy enough to turn up at Sunday tea-time, or even on a picnic. These packet cakes don't want to make a big fuss and will cheerfully make do with a bit of a wrapper, and at the most a thin sheet of cardboard folded into three. They also don't mind a bit of light, good-natured stacking when sitting on the shelves.

Pink icing is intrinsically more fun than white icing, as it is obviously frivolous compared to white icing's implied purity and slightly prim appearance. Being halfway to sinful red, pink is therefore moderately wanton and semi-hedonistic. Any cake looking for a good time is going to pop on its pink icing and red cherry.

A couple of drops of cochineal is all that is needed to make a bowl of pink icing, so a tiny bottle gives years of service. I think most people know that the red food colour cochineal (E120) is made from crushed insects, but they choose to push that to the back of their minds, as it's not too pleasant. That's not going to stop me from going on about it at some length though.

The first and most obvious question is why on earth are these little insects so keen on being filled with bright red dye? Second, and equally obviously, what are the squished insides of beetles doing in my cake?

Actually, they're not beetles but scale insects, which are a little like aphids inasmuch as they live by plunging their proboscis into a plant and letting the sap flow through them, taking what they need. In the case of *Dactylopius coccus*, or the cochineal scale, it is a type of prickly pear cactus. The insect secretes a waxy coat, and any excess sap simply passes out of the back. This is where the red pigment carminic acid comes in: it is an excellent ant-repellent. This comes in handy when some of the nastier ants aren't just interested in your excess sap, but want a main course of scale insect.

It was the Aztecs who first cultivated the cactus and the insects to provide a source of textile dye. When the Spanish arrived, they considered the dye the second most valuable commodity after gold. Two and a half centuries later, the Spanish monopoly on cochineal production was broken when a French naturalist smuggled some cactus pads from Haiti. Today, Peru and the Canary Islands are the main producers. The dye is now used in everything from sausages to lipstick.

Ginger Cake

Has there ever been a cake that likes its packet as much as the Ginger cake? It would rather you tore its bottom and sides off than part it from its extra-large baking case. Just to show how serious it is about remaining wedded to its case, ginger cake saves its stickiest and tastiest bits for attaching to the wrapper. This can often mean that the wrapper is the best bit of a ginger cake, a bit like the crackling is the best bit of roast pork. Scraping it off the wrapper requires a straight knife, not too sharp and not too blunt. Having finally separated the outside from the wrapper it may be formed back into a lump, though this has a tendency to over-compress it, so it's best eaten with the fingers from small heaps in the wrapper.

Battenberg

Battenberg cake steals the show every time. Its nearest rival technically in the two-coloured-sponge arena is marble cake, but this knows better than to go up against the barking mad Battenberg. But where is Battenberg and why are its cakes so pink and yellow, and smell of almonds?

Yet again, the crowned heads of Europe are involved. This time it's the Germans, and if you've just quipped that I must mean the British royal family you'd be right. The German town of Battenberg has given its name to a fair proportion of Europe's royalty, our own included. When Austrian-born Prince Louis of Battenberg married Princess Victoria of Hesse-Darmstadt, granddaughter of Queen Victoria, in 1884, everybody was so pleased that the new Battenberg cake was invented. In 1917, due to World War One Prince Louis relinquished his German titles and took the Anglicised surname Mountbatten.

As everybody knows, a Battenberg consists of two square strips of pink sponge and two of yellow, arranged to form a larger square check. The whole lot is wrapped in a sheet of marzipan and stuck together via that all-purpose cake glue, apricot jam. Why this was felt to be evocative of German royalty I don't know. Perhaps they smell strongly of almonds. Nevertheless, the Battenberg is a splendid cake, and once you become acclimatised to it you will find it hard to resist.

I would be more than a little tempted to pick the Battenberg as my cake of choice in a first-contact-with-aliens situation. It's so cheerful, no matter what wavelengths of light your visual receptors are attuned to. Of course, there is always the possibility in common with some earthlings that they might find marzipan to be toxic, which is fair enough. Although, if they are going to jaunt around the universe, dropping in on people at random, then they have to expect that sort of thing. If they have any manners they'll eat it politely, say what they've come to say, then run back to their spaceship to keel over while searching for an antidote.

And a Sit Down

🫖 Sitting Down

It goes without saying that for a nice cup of tea you need a sit down. Just the same, we always take the belt and braces approach and say, 'A nice cup of tea and a sit down', as this leaves no room for error.

It is often said of people who are engaged in sitting down that they are doing 'nothing': for example, 'Why are you sitting down doing nothing?' They're not doing 'nothing', of course. For a start they are breathing, using their intercostal rib musculature and diaphragm. Their liver is doing any number of the five hundred different things that it is responsible for. The digestive system is busily at work on their breakfast which is contributing to the eleven and a half litres of stuff that flows through it each day. Their heart is pumping up to five litres of blood around the body at any one time, expending in one hour enough energy to raise a one-ton weight by a yard. Their body is renewing its very cellular structure at the phenomenal rate of fifty thousand cells a second. One hundred billion neurons and sixty trillion synapses in their brain are helping them sit there and think about it all, or what is for dinner.

No wonder they'll be needing a nice cup of tea and a biscuit.

When we want to stretch somebody to the limits of human coordination, we ask them to rub their tummy with one hand and pat their head with the other, all while standing up. For most people this simply exceeds their physical limits, even when sober. This is why very few activities require you to do it. The early pioneers of the motor car, for example, avoided control systems that required you to rub your tummy and pat your head simultaneously, settling instead on a steering wheel and some pedals and levers. Interestingly, they still thought you should be sitting down to work all of that. In fact, right across the whole gamut of man–machine interaction we see the sit down as integral, from the operation of sewing machines and military attack helicopters to watching TV and manoeuvring those big lawn-mowers that you can sit on.

Given the fine level of control needed to correctly make and pour tea, to properly unwrap and eat a Club biscuit or to successfully dunk a Digestive, it really isn't tenable that this should be attempted while standing up. Not that we are advocating a sedentary lifestyle. We think people should all get out of the house and go for nice walks and bike rides, that sort of thing. As well as being good for you, you can burn off enough calories to justify a pot of tea and some biscuits and a nice sit down when you get back in.

The Folly of Not Sitting Down

The stand-up buffet is all the evidence required for any evolved society to condemn the practice of standing around trying to relax while eating and drinking. There are simply too many verbs here for anybody to be truly at ease: standing, talking, eating and drinking. Let's not forget spilling, balancing, dropping and swearing as some of the other doing words. On top of that you are probably expected to be talking, listening, mingling and on occasion even clapping. All of this while juggling a glass of red wine, a plate, a fork, a napkin and a selection of delightful morsels, most of which seem to be designed either to pour onto the floor or roll off your plate with all the ease of a handful of steel ball-bearings.

Sometimes hot food is served at a buffet which is bathed in pungent and powerfully staining sauces. Not only can this stuff scald you but it will leave indelible orange stains on all natural and man-made fibres. It's also effective on tricky, normally hard-to-stain surfaces such as glazed ceramics, glass, polytetrafluoroethane (Teflon), stainless steel and fingers. Any that is left over can be used in those briefcases that spray coloured stuff all over their contents when they are stolen, or to brand cattle. If they can't run to a hot buffet then the caterers will make sure that everybody gets a plentiful helping of pickled beetroot, piccalilli or something apparently preserved in ink.

Modern buffets have cutting-edge crockery and accessories intended to ease your predicament. However, strange plates with recesses or clip-on plastic devices designed to hold your wine glass just confer upon you the capability to spill your food and drink simultaneously.

Why is this inflicted upon us? As with most things we don't like, we are usually told that it is good for us. Apparently it is so that we can mingle with one another. I don't know about other nations but the British don't like to mingle; it's not something we are comfortable with. Huddle, yes; mingle, no. Most British people have mastered from an early age the skill of appearing to be approachable while avoiding all eye contact with other people. Unless they are carrying a tray of drinks.

Mingling requires talking to complete strangers, which limits the topics of conversation. Asking about them can be seen as being nosy, while talking about yourself can be seen as blowing one's own trumpet. So this whole area of interaction is best avoided. Subjects such as how nasty the wine is, how long the queue for the food was, why are there no chairs and what exactly is that stuff which is preserved in ink are all good. These, though, are quickly exhausted and long, uncomfortable silences will ensue during which people pretend to be more interested in their buffet lunch than they really are.

By far the best ice-breaker at these events is some form of minor disaster. If you are organising such a gathering, maybe you can arrange for the sprinkler system to be turned on for forty-five seconds. Or you may like to purchase, at very little cost, some form of old motor vehicle and burn it out in the car park near to where people will be entering the building. Both of these diversions will give people ample and sociably acceptable reasons to talk to one another. Mother Nature may even give you a hand and arrange some form of freak meteorological event like a blizzard, torrential rain, or a pleasantly warm spring day.

Often we are told, should we be stroppy enough to enquire, that sitting down is too expensive, so much so that the only practical course of action is to stand. Typically at such cut-price stand-up affairs, we are taunted by a huge pile of stacked chairs at one end of the function room, or in an adjoining room, often with tables too. People are frequently tempted to get some of the prohibited chairs and snatch some illicit sit downs. They probably would if it weren't for the fact that their hands were full of glasses, plates, forks and so on.

Sometimes people are driven to perching on stairs, doorsteps, window sills or even serving tables, risking certain chastisement from the caterers. This is all fairly demeaning and most will resist the temptation, preferring to suffer along with the crowd, their dignity intact. People sometimes complain, but only to one another, so it doesn't really get them very far. Most simply put up with it, afraid that they will be accused of not being sophisticated enough to cope with the ordeal of a stand-up buffet, or stigmatised as a non-mingler.

All proceeds to plan right until the point when tea, biscuits and cakes are served. This is enough to tip most people over the edge, and they will seek out a sit down at all costs. While they were happy to spill red wine and coleslaw down their suits and over their shoes in the feigned pursuit of chit-chat, tea is a much more serious business. To be fair, it's usually cake that causes the problems. Biscuits don't mind perching on the saucer, even though the chocolate-covered ones might melt against the side of the hot cup. Cake, being cake, demands its own little plate, and most people, having been born with a strict limit of two hands, are unable to cope. Some people will just up and leave, maybe taking their cake and tea with them. They will wander forlornly around the entire establishment and venture into the grounds looking for a place to sit down. They could turn up virtually anywhere: cupboards, lavatories, even wandering around in the street.

In such crisis situations, unlikely bands of people will gather, all united by a common struggle. This is the classic plot line for disaster movies such as *The Poseidon Adventure*, *Earthquake*, *Daylight* and *The Little Mermaid*. Groups of displaced people will trail around together, holding open doors with elbows for the other cup and saucer and cake plate-laden attendees, all trying to find a decent sit down. It may take weeks for the caterers to find all of the cups and saucers, some of which may be up to a quarter of a mile away from the original buffet lunch.

Wifey says

Yes, yes, yes, I know you're right, but I like a nice buffet. We had one at our wedding, after all, and that wasn't wretched at all . . . was it?

Sit Down Technique

The main aim when sitting down with a cup of tea is to relax. Any distractions or issues that may interfere with this must be ruthlessly eliminated.

The first requirement is that you are safely and comfortably seated. A chair or settee is almost always the best choice for a sit down as they have been designed specifically for that purpose. Always try to choose one that isn't clapped out with missing springs, incorrectly plumped cushions or bits of wire or cane that jab into your important sitting down areas. Make sure it's situated on level ground and not likely to tip over. If your seat is some form of folding or camping chair, ensure that it has been correctly erected. If you can't guarantee this then you may as well video your sit down, just in case you can sell it to one of those TV programmes that feature half an hour of people falling over. Actually, if you are going to all that trouble, you might want to locate your chair in a paddling pool while cuddling a cat against its will, and get a friend to ride their motorbike into you.

If chairs aren't available and you are forced to perch on the edge of a low wall or fence then always check for structural integrity. There is nothing less relaxing than having your lower body unexpectedly buried in rubble or splintered planks disappearing up the back of your jumper. Moisture is also an issue, especially on moss-covered walls, and unless you take precautions such as sitting on a waterproof coat or plastic bag, not only will the experience be unpleasant but those following you may question your ability to control your bladder functions.

Finally, you may be forced to consider a low step or even the ground itself. Try to ensure that you can comfortably get up again once the sitting down has come to an end. If this doesn't seem likely then try to establish an escape route by which you can crawl off on your hands and knees until a suitable standing-up location is reached. When sitting on the floor, be prepared for other people to tread on you, walk backwards over you and just generally treat you as a second-class citizen. Psychologists may put this down to submissive body language due to your prostrate position, but really it's because other people can't see you down there.

Your next most pressing issue is where to set down your tea and biscuits, and once again stability plays a major role, as does convenience. Some people will often trade one off against the other, choosing the arm of a chair despite its being too narrow or rounded to support their sundry cups and plates safely. Others will choose a solid nearby table or shelf, which, although stable, requires that they lean wildly out of their seat, thereby compromising the first requirement of seat stability. Worse still is having to stand up slightly to reach your cup, thus briefly terminating the sit down state itself. Armchairs with nice big wide flat arms are a boon to anybody seeking a self-contained sit down. My Aunty Dot used to have a three-piece suite in black vinyl which had big flat wooden fingernail things on the ends of the arms like built-in coasters. But this was Essex in the 1970s. Perhaps Western civilisation has only ever surpassed this degree of sit down convenience with Jimmy Savile's *Jim'll Fix It* chair, though this seemed mainly full of cigars delivered through flaps by bits of old coat-hangers. It only did this very rarely, no doubt due to the high probability that it could have had somebody's eye out.

Often the best option is a small table, perhaps from a nest of tables, that can be situated immediately adjacent to your seat. In some households, the competition for these may be fierce and when combined with issues such as line of sight to TV screens can create certain optimal chairs. Such prized seats are typically claimed by either the alpha male or the cat, whichever has the higher social ranking.

24 Moving Vehicles

The wheel is often cited as the most significant invention in human history (or fire or electricity or boats or something). Whatever it was, whenever we come up with some new form of transport, it's only a matter of time before we try to work out some way of drinking tea in or on it. Be it an ocean liner or a jumbo jet, it seems that we enjoy rising above the tawdry details of the engines and drive shafts propelling us to our destinations by having a nice cup of tea and a sit down. Often we'll read a book or the paper while we're at it. In fact, you might be sitting on a train or plane reading this and thinking about having a cup of tea. Perhaps somebody else somewhere is thinking about a man who is writing a book about somebody else on a train thinking about tea. Perhaps it's that bloke over there by the window. Give him a bit of a look; he'll soon stop it.

Trains

Einstein used to think about trains a lot. They used to crop up all the time in his 'thought experiments'. Einstein would try to deduce what would be observed by various people should they be aboard trains travelling at, or near to, the speed of light. Mainly, it would be lots of weird stuff involving people on the train having a different perception of time passing to that experienced by those in the station. Nothing too revolutionary there, then. But what would happen to their tea at such colossal speeds? I would be surprised if they didn't spill it, much like myself on the 8.15 King's Cross train, which I take from time to time. In fact, Einstein would have probably have needed to imagine a few serviettes in there as well, and some of those little three-packs of Custard Creams would be nice while he's at it.

Even with the new electrified line to London, there are still enough jolts and lurches as the train makes its progress that anybody holding tea has to enter an almost trance-like state if they are to avoid throwing it all over themselves. Much like some form of Eastern martial art, tea drinkers must develop keen senses and agile yet graceful movements. Sensing the motion of the train below, they must react quickly yet smoothly to the rocking and swaying. The drinker must become at one with the cup *and* the train, and in doing so create harmony between the two. Of course, knowing in advance when it's going to cross a set of points is also an advantage.

Grand masters of tea drinking on trains will remove the plastic lid from their cup as soon as their tea has brewed. Novices or habitually rigid people tend just to remove it for sips, which they take typically when the train chooses to cross some points. Drinking tea on trains always turns my mind to shaving with an old-fashioned cut-throat razor while surfing. I don't know if Einstein used to think about that. Probably not.

Coaches

As a young man I used to travel from one side of the country to the other by coach, Norwich to Wales, in a mere nine and a half hours, with an hour and a half stopover in Victoria Coach Station, fending off the pigeons with a rolled-up copy of the *New Scientist*. Coach travel, even 'luxury' coach travel, seems like something that human rights protesters might want to take a closed look at. Should you happen to be one of those unlucky people whose femurs are longer than the spacing between the coach seats, then conventional sit downs are ruled out. In order to fit into such a confined space, it becomes necessary to fold into three, with the legs drawn up so your knees are level with your teeth. Smashing your face into your knees as the coach slows down or accelerates is all part of the rhythm and majesty of coach travel.

Deploying your seat-back tray in readiness for a warmish drink is fairly tricky, as it is directly behind your knees. Moving your knees to one side means that you'll probably bash them against the knees of the person next to you. Mind you, by now your close proximity to one another will mean that you've already swapped your entire complement of bodily microbial flora, and have learnt to breathe in as they breathe out to keep the air pressure equalised, and stop your ears popping. In fact, after three hours you'll have exchanged germs with the entire bus, all of which will be fighting it out with your beleaguered immune system to see which is going to make you ill for the next week and a half.

If you are able to get your hand physically into your pocket to rescue enough money then you can purchase your paper cup of instant tea. Experienced coach travellers, who have normally already bagged the window seats, will have readied their refreshments money before getting on. You can spot these people as they may be seen clenching a couple of pound coins between their teeth, and hoping that their knees don't propel them down their throat.

Under normal circumstances you wouldn't contemplate drinking coach tea. However, you will be in a highly suggestive frame of mind. This will have been brought on by ninety minutes of a loud yet incomprehensible soundtrack for a video which is being displayed on a TV screen the size of a beer mat forty feet away. This is the type of thing the CIA used to subject South American dictators to when they had been naughty or were trying to hide in their palace compounds. After an hour and a half of it, struggling to work out if the movie is set in space, under the sea or maybe in the Wild West, you'll happily take anything that is offered to you as you strive to keep your higher brain functions from shutting down permanently.

Finally, as the coach draws near to its destination it will often toy with its weary and disorientated passengers by taking a convoluted round-the-houses approach, often passing the same point several times, and cheerfully plunging itself into unnecessary queues of traffic. Taking it out on the driver is ill-advised, as his state of mind is questionable, with him being a chain-smoker who has just gone three and a half hours without a cigarette.

When the passengers eventually disembark their brain deprogramming is complete. If you were looking to build an army of brainwashed clones to wreak havoc on an unsuspecting world then it might be an idea to hang around Victoria Coach Station and scoop up people as the get off the coach from Norwich. As a bonus, they won't be too choosy about their tea either.

Planes

Airliners are essentially large flying coaches, capable of speeds of 500 miles an hour at heights of 37,000 feet above the earth's surface. The safety talk before take-off is designed to remind you of this, and of what will happen should things go wrong. Of course, most people have listened to the safety talk countless times and don't pay any attention. In order to keep people focused on the details of the talk many stewardesses have taken to wearing bizarre and improbable make-up as a shock tactic. Drawing eyebrows in odd places and painting on mouths which are much larger than normal can make them the centre of attention. However, this often backfires as you try to imagine what their face really looks like under all that stuff, rather than listening to where all the doors and yellow inflatable things are. Everything else about the flight, including the tea, is designed to divert your attention from the fact that you are on a plane.

One of the cleverest techniques at the disposal of airlines for keeping passengers absorbed in concentration is food miniaturisation. This achieves two things. First, your seat, although being merely a glorified coach seat, appears much bigger as your brain struggles to make sense of the miniature bread roll now in your possession. Looking just like a normal bread roll, this chap has been scaled down to a mere one-fifth of its normal size. The same applies to chops, chickens, peas and apple pie with custard. All painstakingly reduced in size, using advanced jet-age catering technology.

Their second cunning trick is to supply a plastic sachet which contains hundreds of smaller sachets, rather like the catering equivalent of a cluster bomb. Cataloguing and finding somewhere to put all of the little

Homeostasis is our body's ability to keep a constant internal environment in terms of chemical balance and temperature. No matter if we are in a rainforest, on the Arctic tundra or somewhere in Bedfordshire sitting on our behinds watching the telly, our body maintains a core temperature of thirty-seven degrees Celsius. But before we get too cocky and start slapping one another on the back for being miracles of biological engineering, let's consider how useless we are unless we've recently had a decent cup of tea.

Some activities deplete our tea reserves faster than others, and by studying exactly which ones are most draining, we can better prepare for the possibility of chronic tea loss. Here is a list of the main culprits:

- Shopping
- Working
- Any form of DIY
- Sitting down
- Swimming
- Driving to the shops
- Mending things
- Housework
- Thinking about previous cups of tea
- Going upstairs then coming back down again
- Visiting other people
- Reading the paper
- Breakfast
- Watching other people do DIY on telly
- Walking to the shops
- Being outside
- Talking to pets in comedy voices
- Being on holiday
- Vacuuming the car
- Days beginning with the letter S
- Having people visit you

In fact, most things I could think deplete our tea reserves. Among the few things that don't increase the need to drink tea, however, are tea advertisements. Perhaps it is because our favourite brand of tea is drunk by plasticine birds. The sight of birds drinking tea just doesn't trigger the brain's tea response. I'm not really sure why tea needs to advertised at all. It's a bit like running adverts to encourage us to breathe more.

sachets that spill out when it is opened keeps you occupied for ten minutes. Among it you'll find your knife, fork, spoon, teaspoon, coffee whitener, sugar, sweetener, toothpick, milk pot, salt, pepper, serviette, lemon-scented clean-up wipe, some more salt and pepper and maybe a little thing containing jam. Some people who are still used to travelling by coach are dazzled by such booty, and despite having no need for most of it now, or indeed later, insist on stuffing the extra salt and peppers, sweetener, toothpick and coffee whitener into their flight bags. They then carry most of this around with them for the next fortnight looking for an opportunity to use it. Perhaps the salt could be utilised to despatch a small slug or clear a few square centimetres of path of snow and ice. The pepper could be used to divert a medium-sized cat from one small potted plant. The coffee whitener and sweetener, however, are next to useless unless you want to tamper with somebody's tea maliciously.

When the tea finally makes its appearance, it does so against its will, having been made with water that has 'boiled' at a much lower temperature than 100 degrees due to the cabin pressure. It also takes an eternity working its way down the rows of passengers only to run out at the chap in front of you. This ensures you get an extra-weak cup out of the new pot that turns up ten minutes later.

By the way, any attempt to take the miniature bread rolls with you when disembarking will meet with failure, as they can survive only in the rarefied environment of an airliner. Taking them into the everyday mortal world will cause them to shrivel up, like alpine flowers plucked from a high mountain or some other lovely metaphor to do with fairies. It's kinder to leave the bread rolls, even the unpleasant wholemeal ones, in their natural environment.

🫖 Tea in Public

Some people seem to need to drink cup after cup of tea in an endless chain just to remain functional. For such people, simple undertakings such as a visit to the shops are fraught with the spectre of ten minutes without a cup of tea. Often they will imbibe whole pots of the stuff before venturing outside in a bid to load their entire system with tea. Of course, there is always the prospect of using some artificial aid to unscheduled tea drinking such as a thermos flask, or one of those little element things that plug into a car cigarette lighter for boiling up water. But, for most, resorting to such things is an all too graphic way of admitting they have a problem. They would rather battle on, grabbing a cup of tea whenever and wherever they can.

By far the most socially acceptable way of obtaining tea in public is to visit some form of café, tea shop or in-store restaurant. Here you can enjoy tea with other tea drinkers in a supportive environment. Clever use of tables and chairs creates areas where you can sit down, and a range of cakes, pastries and till-side biscuits can help to make tea drinking more of a social event and less of a biological imperative.

If you think this is something that you might like to try, or if you are keen to meet other people who drink tea openly in public, then there are a few things you should know. The first and most obvious is price. Most tea shops are family affairs run by people who also share an interest in tea and sit downs, and in general you'll be well treated. However, at larger concerns, such as in-store cafés, you might find the less welcoming face of the tea business. Forced to wear ill-fitting and unfashionable uniforms, many youngsters find themselves serving tea for the minimum wage. As a tea drinker you don't have too much to worry about as it's quite difficult to mess up pouring hot water into a pot, and in general they won't try to force you to buy curled up lasagne, peas and chips. They might, however, simply depress you a little with their miserable conduct. They may also desert their posts, leaving you to stand there like a lemon at the till, with a tray bearing no more than a couple of teaspoons and a packet of shortbread fingers.

If you find anyone wanting to charge you more than two British pounds for tea then you should move on to another establishment. When all is said and done tea is a few dried leaves, a bit of hot water and a dash of milk. In fact, anything over eighty pence and you should begin to carp on about it being a disgrace. Failure to do so may result in your being mistaken for a tourist.

Second, you need to check on quantities. It's no good paying, say, £1.50 for an individual pot of tea only to find that it holds just a single cupful. There really is very little point in making teapots so small. Again, unless you want to look like a tourist, demand a second pot of boiling water, to top it up with. It's worth noting that most individual pots will actually pour more of your tea onto the table than into your cup, especially the little stainless-steel ones, so you really can't afford to start off with short measures. Also, watch out for shallow cups or those with overly thick sides, or, worse still, both. These are for small cups of coffee, not for big cups of tea.

Beware of those establishments that constantly froth up jugs of milk using the steam wand from an espresso machine (unless you actually enjoy the sound of a jet fighter with its afterburners on reheat, just a few metres from the back of your head). You may very, very occasionally have your tea made with hot milk left over from the deafening coffee palaver, either by accident or design. This is morally and technically wrong, and you are within your rights to cause an unpleasant scene should you choose to do so.

Milk is always going to be an issue. Ideally you will be given a small jug of chilled, pasteurised milk. You might be given access to a shared jug of milk, which is fine if you are not in a teapot scenario. Occasionally you'll need to grapple with those little plastic pots of milk. Avoid the brown ones: yet again they are for coffee. Also try to avoid dual-purpose for 'coffee and tea' pots, as these tend to be something other than milk. That's fine for coffee but not really for tea which can come out a bit greasy. If you don't actually get to see the milk but in some way have ready-whitened tea dispensed straight into your cup then leave immediately, and request that the local constabulary cordon off the area.

Another thing to look for is a supply of proper teaspoons. Metal teaspoons are a good indicator that you can expect something that at least approximates to tea. Plastic teaspoons are well meaning but indicate that the staff may not take the business of tea quite as seriously as you do. Anywhere that provides those long pointy stirring things will likely as not have a very cavalier attitude to tea and sit downs, and will be more comfortable serving you a large cardboard bucket of cola-flavoured ice. If you are unsure which end of the stirring thing is for holding and which end is for stirring, don't worry. It doesn't matter. Besides, this is the least of your problems: you should be more concerned about possible puncture wounds should you trip and fall on top of it while carrying a scalding-hot paper cup of tea back to your uncomfortably small plastic seat.

The quality of the tea is something that you might care to be concerned with, and often the brand of tea will be displayed or will be obvious from the tea bag supplied. If you are somewhere that serves tea from behind the counter out of a huge teapot then you should just drink it down with gusto, whatever it is like. Not only is it probably very strong and a bit stewed but it's no doubt going to be very effective. Finding out what sort of tea is actually in there is purely academic. If they also happen to sell bacon sandwiches then you should have one of those too. Ideally, I would like to see some form of standard sign outside these establishments saying, 'We serve tea out of an enormous teapot. Really, it's huge.'

The next step up is obviously the tea urn, to which the above also applies. Sometimes you will be given all sorts of fancy tea bags to choose from, which is all well and good, but such opulence usually comes at a price. The rule of thumb is for every extra variety of tea they recite, expect to add another ten pence to the price of a cuppa. At such an establishment you should always take the fight to them and ask for a blend of tea that they don't stock before grudgingly accepting one which they do. This will create a stabilising air of mutual pomposity in which to carry out your tea-purchasing transaction.

Vending Machines

The vending machine is the beverage equivalent of a fruit machine. If you are lucky, you'll get something you can drink delivered into your cup. If you are unlucky, you'll get something unknown poured over the back of your hand. Anybody who has had to depend on a vending machine for their tea will be carrying around the emotional and sometimes physical scars of experience. Let's face it, anything that produces tea, coffee, vegetable soup and lime squash while making a noise like a bin lorry compacting rubbish should be viewed with deep suspicion.

Many vending machines have their own idiosyncratic twists. The refusal to dispense drinks into anything but their own flimsy plastic cups is all too common. Once the cup is removed from the sanctuary of the machine, it quickly loses all structural integrity. This is much like a milk carton whose top has been completely opened and then recklessly filled to the brim with boiling oil. Try sticking your own mug in the dispensing bay of one of these guys and it will receive a small squirt of something foul while spraying you with scalding-hot water as the whole machine shuts down to await the attentions of its 'local' service engineer.

The engineer, of course, has three similar incidents to attend to this morning in his 120-mile call-out area.

Should you find yourself present when the engineer does finally turn up, whatever you do, don't look inside the machine. To do so is to gaze upon a forbidden nightmare world of pipes and fluid, far beyond our everyday comprehension. It's much like being the hapless witness to an alien autopsy. These people usually turn up with a couple of buckets and wearing waterproof footwear for a reason. It puts one more in mind of farmyard animals giving birth than a nice cuppa.

There is, of course, a certain starship captain who always gets his tea from his own personal vending machine built into his office wall. I suppose he thinks it's glamorous to have his own vending machine. As he only seems to drink Earl Grey then he is pretty safe as it all tastes like dilute aftershave, even if it has been molecularly assembled just for him.

Christmas

Christmas is that special time of year between 6th November and 31st January during which, while remembering the birth of Christ, we are encouraged to spend as much money as we can afford. And then some more. Of course, if you just bought or received this book then that's perfectly fine.

It is also the time of year when whole communities come together with a shared purpose and vision for the festive season, which is to make their street visible from outer space. Any visiting aliens who were hoping to impress us with their UFOs bedecked with twinkling lights didn't reckon on Britain in December. I expect they all just park up on the moon over Christmas and do all those little jobs they've been putting off all year.

Tea, biscuits and cakes all play their part in the festivities. Back in the 1930s, tins of biscuits were all the rage as Christmas gifts. Nowadays, we still give tins of biscuits at Christmas, but rarely as your top, leave it until last, phone your mates up and boast about it sort of present. One of the most popular biscuit tins is the Danish Butter assortment. This, to me, is an enigma. What exactly is assorted about them? The Danes only appear to know how to make one type of biscuit, and in a feeble attempt to disguise this fact they make it in various shapes. Alas, most of the shapes are roughly circular, so any difference is far from obvious.

But the more troubling matter surely has to be Denmark's track record in biscuit baking. Granted, they are well known for their pastries, although it seems that everybody else makes them on their behalf, much in the way that the Spanish have franchised out their omelette business. There is also a lot of bacon of Danish origin. Biscuits, however are something that they only seem to crank out at Christmas. Presumably the Danish fleet of biscuit factories remains mothballed for much of the year and gets recommissioned each winter to produce a tide of butter biscuits. It also seems likely that the Danes put in a sizable order for butter round about mid-September, which could be a handy piece of information if you happen to run a dairy.

Many other well-known biscuit ensembles don a tin at Christmas, in much the same way that we put on our best jumper or frock. They are still the same old lovable biscuits, plus you have the bonus of a new biscuit tin. I always think it's nice to take the uneaten selections into the office at the end of January, just as the weather turns really nasty. By now, many people are subsisting on gruel and stale bread, having remortgaged their homes to pay for all the consumer electronics they bought at Christmas. During such times of hardship, a small foil-wrapped biscuit with a steaming cuppa can seem like the very lap of luxury. Perhaps it will help them look on the bright side: if their home does get repossessed, they can always live inside their new TV, most of which are now the size of small caravans.

Christmas simply wouldn't be Christmas without mince pies. These have seen a great deal of innovation over the years. The main advance has been the replacement of dangerous and unpredictable homemade ones with professionally made shop-bought ones. Christmas used to be a time when a bizarre arms race took place between Nanny Nicey and my aunties to create ever more durable and impervious mince pies. This would ensure that a small production run of mince pies would take weeks to work through, unless my dad was allowed unsupervised access to them. Nanny Nicey always insists that pastry tolerance is the cornerstone of any successful marriage. I suppose the same could be said of Wifey, given that she's never made pastry. She once made soda bread, which came out quite firm. I was tempted to phone up NASA and see if they could put the recipe to good use. Wifey said it was because she couldn't get hold of proper buttermilk.

Still, as a child I could sleep soundly at night, knowing that if the much-anticipated nuclear war broke out, we could improvise an effective fall-out shelter using upturned mince pies. Occasionally we would visit somebody who made mince pies with an even thicker and heavier-set pastry. After such visits, we were all supposed to feel thankful that the ones we were used to at least were rendered semi-pliable by scalding-hot tea.

⦗27⦘ Is it the End?

As a notorious biscuit enthusiast I'm often asked by people what happened to certain biscuits: 'Can you still get . . .?', 'Do they still make . . .?' and so on. I don't mind that at all, especially if I know the answer. Often a question such as 'Where can I get Lemon Puffs, I've not tasted them for thirty years?' can be answered by directing them to their local supermarket. They simply forgot to buy them for the last thirty years.

But there are others who are not so lucky, asking after McVitie's Royal Scot, Huntley and Palmer's Milk and Honey or Breakfast biscuits, Butter Osbornes, Banjo Wafers, Barmouth biscuits, Yoyos, Chocolate Garibaldis and even Abbey Crunch. Where are all these wonderful biscuits? Well, they are simply recipes and memories now. But what happened to them?

The chap eating his Lemon Puffs after a thirty-year hiatus doesn't worry that his long absence might have contributed to their downfall. For some biscuits, recipes were tinkered with and products lost their appeal. Others became uneconomic due to old production plants wearing out or the increasing cost of certain ingredients. With some brands, company mergers caused factories to shut and product ranges were rationalised. These are all factors that apply to virtually everything we consume; simple matters of supply and demand.

We have created a subtle and insidious rod for our own backs in the name of progress. Our love of the motor car is responsible for many of the changes we have seen in retailing and the products we buy. Large out-of-town shops are easily reached; we park there for free and fill our cars with bag after bag of shopping. By contrast, many years ago, I remember going shopping with Nanny Nicey, being dragged up and down the high street, waiting our turn at the butcher's, greengrocer's and the bakery.

Choice became a matter of how many shops you were prepared to visit, how far you wanted to walk and how much you could carry. No wonder I was quite old before I tasted a melon. So, yes, supermarkets with car parks were a boon, and people quickly took to the idea.

Now, though, we are reaping what we have sown. Town centres, for centuries the market-place for the local produce of a community, have been drained of their vitality. Bakers struggle to sell bread, cakes and pastries, having only a small passing trade of people who have come to visit their building society or to buy a birthday card. The outskirts of our towns have changed, too. Sprawling new estates, their detached houses packed closer together than terraced houses ever were, have no need of corner shops. They have been designed for the car, which demands ever more parking space. Gardens, an expensive waste of parking space, have dwindled to small postage-stamp-sized plots just big enough to accommodate a rusting barbecue. Estates are conveniently built next to a brand-new supermarket, which in theory can be reached on foot by eccentric pedestrians.

Vast stores create an illusion of choice so convincing that, if we can't find what we are looking for, we assume it's no longer made. As a result, we are eroding the diversity of our shopping experience. The retailers, of course, are only responding to our needs, and we can't really be too harsh on ourselves for wanting an easier life. As we rely on fewer and fewer chains, the range of products available to us becomes ever more refined and deliberated over by an ever-decreasing number of people.

Are we condemned to a gradual atrophying of real choice? Well, no, not at all, if that's not what we want. Already we are seeing consumers choosing to buy organic and Fair Trade products, and stores catering to this. Manufacturers who acquire smaller firms can often offer them the benefits of a larger European or even global distribution network for their products. Newly acquired products from around the globe can find themselves on our shelves alongside their established stablemates.

What can we do to help? Exercise our choice by trying new things, and look after the old favourites that you've not had in a while by buying some every now and again. Leave the car at home, and try walking to the corner shop for a few odds and ends. It may be frequented by elderly ladies, but they have a pretty good eye for a biscuit, and they'll make sure the shop-keeper gets all the good ones in. When you are next in town visiting the bank or buying a birthday card, pop into the bakery and get yourself some nice sticky buns, or some lemon curd tarts. You never know, you might even be able to get a nice cup of tea and a sit down while you are there. Lovely.

Acknowledgements

Our grateful thanks to all those who have helped with this book. First our agent Antony Topping for insisting that we do a book, and for all his help once he talked us into it. A special thanks to Denise Wilton for her lovely cup of tea, armchair and biscuit tin logos. To all those manufacturers who lent their support including United Biscuits, Fox's Biscuits, Burton's Foods, Bahlsen, Thomas Tunnock Ltd. To Barkers Bakery Ltd, Activehotels.com, Belly Busters Cafe for their assistance for the photography.

To all those who helped with the long and bizarre journey from office biscuit tin to book. Tony Wardell, Andrew Douglas, Eddie Hobson, Adam Reynolds, Rob Manuel, Joel Veitch, Nick Parker, Stephen and Mandy Borrill, Richard & Judy, Good Food Live, B4TA. To all the team at Time Warner Book Group, for their warmth and enthusiasm, and especially Tom Bromley for making the tea amongst other things.

Finally, of course, to all the biscuit-hunters, contributors and readers of NiceCupOfTeaAndASitDown.com whose input makes us both happy and proud at the very least twice a week, and remind us that we are actually very normal, especially Brian Barratt, Biscuit Man, James Fussell, Keith O'Kane and Maddalena Feliciello.

Shivers ran down the back of her neck at the outraged expression etched on Judah's face. She understood why Sean had bailed, but she wished he'd stuck around for moral support.

Judah scowled at her. "Can you really explain, Autumn? Because it appears that you're running around trying to dig up dirt on me and my business. This is serious stuff."

Shock roared through her at his accusation. "Surely you don't believe that. I would never do anything to cause you pain, Judah."

His eyes widened. "Are you kidding me? You have no idea of how much you once hurt me, and it appears that you're not finished twisting the knife." For a moment it seemed as if steam might come out of his ears. "Fishing is my life. My career. It's the only reason I get up in the morning." His voice rang out with outrage. "It's all I have in this world. If it's taken away from me, I really won't have anything left."

Chapter Four

Judah bolted out of Northern Lights without even waiting for a response from Autumn. So much emotion had risen to the surface in their encounter, he'd felt as if he was on the verge of an explosion. He knew that retreating from the situation was the only sensible option. He had so much built up inside of him that he was struggling to control. It had been this way ever since the accident, and although he was getting better at controlling his outbursts, he was still a work in progress. Judah didn't want Autumn to be on the receiving end of his anger. He would have a hard time living with himself if he continued to lash out at her. During the many years they had spent together, he could only remember one time when they had raised their voices at one an-

other. Judah had stuffed down the memory of Autumn breaking up with him because it hurt too much to relive it.

His brown-eyed girl. That's what he had lovingly called her. Seeing her after all this time had dredged up a lot of memories.

He strode away from the establishment until he reached the fenced-in promontory where he could look out over the vast valley of Serenity Peak. The gleaming water sparkled below. Judah watched as a flock of birds dipped down to capture their fish of the day. The natural beauty of Alaska had a way of soothing his soul as nothing else ever could. Slow, deep breaths, he reminded himself.

Serenity Peak, Alaska, had once been his haven. In the last few years it hadn't served that purpose whatsoever. Not after the accident. If it wasn't for his home and the memories of his wife and son that would always be imprinted within those walls, he would've picked up and moved ages ago. His fishing career was all he had left, along with a few loyal friends like Sean and Brody.

"Judah." He let out a soft groan as Autumn's voice washed over him. She'd followed behind him without his knowing it. Judah didn't trust himself to turn around and

face her. He was too emotional right now and Autumn was one of the few people who could make him feel vulnerable. He'd worked hard to develop his tough guy image.

Judah heard the crunch of footsteps in the snow, right before he felt her slight touch on his arm. He wanted to jerk away from her nearness, to run as far away as possible from her warm, brown eyes and the tender timbre of her voice.

"Judah. You completely misunderstood my conversation with Sean."

He whirled around to face her. "So you're not working for the *Tribune* on a story about the commercial fishing industry? Did I get that wrong?"

"No, you didn't. I am," she admitted. "But I'm in no way focusing on you and Fishful Thinking as part of my article. As you know, there have been allegations floating around the area about reporting irregularities and fraud. My assignment is to write about the local fishing industry and report on it for the *Tribune*. My focus is on all the fishermen from this area, not just you."

A little of his defensiveness fizzled out. "I just hope my operation doesn't get dragged

under. My professional reputation is at stake." He wanted to make it clear to Autumn that he wasn't going to sit by idly and allow her publisher to tarnish his name.

His gaze strayed to her trembling lips. "I'm hurt that you think so poorly of me. Why would I ever do that to you? I'm a professional journalist, not some hack."

Judah scoffed. "I've asked myself the same question about a lot of people here in Serenity Peak over the last four years. I reached the conclusion that there aren't always good reasons for human behavior." Judah could hear the bitterness ringing out in his voice. When had he let it consume him so wholeheartedly? Had losing Mary and Zane forever hardened him?

Autumn shook her head, causing her light brown hair streaked with gold to swirl around her shoulders. "You know me, Judah. Or at least you used to. That's not my style."

Judah wished he could believe her. So many years stood between them. Time hadn't stood still. It seemed as if they'd lived a lifetime without one another. In many ways they were strangers.

"We don't know each other any longer. Not

really," Judah said. Just saying the words out loud caused a little hitch in his heart. Never in a million years had he ever imagined they would be living such separate lives. If anyone had asked him back then, Judah would have predicted they'd be married and raising a house full of kids together. He shoved the thought down. It was incredibly disloyal of him to even think such a thing when his life had revolved around Zane and Mary.

Autumn's expression crumpled. She frowned at him. "I don't believe you can ever truly stop knowing someone you were once close to the way we were. And it might sound strange, but I'd like to think we can still be friends. I'm back for good, Judah. We're going to be in each other's orbit."

A ragged sigh slipped past his lips. "Maybe not. I don't get out much these days. I tend to stick to my own company."

"Sean mentioned that to me." She bit her lip. "Judah, it might not be any of my business, but you were always such a big part of the Serenity Peak community. The Judah I used to know was woven into the fabric of our hometown. He wasn't antisocial. Or angry. You were a leader in every facet of this town."

Judah bristled. Clearly Autumn didn't understand what he'd been through. The accident had forever changed him. He no longer cared about being at the center of all the goings-on in Serenity Peak. Too much hurt rested on his heart. But what did she know about it? Autumn hadn't lived in town for ages. She hadn't lived through tragedy as he had.

"You're right. It really isn't any of your business. I'm sorry I don't measure up to the younger version of myself." Anger vibrated in his voice.

Autumn's jaw dropped, and before she could say another word, Judah turned on his heels and strode toward his truck. He revved the engine and took off with a roar, letting his vehicle get the last word in. Even though he told himself not to do it, Judah looked in his rearview mirror to get a final glimpse of Autumn. Something tugged at his heart at the sight of her standing in the same spot where he'd left her. Her gaze trailed after him, her arms folded stiffly across her chest.

He swallowed past the bile rising up in his throat. Why had he been so curt with her? So mean and short-tempered? What was it about

Autumn that always left him wrestling with a host of emotions he would rather not face? Judah quickly looked away from her and focused on the road up ahead.

She had pricked at something inside of him he'd been struggling with for the past four years when he'd lost his family. Autumn's words had reminded him that he hadn't always been this way. He'd been kinder and gentler. A huge question came into sharp focus. Where had the old Judah gone and would he ever find his way back to the man he'd once been?

Dear Lord. Give me strength. Autumn repeated the words over and over again after she headed back inside Northern Lights. She'd almost followed after Judah to give him a piece of her mind for being so rude to her. *Mind her business!* He'd acted as if she was a nosy town busybody instead of a concerned friend. She let out a sigh. Not that he considered her a friend anymore. Judah had made that simple fact perfectly clear. Tears pricked her eyes and she furiously blinked them away. Although she'd fallen out of love with him many years ago, she still cared about him.

Seeing him so broken caused an ache inside her chest. It was part of her nature to be a problem solver. She hadn't meant any harm.

As she walked into her brother's office to gather her purse and coat, Autumn noticed Sean sitting back at his desk talking on the phone. Seconds later he ended his conversation, quickly turning his attention in her direction.

"Are you okay?" Sean asked as he scanned her face.

Autumn let out an indelicate snort. "I thought you didn't want to get involved."

Sean rolled his eyes. "I don't, but I can still check on my baby sister can't I?"

"I guess," she said in a low voice. Her conversation with Judah had been full of tension and she had no idea how to shrug it off. Being at odds with people always left her unsettled. It would take her a bit of time to calm herself down.

"Don't take this the wrong way, but you look as if you were whirled around by a tornado. What happened?" Sean asked.

Autumn placed her hands by her hips. "I don't know how you and Judah are best friends," she exploded. "He has a huge chip on his shoulder and he seems to think every-

one in Serenity Peak is out to get him, including yours truly. I just came back to town and he's acting as if I have an axe to grind with him."

Sean rubbed his temple. "That's about right. Try not to get too upset about Judah." Sean made a face. "He's really been through a lot, Autumn. Losing Mary was bad enough, but his only child as well. Zane was his mini me. That nearly killed him." Sean made a hissing sound. "And these whispers about Fishful Thinking being part of the fraud probe are tearing him apart. He won't admit it, but I can tell. He tries to be strong, but I can see the fault lines."

Autumn nodded. All of the anger she was holding onto began to dissipate. Judah had suffered major trauma. Of course he was bitter and angry. Who could blame him for wanting some distance from the townsfolk? Or brooding over his losses? She felt a bit ashamed that she hadn't been more sensitive. The interaction between them was complicated by their history. She should have known better than to try to give him advice, even though it had been well-meaning.

"I wasn't here when the accident happened,

but I can imagine how devastating it must've been," Autumn said. "The truth is, Judah and I don't know each other anymore. I said some things that he most likely viewed as overstepping." She shrugged. "I should have kept my mouth shut."

Sean quirked his mouth. "These days it doesn't take much to rattle him. Maybe you should just steer clear of Judah." He jutted his chin in the direction of her belly. "Your focus should be squarely on my niece or nephew."

"I can't argue with you about that." She rubbed her palm over her stomach in the hopes she would feel some movement. "I'm going to drive over to Sugar Works to see Violet." Autumn took a quick glance at her watch. "She's expecting me shortly." Just the thought of seeing her close friend after such a long time apart almost made her forget about Judah's bad attitude.

Sean smiled, showcasing a sweet set of dimples. "That'll be good for you. You won't believe all the changes over there."

Autumn grinned at her brother. "I can't wait to see," she exclaimed, waving as she exited the room. Paying a visit to Violet and the birch syrup company would serve as a per-

fect distraction from her run-in with Judah. She had to face facts. He wasn't the man she'd once known and loved. Time and circumstances had forever changed him.

Love and light was her new motto. With a baby on the way and a new life to build in Serenity Peak, Autumn had to focus on those things. If she did well with this story on the local fishing industry, the *Tribune* might keep her on their payroll long-term. That would mean that she would be able to support herself and the baby. Although her ex had offered her child support, she didn't want to solely rely on those funds. She was determined to show her child that she could stand on her own two feet and make a good life for them in Alaska.

Fifteen minutes later, Autumn was approaching the turnoff on the road that led to Sugar Works. The gold and cream sign surrounded by birch trees and snow was graceful and beautiful.

Serenity Peak was a town that had been formed as a haven for people seeking peace and refuge from their troubles. As a result, many of the local businesses centered around wellness and artistic endeavors. Sugar Works specialized in creating all-natural birch syrup

that was low in sugar and additives. The company had become so popular that the family had branched out to gift baskets and self-care items sold in a store on the property. From what Autumn gleaned from her conversations with Violet, Sugar Works was one of the most profitable companies in Alaska. The business employed a large number of locals, which energized the local economy.

Autumn navigated her truck toward the two-story log-style home. A feeling of nostalgia washed over her. This house was as familiar to her as her own. She'd spent countless hours here hanging out with her best friend. The Drummonds had always been welcoming and kind to her. As soon as she stepped down from the truck, she spotted Violet striding toward her and wildly waving her arms.

"Autumn!" Violet called out as she came rushing toward her with arms extended in greeting.

"Vi!" Autumn said as Violet enveloped her in a welcoming hug. A lemony scent rose to her nostrils. Violet's long hair brushed across her cheek. Autumn didn't ever want to stop embracing her best friend.

When they finally pulled apart, Violet reached for her hands and took a step back.

"Let me get a good look at you." She began nodding her head and smiling. "You look fantastic. Other than a little bit of a baby belly, you're the same as always. Pregnancy really suits you."

Autumn grinned. "I haven't even dealt with morning sickness. How about that?"

"You're blessed. When I was pregnant with Chase I couldn't keep a thing down. It made for a pretty miserable nine months, but I wouldn't trade him for anything in this world."

"Of course you wouldn't. He's a keeper," Autumn said. "Is he around? I'd love to give him a hug." Chase was Violet's only child. At nine years old, he was a warm-hearted, decent kid who'd always been close with his mom. The only static between the two had revolved around Chase never knowing his father. To this day, even Autumn wasn't privy to all the details about Violet's relationship with Chase's father or why his identity was such a closely held secret.

"He's over in Kodiak with some friends for a birthday getaway. He'll be back in a few days though." She shoved her hands in her jean pockets. "I'm trying to give him some freedom since he always accuses me of being a helicopter mom."

"You're a great Mom, Violet. If I'm half as devoted as you are my child will be quite fortunate."

Violet fanned her face with her hand. "You're going to make me cry. Now, how are you getting acclimated to Serenity Peak? It's been a minute since you lived here."

"So far so good, except I had a slight run-in with Judah at Northern Lights. He overheard me talking to Sean about my *Tribune* piece and he got really heated. For some reason, he assumed I was going to link him with the fraud allegations swirling around," Autumn explained.

Violet ran a hand through her strawberry blond hair and made a tutting sound. "It's a shame the two of you are at odds. If you're writing a piece about the local fishing industry, there's no one who can better assist you than Judah. That guy knows his stuff."

Violet was right. Judah was a fourth generation Alaskan fisherman. He'd come out of the womb knowing the ins and outs of the industry. If things weren't so strained between them Autumn wouldn't think twice about asking. But after their run-in she wasn't sure if he would be receptive to helping her.

"I don't know, Vi. He wasn't giving out

good vibes, if I'm being perfectly honest. Once he found out I was working with the *Tribune*, he got really heated." She chewed on her lip. "Anyway, wouldn't it be a conflict of interest to get help from someone who might be implicated in the investigation?"

"You're an ethical person, Autumn. And so is he. He's innocent until proven guilty. I have no doubt that if you uncovered something shady, you wouldn't bury it."

Autumn shook her head. "No, I couldn't ever do that. Not even for Judah."

Violet locked gazes with Autumn, and although no words were exchanged between them, Autumn knew her friend understood. She had been an up close and personal witness to Autumn's love story with Judah. More than anyone else, Violet knew how difficult it had been to end their relationship.

"How's Skye doing?" Autumn asked, swiftly changing the subject. She had no desire to dwell on the situation. As a journalist, she needed to figure out a way to make the research angle work so her article was stellar.

"She's okay," Violet answered. "It's taken her a long time to move past what happened with Tyler." Violet clenched her jaw. "For the

first year she was miserable, so it's nice to see she's emerging from the fog of depression."

Autumn's stomach lurched. She hadn't realized how bad things had been for Skye and it made her feel guilty for not being in Serenity Peak to help. "I can't imagine how difficult that was for her. She built her whole life around him and the idea of becoming his wife." Autumn watched as her best friend blinked back tears.

Autumn placed her arm around Violet and pulled her close to her side. Due to the ten-year age gap between the two sisters and the loss of their mother when they were young, Violet had served as Skye's surrogate mom. They'd always been exceptionally close.

"So, are you still writing an article about this place?" Violet asked, gesturing with her arm toward the expanse of land where the birch trees grew. "I've been looking forward to it ever since you mentioned it. Sugar Works has been doing well, but media attention is always a good thing."

"Of course I am. Not only was I eager to lay eyes on you, but I have my camera with me to take some pics to go along with my article." Autumn patted the camera bag she'd strapped over her shoulder. The idea of cap-

turing Sugar Works for a lifestyle feature was exciting.

Violet clapped her hands together and grinned. "Well then let me show you what's new. A lot has changed here in the last two years."

Autumn let out a low whistle as she looked around the property. "I knew Sugar Works was doing well, but you've really expanded your operations." She spotted a few new buildings in the distance. Violet looped her arm through Autumn's as they headed toward a small structure with several cars parked in front and people walking around. A sign reading "Sugar's Place" hung from the porch awning. A sweet bright green rocking chair sat near the entrance.

"This is our general store, named in Mama's honor. Come on inside and check it out," Violet said.

Sugar Drummond, Violet's mother, had been the heart and soul of the family. A random bout with the flu had led to her sudden death eleven years ago. Loving and lively, Sugar had conceived the idea for Sugar Works years before she passed away. Her husband, Abel, got it up and running in her memory. Sadly, Sugar hadn't been around to savor the

success of the wildly popular birch syrup company.

Once Autumn stepped inside the shop she was immersed in the down-home vibe of the establishment. A vintage Welcome to Alaska sign hung by the entrance. The smell of birch syrup and lavender permeated the space. Beautiful items were displayed in every nook and cranny. A vase of forget-me-nots sat at the checkout desk.

"You've outdone yourselves," Autumn gushed. "This place has so much charm."

"Thanks," Violet said with a grin. "I think Mama would be proud."

"Of course she would," Autumn said as she picked up a lavender sachet and raised it to her nose.

"Autumn!" Skye raced toward Autumn. Just before she reached her, Violet stepped between them.

"Easy there, sis. Baby on board," Violet cautioned. "You were coming at her like a runaway train."

"I'm sorry," Skye said, appearing sheepish. "You know me. I always get a little carried away."

"But your heart's always in the right place. I'm excited to see you too," Autumn said,

leaning down and pressing a kiss on Skye's temple.

Skye, with a mane of curly blond hair and big blue eyes, had always been the town charmer, ever since she was a little girl. Although she had a reputation for being spoiled, Autumn knew that her loved ones had only been trying to fill the void left by her mother's death. Perhaps they'd gone overboard, but Autumn believed in Skye's potential.

"Daddy's coming right behind me," Skye said with a wide smile. "He's even more excited than I am if that's possible."

Within seconds Abel appeared—a big bear of a man with a long grizzled beard and small spectacles that didn't seem to fit his round face. He'd always been a larger-than-life figure in Serenity Peak. Autumn loved him like a favorite uncle. With an ambling gait he came over and clasped her hands in his. "Welcome back, sunshine. It's been a long time coming."

She blinked back tears as Violet, Skye and Abel fussed over her. Being with the Drummonds was a second homecoming for Autumn. This wonderful sense of community was a huge reason why she had chosen to move back home and raise her baby here. New

York had been vibrant and pulsing with life, but it had never felt like a warm embrace. Not like Serenity Peak where she was woven into the fabric of the town.

Autumn snapped photos and jotted down notes while getting a tour of the renovated property. After saying her goodbyes she began the drive back to Cecily's place. The idea of getting assistance from Judah continued to flit through her mind as she drove the scenic route that gave her stunning views of the mountains. Just because it might be awkward to ask for his help didn't mean she shouldn't do it, Autumn reckoned.

Making a good impression with the *Alaskan Tribune* was vital to her long-term employment here in Alaska and she was struggling to flesh out this piece. Supposedly there was a federal investigation going on, but she hadn't found any information regarding it.

There were no lengths she wouldn't go to in order to provide for this baby. All she wanted to do was bring her child into the world and provide a wonderful life for the both of them.

Autumn was going to reach out to Judah and offer him an olive branch in the hopes of getting his assistance on her article. Things weren't going as she had expected. She couldn't

deny it would be tricky to get Judah to agree. Being around Judah had a way of making Autumn think about things she'd put in her rearview mirror ages ago.

She couldn't allow herself to get consumed by Judah and all of his issues, even if a part of her longed to help him heal.

Chapter Five

A few days after Judah had butted heads with Autumn at Northern Lights, he was at home working in his yard. The previous night's flurry had yielded a few more feet of snow in an already wintry February. For Judah, the crack of dawn usually signified an early departure from the marina for Fishful Thinking and its crew. Heading out on the Bay in the wee hours of the morning always reaped the best rewards. Since it was Sunday he'd been able to sleep in this morning, which was an unusual treat for a fisherman.

Even though Judah no longer considered himself a man of faith, he had arranged to shut down operations on the Lord's day so his crew could worship and spend precious time with their families. Sunday had always

been one of his favorite days to hang out with Zane and attend services together as a family. Even though he didn't worship any longer, it didn't mean others couldn't. If they wanted to waste their time in church, who was he to argue? All he knew for certain was that God had abandoned him in his darkest hour.

The sound of crunching tires on the snowy ground drew his attention to the tree-covered lane leading to his property. Someone was turning in to his driveway. These days Judah didn't get many visitors out here with the exception of a handful of folks he could still tolerate. Sean, Brody and his nephew, Ryan. Even Leif had stopped coming around since they had reached an impasse with Judah refusing to listen to his brother's side of the story, and Leif not apologizing for being disloyal. Judah had gone over it so many times in his head, but he still couldn't reconcile the fact that his brother still associated with some of the town residents who spread the rumors about Mary being under the influence at the time of the accident. It served as yet another devastating blow.

Sean's red truck came into view. He could see Autumn's face as she steered the vehicle toward him. He would know the graceful

tilt of her head anywhere, combined with her sun-kissed brown hair and striking features. After all this time she was still indelibly imprinted on him even though more than a decade stood between them.

What was she doing here? He battled against a feeling of irritation. He didn't feel like dealing with people today. Especially Autumn. She had a way of getting under his skin and burrowing there. That knowledge wrecked him. He couldn't even allow his mind to go there.

"Hey there, Judah," Autumn called out as she shut the truck door and made her way toward him. In her berry-colored parka and jeans, he barely noticed her baby bump. Autumn's athletic physique hid her pregnancy from casual observers. In her high school days, she'd played basketball and soccer, leading her team to championships in both sports.

"Autumn," Judah said, putting his shovel down. "What brings you out here?"

"A peace offering," Autumn said, holding up a small basket overflowing with items. "I didn't like the way we left things the other day. It didn't sit well with me."

"Thanks, but it wasn't necessary to bring me anything," he said, taking the basket off

her hands. It was filled with all kinds of treats—hot chocolate, scones, muffins and birch syrup. The aroma of the baked goods caused his stomach to grumble. He looked up at Autumn. "Did you bake these yourself?" he asked. Judah felt a smirk tugging at his lips. Autumn had never been a baker. Maybe now with the baby coming she'd been honing her culinary skills.

"I sure did," she said with a huge smile. "Not to brag, but I'm a pretty good baker these days. I took some lessons from a semi-famous New York baker and learned the craft." Autumn was beaming so hard Judah didn't have the heart to make any jokes. The image of Autumn baking up a storm in a trendy New York City loft apartment flitted through his mind. Her life, he imagined, had been very different than the one he'd led in small town Alaska. Miles apart from the one they had dreamed about living as a couple.

"Well, if they smell as good as they taste, I'm in for a treat," Judah said, surprising himself with his civility. His dad had always said Autumn brought out his sweet side. Judah was far more content these days being reserved.

Autumn shoved her mittened hands inside

her jacket pockets. "Judah, do you think we could talk? I have something to ask you."

Judah raised a brow. He was on high alert now and a bit annoyed. Of course Autumn hadn't just swung by to make nice with him. Something else was on her agenda. He let out a little huff of air as a feeling of disappointment swept over him.

"What is it?" he asked. "You don't need to beat around the bush. Just spit it out."

Autumn planted her hands on her hips. "And you don't need to be so gruff with me."

For a few beats they simply stared at one another, neither one giving an inch. It reminded him of the past and the numerous times they'd butted heads with one another. Neither one of them had ever wanted to give in to the other due to their strong wills. Each and every time they had ended up laughing it off and repairing the situation with a tender kiss. Something inside of Judah slightly softened. The ties he shared with Autumn always seemed to rise to the surface even when he tried to stuff the memories down. She wasn't like anybody else in Serenity Peak, so he had to make concessions for that fact.

"It's pretty cold out here. Why don't you come inside and I'll make us some of this hot

cocoa?" he suggested. Although he knew Autumn was a capable woman, Judah felt protective of her. *Old habits were hard to break,* he thought.

Autumn shivered and crossed her arms around her chest. "Don't mind if I do. It's downright frosty today. One thing I haven't quite missed about Alaska is being chilled to the bone."

"Watch your step," he instructed, reaching for her elbow as they walked across a slick patch of snow. He made a hissing sound. "I need to put more salt down on this ice." Judah reached into the big bucket by the side of the house and retrieved a cup full of salt that he sprinkled over the ice.

He wasn't going to have Autumn fall. Not on his watch. She was carrying precious cargo.

Once they made their way inside, Judah headed toward the kitchen and set the basket down on the counter. He put the kettle on then turned back to Autumn. "Make yourself comfortable. I can get a cushion if you need one."

Autumn chuckled. The rich sound of her laughter filled up his kitchen. "I'm good, Judah. Hopefully I won't need any cushions until I'm in my final stretch."

Pregnancy was treating her well, he thought. She looked like pure sunshine.

"Just making sure," he said, reaching into his cabinet to pull out mugs. When the kettle squealed Judah began filling the cups with cocoa then pouring hot water and milk on to the powder. He placed a mug and a spoon in front of Autumn then slid into a chair.

A feeling of nostalgia gripped him as he stirred the cocoa. "You never met my son, but he loved hot chocolate. He once drank so much of it on Christmas Eve he stayed up half the night with a bellyache." Judah surprised himself by laughing at his recollection of Zane. Words couldn't describe the ache of missing his beautiful boy.

"I actually saw him on one of my visits home. The two of you were going into the five-and-dime on Main Street. I should have said hello, but—" her voice trailed off.

"I get it," he said, bringing his mug to his lips. He didn't say it to Autumn, but he wasn't sure that he would have stopped to talk to her either if he'd spotted her. Especially if Mary had been present. His wife had always been a bit jealous of what he and Autumn had shared. Judah had never been able to fully

convince her that Autumn was his past while she was his future.

"It made my heart soar to see the two of you together. You seemed like such a natural at fatherhood. Your body language and the way he was gazing up at you spoke volumes." She fiddled with the rim of her mug. "I hope it's okay that I'm sharing this with you."

A thick lump sat in his throat and he coughed to try and clear it. "It's okay," he conceded. "I try not to think about him too often, but at moments like this his presence looms large."

Autumn looked at him with wide eyes. He sensed she wanted to say something but was biting her tongue. Folks tiptoed around him a lot, so he easily recognized the signs.

"What?" he asked. "You don't need to hold back with me. I don't break easily." Otherwise he would have shattered by this point, he wanted to add.

She locked eyes with him across the table. Her gaze felt so intense Judah was tempted to look away.

"I can't imagine how hard it's been for you to mourn the loss of your family, but I'm sure you have so many beautiful memories of Zane." Her tone oozed compassion. "If you

let them, those thoughts will nurture you. I know it's not the same, but when my Gran passed away I had so many keepsakes to remind me of how much she loved me." She looked around her. "I noticed you don't have any pictures of your son or Mary hanging up."

Judah put his mug down on the table and took a calming breath. Autumn no doubt meant well but Judah knew pictures wouldn't ease the sting of all he'd lost. What good would it do other than torment him? Their faces were already imprinted on his soul. Wasn't that enough?

"Someone once told me that there's no one way to grieve. This is my way. I don't like visual reminders." He stirred his drink. "I don't know if it's the healthiest way to deal with it, but it's the path I've chosen to walk."

Autumn seemed chastened. "I'm sorry," she blurted out. "It's not my place to tell you how to mourn."

Judah didn't correct her. He'd gotten a lot of advice over the years. All it did was make him wish he could just burrow inside his house and never leave. In the space of four years he'd lost Zane, his father and Mary. A triple kick in the gut. Even now, as he was

emerging from the darkest recesses of loss, he still wondered why God had let it all happen.

"So…you said that you swung by to ask me something? I think you've kept me in suspense long enough." He looked at Autumn over the rim of his mug as he finished the dregs of his cocoa.

Autumn nodded her head as long strands of her hair swirled around her shoulders. It was hard for him not to notice everything about her—the graceful slope of her neck, her fully rosy lips and the little freckles dotting her cheeks. She drummed her fingers on the table and bit her lip. His stomach did a little flip. He knew the signs of nervousness in Autumn.

"I need your help, Judah, with my article. I've wracked my brain and you're honestly the only one who can help me out. Please say yes. My future in Serenity Peak is riding on this story!"

Judah's expression reflected shock and a fair amount of dismay. Autumn held up her hands before he could respond and shoot her idea down. Some instinct warned her that he wasn't going to agree to help her. "Just hear me out. You're an expert in the field, Judah.

An authentic Alaskan fisherman. So much is at stake. I need to knock this assignment out of the park and I'm already feeling a bit in over my head."

She was beginning to ramble. Asking for this huge favor after all their years apart was humbling and a bit pushy. At times she wasn't even sure if she knew the man sitting across from her. Tragedy had forever altered his life. Perhaps this really wasn't a good idea even if she was desperate.

"I know this might seem awkward because of our past—" she began.

"That's not a factor," he snapped, cutting her off. "Our relationship was over a long time ago. We've both moved on with our lives."

"So you'll help me?" she asked. A sense of relief swept over her. If she couldn't deliver this article, she might be let go. In her situation as a single soon-to-be mother, stable employment was a huge factor in her ability to start over in Alaska.

"I didn't say that," he said, sighing. "What kind of help are you talking about?" Judah asked, furrowing his brows.

"To be honest, I'm a bit in over my head. I'm hitting a few brick walls with setting up

interviews with local fishermen and the clock is ticking," she admitted, feeling sheepish. She'd never been so frustrated in her professional life. It felt as if she was spending all her time chasing down folks who didn't want to talk to her. This assignment was proving to be way more challenging than she'd imagined.

"Meaning?" Judah pressed. He sat back in his chair and folded his arms across his chest.

Her shoulders slumped. "No one seems interested in talking to me, and I have a deadline looming. Doors are literally being slammed in my face. I guess twelve years away from my hometown makes me a stranger."

"That's not surprising, Autumn. You've been away from Serenity Peak for a long time. Don't take this the wrong way, but I'm sure they're wondering if you can be trusted." He let out a brittle laugh. "Folks in the fishing industry don't want to get tangled up in a federal investigation or say the wrong thing on the record. And I can't say that I blame them," he muttered.

"First of all, the article is a three-part series. The focus of my work isn't solely on the allegations of fraud. I'm determined to write about local fishermen and how they've shaped Alaska. But I need to speak with actual fish-

ermen to pull this off. You could make those introductions for me, Judah. You're very well respected in your industry," Autumn said. "And if you could take me out on your vessel just so I can understand the mechanics of how it all works with reporting the catch, I'd be ever so grateful." She knew it might seem pushy, but she figured she'd go all out. The worst he could do was say no, which at this moment seemed quite possible.

Judah ran a hand over his face. She could tell he was thinking things over.

"I'll make a few calls and see who I can reel in," he conceded. "No pun intended." She let out a little whoop of excitement.

He held up his hand. "Don't get too revved up just yet. There are a few folks I don't get along with so you might have to make those contacts on your own. But if my friends come through, you'll definitely have enough to write an article or two." The frown etched on his face hinted at things Autumn didn't dare ask about. From the sounds of it, Judah wasn't on good terms with a number of Serenity Peak residents. She had thought that the fishing community was an exception.

Autumn stood up from her chair. "Well, I'm going to dash before you change your

mind." Judah walked with her to the door. She reached for her parka on the hook and put it on before sliding her feet into her comfy winter boots, then turned back toward him.

As gratitude bubbled up inside of her, Autumn threw herself against Judah's chest and wrapped her arms around him. A woodsy scent rose to her nostrils. For a moment she felt transported to a place and time when she'd felt safe and protected in his arms. After a few seconds she released him, immediately noticing the tension on his face. Regret washed over her. She'd acted on impulse and created a terribly awkward situation between them. Judah's body language was stiff and uncomfortable. Clearly, she had crossed a line with him.

Why was it so difficult for her to accept that time had altered their once close relationship? And she didn't mean romance. They had been friends well before they'd fallen in love. A strong foundation of friendship had paved the way for a tender romance.

"Well, thanks again," she said lamely, beating a fast path out of the house. A fierce wind whipped across her face as she made her way back to the truck. Frankly, she needed the chill to cool her heated cheeks. Embarrassment threatened to swallow her up whole.

When she got behind the wheel she paused for a moment to cover her face with her hands. *Why had she hugged him?* It had been a rash and foolish act. She'd been so relieved to know he'd be helping her that she'd fallen into old familiar rhythms. Those days were over and done with.

Now she felt all turned upside down. She hadn't expected to feel such a rush of nostalgia. Being in close proximity with him had sparked something inside of her that she needed to snuff out as quickly as possible. Maybe it was a terrible idea to have asked for his assistance. It meant they would be thrown into one another's path.

Get a grip! she scolded herself. You're not a moon-eyed twentysomething anymore.

Autumn had come back to Serenity Peak with a single-minded purpose. Everything in her new life revolved around creating a solid foundation for her precious child and ensuring that she had the ability to put bread on the table. She harbored dreams of buying her own home for the two of them. She couldn't live with her sister indefinitely. And she wasn't going to take her eyes off the prize by getting distracted by Judah Campbell. He was grappling with his own serious issues.

Even though it had been twelve years since they had been a couple, Autumn couldn't ignore the sudden rush she'd experienced in those few moments back at his house. It served as a reminder that she needed to keep a professional distance between herself and Judah.

Judah watched from his front window as Autumn drove down the lane and out of his sight. Her unexpected visit had been full of surprises. He began performing his breathing exercises in order to calm down his rapidly beating heart. He'd been holding on fairly well until she'd sucker punched him with an out of the blue hug. Having Autumn pressed up against his chest had thrown him completely off-kilter.

He couldn't think of the last time he'd had such close physical contact with anyone. Part of being removed from the social whirl in Serenity Peak meant he wasn't shaking hands or sharing hugs with the residents. Judah hadn't missed the close contact with human beings until a few minutes ago. Everything about Autumn's nearness had awoken his senses. The lemony scent of her shampoo, the softness of her hair and the way the top of her head skimmed his chin.

And he had almost said no to her request. The words had been on the tip of his tongue when something inside him reversed course. She had a baby to raise and it wouldn't be much trouble to smooth the path for her with his fishermen friends. Taking her out on his boat might be a tad more difficult. Judah really didn't want that type of closeness to Autumn. As he'd just learned, that's how things could easily go astray.

Ever since he'd first seen Autumn at the pier, thoughts of her had permeated his waking hours. And perhaps some of his dreams as well. Thinking about her and their past relationship made him feel incredibly disloyal to Mary. His wife had loved him with such unbridled devotion. And he'd loved her in return—in a different way than he had loved Autumn, but it had been real and strong nevertheless. Autumn Hines had always had a hold on him. She had shattered his heart once before and left him gutted.

Only a fool would go back down that road again.

Chapter Six

"Are you sure it's a good idea to work with Judah? That just seems like you're asking for trouble." Her brother was looking at her with a mix of surprise and concern. They were standing in Northern Light's kitchen as Sean packed up meals for senior citizens in town. It was his way of giving back to a community that had always sustained him. "From what I saw the other day, the two of you are bound to clash."

"I'm hoping it'll be okay," Autumn said. "I've made dozens of calls for interviews and so far, no one has called me back. Hopefully that'll change when Judah gives me his personal contacts." She wrinkled her nose. "Otherwise my assignment might not even get off the ground. I need to make this work."

She wasn't going to admit to Sean that she was thinking along the same lines about Judah. It hadn't escaped her notice that her ex-boyfriend was a bit all over the place. At times she saw flashes of the man she had once known, but those instances were few and far between. Autumn had to believe he was simply trying to readjust himself after the trauma of the accident. She was willing to extend him grace.

"Don't say that I didn't warn you. I love him like a brother, but he's not the guy you remember. He's difficult." To her ears, Sean sounded judgmental.

"It's understandable," she snapped. "He's been through unimaginable trauma."

Her words crackled in the air between them. Sean raised a brow as he gazed at her. She instantly felt badly about her tone. She wasn't sure why the thought of Judah being criticized made her so prickly.

"I know, bug. I was here," Sean responded in a low voice. "I've seen him through some dark days. I'm team Judah 24/7. But I have to be honest, especially with my little sister."

She reached out and placed her arm around his waist. "I'm sorry, Sean. I don't know where that came from." He looked down at

her with an all-knowing expression. She had the feeling he was biting his tongue. Autumn didn't have to guess what Sean might have wanted to say. He no doubt thought she was sticking up for Judah because of what he'd once meant to her.

"Switching gears, could you run these meals out to Ida? I'm headed in the other direction of town with these additional food deliveries so you would be doing me a giant favor."

"Of course. It would be my pleasure. Miss Ida is my favorite teacher of all time." Ida Mayweather had taught fourth grade in Serenity Peak for over forty-two years. She was beloved by all. A recent health condition had left her unable to drive and housebound. Sean made sure to send over food on a regular basis as well as groceries.

Autumn bagged up Ida's meals and headed outside to the lot. Once she was in the vehicle she turned the radio on and began singing along to her favorite ballads. Some of these songs she hadn't heard in years. What a nice feeling to be able to enjoy the simple pleasures of life. With the end of her marriage, her husband's infidelity and this move back to Alaska, Autumn's stress level had been incredibly high.

Miss Ida lived out by the mountains near the famous Serenity Peak hot springs. The hot springs were a hidden gem in town. Its natural beauty was unmarred by any type of construction or developments. Pure, unspoiled Alaskan land. When Autumn had been a teenager, going swimming in the hot springs on the coldest day of the year had been a rite of passage.

When she reached the moose crossing sign, Autumn steered the truck off the main road and drove down a snow-packed lane. There weren't any neighboring houses for at least a mile, which made her worry about Miss Ida's safety. What if she fell or a fire started in her kitchen? Would anyone be near enough to help her in time?

Once she spotted the Welcome to Ida's Place sign hung on an ancient white spruce tree, Autumn knew she had arrived at her destination. It had been ages since she'd come all the way out here. A sweet memory washed over her as she stepped out of the truck and gazed across the property. Autumn and her classmates had once been invited to an end-of-the-year picnic at Miss Ida's house. To this day she could still remember the chocolate cake and the gaily decorated picnic tables in

her yard, as well as the excitement flowing amongst her peers.

The sight of Ida's house peeking through the trees caused the corners of Autumn's mouth to turn upward in a gigantic smile. The powder pink color was unusual for Alaska, but it was pure Ida. The home was cozy and unique. She had once famously said, "You don't get anything in life by being a cookie cutout of everyone else."

She walked up to the house and gently knocked on the front door, admiring the beautiful wreath with dried bluebonnets laced with baby's breath. Miss Ida had always been wonderful with crafts and making beauty out of ordinary objects. When the door swung open, Autumn had to stop herself from letting out a gasp. Judah was standing in the doorway looking very at home. He was laughing about something, and for a moment, there was a glimmer of the old Judah. His handsome features and straight white teeth were on full display. She wondered if she should retreat. Clearly, she was walking in on a tender moment between Judah and Ida that she didn't want to spoil.

"Who's at the door?" Miss Ida called out from behind him.

"It's Autumn. Autumn Hines," Judah answered, his gaze never straying from her own.

"I just came to bring Miss Ida some meals from Northern Lights," Autumn explained in a low voice, pressing the bag against his chest. When she tried to turn around and leave, Judah reached out and lightly grabbed her arm. He turned her right back around to face him.

"Where do you think you're going? Ida would have a fit if I let you leave." A hint of a smile rested on his lips. "And I would get the blame."

"Don't stand on ceremony. Let the girl in," Ida barked from inside.

"The queen has spoken." Judah shook his head and waved her inside, quickly closing the door behind her. At this point she knew better than to argue with the Queen Bee. After quickly shedding her winter parka and boots, Judah led her into the adjoining room.

As soon as she stepped into the living room, Miss Ida came into view. She was sitting in a love seat with a crocheted blanket draped over her torso and legs. She was wearing a pretty green sweater dress. With small spectacles, a heart-shaped face and a head full of gray hair, she hadn't changed all that

much. Just a few more lines on her lovely face. As always, she was adorable. Delilah was laying down next to Ida's chair, looking like a pampered pooch.

A fire crackled in the fireplace, providing a sharp contrast to the frigid temperature outdoors. Warmth immediately enveloped her as soon as she'd crossed the threshold.

"Miss Ida!" Autumn flew to her former teacher's side and bent down to give her a tight hug. The scent of eucalyptus rose to her nostrils, bringing back another wave of memories.

"Autumn, I think it's high time you stopped calling me Miss Ida. Just Ida from now on," she said, wagging her finger at her. "We're all grown folks now."

"Will do," Autumn said sheepishly. Judah was looking on with interest. He was practically smiling! If Ida was responsible for his lighthearted mood, then she was all in favor of them hanging out together on a regular basis.

"Oh, it's been a long time," Ida said, dabbing at her eyes with her finger. "I've missed you. And from what I hear from Sean, you're expecting a baby. Isn't that wonderful?"

"I am," Autumn said, placing her hand on

her belly. Although he didn't utter a word, Judah's eyes were trained on her stomach. *What was he thinking?* she wondered. About his own son who was no longer here? She couldn't imagine the painful road he'd walked.

"Bless you and this baby," Ida said. "Don't tell anyone, but the two of you were among my favorite students."

"No big surprise there," Judah said. "I always knew it," he said, snapping his fingers.

"Oh, you're still incorrigible," Ida said, her tinkling laughter filling the small space.

"So, what brings you here, Judah? Just paying a social visit?" Autumn asked. She'd been trying to stifle her curiosity about his presence at Ida's house, but in the end she couldn't resist inquiring. Sean and Cecily had painted Judah as a near recluse.

"Ida and I have a longstanding date once a month when my schedule allows it. We have lunch or play a few rounds of Scrabble," Judah explained. He winked at the older woman. "On occasion she lets me win." Ida was looking over at Judah as if he'd hung the moon.

And here Autumn had been under the impression that Judah only had a few friends in

town. She considered it a good sign that he was branching out by regularly visiting Ida.

"I'm so blessed to have you making time to come see me," Ida said. She was gazing at Judah as if butter wouldn't melt in his mouth. "It gets lonely out here."

Autumn's felt a pang in her heart upon hearing her former teacher's words.

Judah reached out and lifted her hand up, pressing a kiss on her knuckles. "You know you're the only girl for me, Ida."

Ida gently swatted him with her hand. "Don't toy with me, Judah Campbell. You're still as charming as ever and twice as handsome. Isn't he, Autumn?"

Autumn shifted from one foot to the other. Ida meant well but she'd placed Autumn in a terribly awkward situation. "Yes," she admitted as a small sigh slipped past her lips. "He really is." She was telling the truth. Judah had always had an abundance of charm… and his good looks were obvious to any female with a pulse.

Judah looked over at her, and for a few moments their gazes locked and held. Something flickered between them that hummed in the air around them. Goosebumps pricked the back of her neck. She looked away after

a few seconds, wondering if Ida had noticed anything. Perhaps she was imagining things. Nothing existed between her and Judah except their tangled past. And she didn't want anything either. All she dreamt about these days was holding a smiling baby in her arms.

"I was telling Judah how much I miss going fishing with my Clinton," Ida said with a sigh. "Those were the days." Clinton Mayweather hadn't been an Alaskan fisherman, but fishing had been a pastime that provided him with a great deal of happiness. Oftentimes he was accompanied by Ida when she wasn't in the classroom. They had shared a love story for the ages.

"He was such a sweetheart," Autumn said. Clinton had worked at the small post office in town, and he'd known everyone in Serenity Peak by name. Autumn smiled at the memory of the older man who had been short in stature but in possession of supersize charm.

"Any time you want to head out with me on Fishful Thinking, I'll be ready," Judah said, clasping his hand in hers.

"You're so kind, Judah. Always remember that weeping may endure for a night but joy cometh in the morning." Ida squeezed Judah's

hand. "Be patient. I know you've been at rock bottom, but your joy is coming."

Judah didn't respond but simply nodded and patted Ida's hand. Autumn couldn't be sure, but she thought there was a sheen of moisture in his eyes.

Bless Ida. She had the best heart. Autumn hated to think that someone as lively and wonderful as Ida might be lonely in her everyday life. The older woman had so much to give the Serenity Peak community.

"Why don't we have some of my almond Bundt cake? It's one of my best recipes if I do say so myself. I can put a kettle on and make tea," Ida suggested.

"You don't have to ask me twice," Judah said, patting his stomach with extra emphasis.

Autumn knew she should be heading back to town to focus on work, but she couldn't resist Ida's invitation. It wasn't hard to see that the older woman was feeling a bit isolated and in need of company. "I never say no to cake," Autumn teased. Ida's face lit up, which caused a warm and fuzzy feeling to spread through Autumn's chest.

After heading to the kitchen where Judah slid the bag with Ida's meals into her fridge, Ida began cutting generous slices of the cake.

As they settled down at the table, Autumn thought the kitchen had a serene ambiance. It reminded her of why she loved Serenity Peak so much. Ida had welcomed her back with open arms despite the fact that she'd been gone for twelve years. Watching Judah's rapport with Ida was the biggest revelation of all. Despite his traumas, he was still able to smile and be joyful. He was helping others. Trying to put one foot in front of the other.

As she bit into the almond cake, Autumn let out a sound of satisfaction as the mix of flavors hit her tongue. "This is delicious, Ida," she said. "If you ever get bored at home you could open up a bakery in town. Customers would be lining up outside the doors to experience this." She closed her eyes and savored the last morsel of the cake. When she opened them, Judah was looking over at her, his gaze intense.

"You think so?" Ida asked. Her tinkling laughter filled the air. "Clinton used to always tell me that he fell in love with my baked goods before he became smitten with me."

For the next half hour, they chatted recipes, baby names and discussed upcoming town events. The twenty-fifth annual town festival was coming up and Ida let it be known

that she wouldn't miss it for the world. Judah didn't talk much but he listened intently, saying a few words here and there.

"I hate to eat and run," Autumn said, reluctantly standing up from the table, "but I've got to head out."

"Me too. I've got a delivery to make," Judah said, a regretful expression stamped on his face. "As always, I had a great time, Ida. I'll be back soon, way before you even have a chance to miss me."

"Not possible," Ida said with a sigh. "I miss you already."

After putting her coat and boots back on, Autumn said her goodbyes to Ida, again promising to come back to visit soon. Judah and Delilah trailed behind her as she stepped back outside into the cold.

"So, I've been in contact with a few buddies of mine. They're willing to talk to you and give you an overview of the problems we fishermen are facing these days." He shrugged. "Hopefully it will help. Most fishermen want to be featured in a positive light and have a spotlight shone on our endeavors."

Her heart leapt at the news. "Oh, Judah. That's wonderful. I really appreciate it." She was so relieved at Judah's announcement that

she wanted to shout in celebration. Being a journalist meant the world to her and she would have been devastated if the assignment fell apart. It wouldn't bode too well for her standing with the *Tribune*.

"If you give me your cell number I can send them over as contacts."

"Sure thing," she said as she pulled out her cell phone and began exchanging information with him.

All of a sudden Autumn experienced a startling sensation in her stomach that caused her phone to slip from her hand to the ground. She let out a little cry and tightly gripped Judah's arm.

Judah became alarmed as soon as Autumn clutched him as if her life depended on it. The expression etched on her face was hard to read. Pain? Surprise? For the life of him, he wasn't sure what was going on but his pulse began to race.

"What's wrong?" he asked, fearing the worst. Because of what he had been through, Judah knew his mind often went to a worst-case scenario. He was still primed for disaster. Maybe he always would be.

"I'm sorry for grabbing you. I was just star-

tled," she said, her eyes filled with wonder. "Oh, my stars. I—I think the baby just kicked me for the first time." She let out a shaky laugh. "It was the oddest feeling, but amazing at the same time."

She looked more radiant in this moment than he could ever remember. Joy lit her up like a beacon. He bent down and picked up her cell phone, quickly handing it back to her. It gave him a brief opportunity to catch his breath. He felt relief flow through him that she wasn't in harm's way. Of course she was excited. A baby's first movements were worthy of a celebration.

Autumn lovingly ran her hand over her abdomen. Judah couldn't quite manage to take his eyes off Autumn's perfectly rounded stomach. How many times had he placed his palm on Mary's stomach so he could feel Zane's kicks?

At this moment all he wanted to do was reach out and feel the baby kicking. It was such a beautiful affirmation of life. For so long now he had been almost afraid to live, scared of doing anything that might be viewed as enjoying himself or moving forward. Sean thought it was survivor's guilt. Maybe his best friend was right in his assess-

ment? Lately he'd been taking baby steps toward finding a measure of happiness in his life. It was one of the reasons he enjoyed visiting Ida so much. She was restoring his faith in the residents of Serenity Peak.

"Go ahead. It's all right, Judah," Autumn prodded. "I don't mind." Autumn seemed to have read his thoughts. That's how it had always been between them. They had shared such a close bond, one he'd once thought of as unbreakable.

Judah tentatively reached out and placed his hand on her parka over her stomach. For a few moments they stood there waiting for something to happen. Disappointment flooded him at the idea that the moment might have passed. Then suddenly he felt movement under his hand. A thumping sensation began to pulse against his palm in rapid succession.

"Do you feel that?" Autumn asked, sounding breathless. Her eyes shimmered with happiness.

He nodded, not trusting himself to speak. A huge lump sat in his throat. At first the movements made him feel as if he was soaring high, until a feeling of such guilt washed over him it made him weak in the knees. This

moment was too much to bear. A reminder of everything he'd lost.

What was he doing? This had absolutely no connection to him or his life.

It was pathetic to get so excited about a baby his ex-girlfriend was bringing into the world. He'd lost his only child. That knowledge would never change and it gutted him.

Judah needed to get away from here as fast as possible. Away from Autumn. Away from this celebratory moment. His emotions were all over the place right now. Grief had a way of working its way into a million different scenarios. Just when he thought he had turned a corner, the ache of loss had seized him by the throat and wouldn't let go.

"I need to make a fish delivery to Northern Lights. I've got to go." Judah forced the words out of his mouth, surprising himself by how steady his voice sounded. He turned away from Autumn, letting out a whistle so Delilah would follow him to the truck.

"Wait!" she called out after him. "What about my going out on Fishful Thinking with you and your crew?"

Judah wanted to let out a loud groan. Taking her out on his boat was the last thing he wanted to do, but he had always been a man

of his word. He turned back toward her. "I'll give you a call so we can arrange something." The brilliant smile he received in return instantly made him regret agreeing to take Autumn out on the Bay. Being around her wasn't good for him. There was such a thing as feeling too much, which was what had happened when he'd touched her stomach. Stuffing his emotions down was much safer territory for him.

His hands trembled as he situated himself in the driver's seat and placed his hands on the steering wheel. At moments like this Judah had always been able to pray. For Grace. Mercy. Peace. Wisdom. Now, he couldn't even find the words. And even if he could, Judah wasn't sure God would be listening to him.

Autumn watched as Judah roared away from Ida's house with his truck's wheels spinning on the snow-covered ground. His desire to be as far as possible from her was obvious. She really didn't blame him. She was certain he'd been thinking of his own son when he'd felt her baby's movements. It had been written all over his face when he'd pulled away from her. She'd never meant to cause him

pain, but it seemed as if that's all she ever did with Judah.

What had she been thinking? Why had she been so inconsiderate as to invite him to feel her baby kicking? She had gotten carried away in the joyful moment and she'd wanted to share it with someone. She was going to have to remind herself that they were no longer friends…or anything else for that matter.

The stunned look on Judah's face had been heartbreaking. And it had been a direct result of the little bundle growing inside of her. With an expressive face like Judah's, it was impossible to ignore his feelings. If only she had kept her excitement to herself. The moment had come out of the blue, leaving her incredibly flustered. There hadn't been time for her to play it cool. The life growing inside her was a constant source of happiness.

Autumn placed her hands on her baby bump. A moment that had brought so much delight to her had left Judah reeling. Sometimes life was so complicated.

Running into Judah this afternoon had been pure coincidence. She had been pleasantly surprised by his sweet relationship with Ida and the way he seemed to experience genuine joy in their interaction. He'd shown her

glimpses of the man she had once known. She hadn't allowed herself to acknowledge it for quite some time, but she'd missed him over the years. His presence in her life had always been strong and steady. As solid as the Rock of Gibraltar.

And now, she was torn between her goals here in Serenity Peak and checking on Judah to make sure he was all right. Was it even her place to do so? She highly doubted he would welcome it. Their past was full of moments where he'd been the one to lift her up when she'd fallen. It was hard to ignore that he was a man who seemed to be in pain. Didn't she owe it to him to try to help?

Keep your focus on the baby and your career, she reminded herself. Sean had tried to warn her earlier today about the complications of being near Judah, but she hadn't wanted to listen. For some reason she always thought with emotion when it came to her first love rather than common sense. Judah was a complication to all of her best-laid plans in Serenity Peak. She needed to remember why she had come back home in the first place and that it had absolutely nothing to do with Judah Campbell.

Chapter Seven

Autumn woke up to the aroma of freshly cooked bacon and eggs. There was no way she could go back to sleep with these tantalizing smells wafting through the house. Her nose and a grumbling stomach led her to the kitchen where Cecily had left her a note along with a covered plate of food.

Good morning. I thought you and the baby might like some pancakes, bacon and eggs. Love, Cici.

The last few days her sister had shocked her with her thoughtfulness. Flowers for no reason. A foot massage. A romance novel written by her favorite author. And now this scrumptious breakfast. It served as a reminder that she needed to try harder to foster a good relationship between them. She devoured her

breakfast, finishing with a tall glass of orange juice. After hand washing her dishes and placing them on the rack, Autumn went into high gear.

It was time to get to work, she realized. This article wasn't going to write itself. Even though she had been a freelance journalist back in New York City, Autumn still felt a little rusty. She couldn't think of the last time she'd actually met someone in person to interview them for a piece. So much was done online or over the phone these days. Butterflies soared around in her stomach. She felt as nervous as a kid on the first day of school.

She dressed casually in a purple cashmere sweater and a pair of jeans. She could barely zip them up anymore thanks to her rounded belly. She'd purchased a bunch of maternity clothes, but she still hadn't worn any of them. Judging by the way these jeans were fitting, it was high time she did.

Thanks to Judah's list of contacts, she was making headway in setting up interviews. This morning she had arranged to meet two brothers—Brody and Caden Locke. Brody worked on the Fishful Thinking with Judah while Caden was a local pilot. Both had longstanding ties to the local fishing community.

They also had generations of fishermen in their family. Since Serenity Peak was on the water and accessible only by air or ferry or boat, fishing had always been a huge industry.

Meeting at Northern Lights wasn't an option. The restaurant was popular and tended to get hectic at this time of day. She didn't want to have to talk loudly over the din of the crowd or be interrupted by acquaintances. Brody had suggested they meet at Humbled, a popular coffee shop on Fifth Street that had a connecting bookstore next door. Owned by Skye's best friend, Molly Truitt, it was a wonderful way to combine a love of books with an appreciation of coffee.

Autumn arrived early and ordered a green tea since she was steering clear of java during her pregnancy. There was a large selection of baked goods—scones, muffins, coffee cakes and an assortment of bagels.

"I highly recommend the lemon blueberry scone," Molly said, smiling at Autumn as she eyeballed the baked goods. "They're the perfect blend of tart and savory." With long brown hair that she wore in a single braid and round-shaped glasses, Molly always came across as more youthful than her actual age.

"I ate breakfast not too long ago, but I can't resist a good scone," Autumn said.

The ambiance of the coffee shop was warm and cozy. The walls were covered with Bible quotes and stunning pictures of Alaska. There were comfy love seats, plush couches and retro beanbags to sit on. The walls had been painted a calming eggshell color with little splashes of pink and baby blue. The vibe was soothing and peaceful, which was perfect for Autumn's mood. It was exactly what she needed in her life.

Autumn took her tea and the scone over to a comfy looking love seat. After sinking down into it she realized that she might have some trouble getting up. Her center of gravity was completely off-kilter these days. A few minutes later the brothers walked into the café. Although she vaguely remembered both from when she'd lived in Serenity Peak, they'd changed quite a bit since they were kids. They were fraternal twins, but to Autumn, they barely looked like members of the same family. Both were handsome men. Brody was just under six feet and more compact than Caden, who was tall with a rugged frame. The brothers had warm russet tones to their skin and kind brown eyes.

"You must be Autumn. I'm Brody. And this is my brother, Caden," Brody said by way of introduction. Both men reached out and shook Autumn's hand before sitting down on the couch next to her love seat.

"Thanks for coming. I really appreciate it," Autumn said. "Can I get you anything to drink or eat? It's the least I could do as a thank you for meeting up with me."

"No, thanks," Caden said. "I think we're all set."

"Judah said you're writing a piece about the fishing industry in the Kenai Peninsula," Brody said. "What in particular did you want to know?"

"I work for the *Alaska Tribune*. This is my first piece for them and it's an overview of the local fishing industry. As you know there's been a lot of ups and downs over the past few years with many fishermen suffering big financial losses."

Brody and Caden exchanged a glance. "Is this about the feds investigating?" Brody asked. "We've heard rumors but nothing specific to this area."

"To be honest, I haven't been able to get any information as to whether the authorities are close to charging anyone or if it's merely

a rumor. As a result, I'm not going to lead with the alleged fraud," Autumn explained. "I'm going to wait for further developments."

"The authorities are keeping it close to the vest from what I've heard, which is why rumors are swirling around," Brody said. "There have been irregularities for years in the fishing industry, but all I know is that the fishermen I work with are above reproach. No one is altering the books or overfishing in off-limit areas."

"That's the frustrating thing," Caden said. "It's not right for a few dishonest fishermen to tarnish the entire profession."

"There have been whispers about Judah," Brody admitted. "None of it is true. I've worked alongside him for five years. He's as honest and hardworking as they come."

Brody was only confirming what Autumn already knew about Judah, although it was nice to know that his colleagues respected him.

"I'm curious though. What do you think is going on?" Autumn asked. Every instinct told her that the rumors about Judah were way off base. But who was behind them?

"There's someone who used to work for Judah. Scott Purdue. He was let go because he was caught cutting corners. He started his

own operation, and so far, it's not doing too well," Brody explained. "I really think he's trying to trash Judah's reputation by starting a whisper campaign against him."

"Makes sense," she said, pausing to type notes on her iPad. It was a lot easier than jotting everything down in a notebook. She wasn't comfortable publishing anything about Purdue without tangible proof, but this information might help her in the future. "I haven't heard anything negative from my source about Judah. All of the whispers are coming from the local community, which is also unusual."

"My guess is it's coming from the same person. He's smearing Judah's name because he's his competition," Caden added.

"Plus, he's angry about being let go. He's not the sort to forget," Brody said, his expression darkening. Both Caden and Brody were firmly in Judah's corner. Their loyalty was unbreakable.

And if there was one thing she knew for certain it was that Judah Campbell wasn't the type of man to commit fraud. He may have changed due to a family tragedy, but his core values remained intact. He came from a lineage of fishermen—proud, hardworking men who had carved out a living for themselves in

a harsh and oftentimes unforgiving climate. As a journalist she had to remind herself to keep an open mind, but she believed in Judah's integrity.

For the next hour Autumn talked about the highs and lows of being a fisherman in Serenity Peak as well as their individual experiences. Although both men were overwhelmingly positive, neither one sugarcoated the drawbacks. Autumn found herself entertained by their comedic stories and equally moved by the struggles commercial fishermen faced. By the time the brothers headed out, Autumn felt like they were old friends. And she now had a bunch of ideas floating around in her head about how to tackle her subject matter. Fishermen were the heart and soul of the Kenai Peninsula. Instead of them being under the umbrella of suspicion, they should be lauded. Praised and respected. Her heart swelled at the idea of writing about such an honorable Alaskan profession.

She would continue to investigate fraud within the local fishing community, in the hopes of exposing the guilty parties in the series finale. And if she uncovered some information to help Judah in the process, all the better.

* * *

The smell of the Bay rose to Judah's nostrils, salty and briny. It was such a part of him now, as constant as the sun that rose every day in the sky. He breathed in deeply as he watched a glaucous-winged gull swoop down low across the water. Judah raised his hand in greeting to a few of his crew members who had arrived and were heading on to the boat.

Judah had surprised himself by phoning Autumn the other day and throwing out some dates for her to accompany him on Fishful Thinking. He still wondered if it was the right call, but it was too late to backtrack now. Autumn was supposed to be meeting him here at the waterfront any minute now. He had already given his crew the heads up so that no one would be taken off guard by her appearance. It was usually just him and the crew. Since she was Sean's sister, Judah knew they would greet her with open arms.

The tomato red truck came barreling into the parking lot before pulling up a few feet away from him. Seconds later Autumn emerged from the truck carrying a small duffel bag. Dressed in an olive green thick parka and a pair of long rain boots, she had come prepared for a day at sea. A black beanie

perched on her head completed the look. For the life of him, Judah couldn't ever remember someone looking so stunning for a day out on his boat.

"I hope I'm not late," she said, sounding out of breath. "I burned some toast this morning and set off all the alarms."

"You're right on time," Judah reassured her. "Are you sure about this? It gets rocky out there when the waves get rough."

"I'm very sure," she said. "I've never gotten seasick a day in my life. This isn't my first time on a commercial fishing boat."

But you weren't pregnant then, he wanted to say. He held his tongue. Autumn was grown enough to make her own decisions. He didn't want to come across as trying to dissuade her even though he worried about her being uncomfortable.

"Let's get started then," he said, walking toward the pier where Fishful Thinking was docked. Judah felt a burst of pride as they drew closer to the boat. To own his own fishing boat and employ a crew had been his dream ever since he was a kid. Autumn had been right alongside him as he'd dreamt big. And he had made them all come true.

"This is a great size," she said, just as he

held out his hand for her to step from the dock onto the boat. He watched as she looked around. "It's beautiful," she said. "Your dad must have been really proud."

"He was," Judah acknowledged. Autumn had been one of his dad's favorite people. They had gotten along so well and fully understood one another. "He often said that he wished he was twenty years younger so he could be one of my crew members." The memory didn't sting like it normally did, but instead settled over him with the warmth of a cozy blanket. "All of this is because of him."

"Not all of it, Judah. It came to fruition because of your vision and hard work. Kurt would never want to take credit for your accomplishments."

Autumn was right. His father had been a humble and generous man who thankfully had lived to see Judah make a success out of his fishing outfit. Missing him was a part of his everyday life, but lately it was more of an ache than the sharp twist of a knife. He had been sick for a while and Judah had known the end was coming, which was a lot better than being blindsided by an accident.

"Just make sure to steer clear of the action," Judah advised. "I don't have a problem with

you observing from a distance, but it's unsafe for you to be too close to the crew. You might get bumped by accident or get tangled up in something. Plus, I'm giving you a life jacket just in case something goes awry." He saw Autumn opening her mouth to protest. "It's the only way I can make this work so I'm not questioning my sanity. Agreed?"

Autumn's frown led him to believe she was going to fight him on the rules he'd laid out. He folded his arms across his chest and held her gaze as she stared him down. She let out a huff of air, then said, "Okay. Your boat. Your rules."

Every time he turned around, Autumn was there, watching him and his crew's every move like a hawk from a safe distance. She had a little notebook where she scribbled things down. Judah wasn't surprised when it got waterlogged and she had to abandon it. She seemed to take it in stride, shaking her head and smiling. He couldn't be sure, but Autumn seemed to be having fun.

"How are you doing?" Judah asked when he had a free moment to check on her. She was looking on as his crew netted herring and arctic char. There wasn't a single detail she didn't seem interested in. He could tell

by her furrowed brow and the look of intense concentration etched on her face.

"This is great," she said. "Being here brings back a lot of memories."

Judah knew exactly what she meant. Back when they'd first started dating, Judah had invited her out on his father's boat—the Alaskan—on several occasions. For Judah it had been a test of sorts to see if she could handle the fisherman lifestyle. Autumn had passed with flying colors and managed to wrap the entire Campbell family around her little finger. She'd even landed the catch of the day, a King Salmon. Leif had crowned her Queen of the Bay. The nickname had stuck long after their excursion ended.

"Those were good times," he said. Judah surprised himself with the admission. He had been head over heels in love with Autumn back in the day. Everything between them had been near perfect, with talk of marriage and kids coming up from time to time between them. Then, without warning, Autumn had broken up with him with little or no explanation. He had been shattered and confused, but he'd been forced to accept her decision. Frankly, he wasn't sure he had ever gotten over it. On the rebound, he'd begun

dating Mary and quickly dived into a serious relationship. Looking back on it, he had still been licking his wounds when things got started between him and Mary. There had been numerous times when she'd called him on it, but he'd blindly denied her assertions.

"Some of the best moments of my life," Autumn continued. "There's something so carefree about being out on the open water. I've really been looking forward to it. It's almost as if we're in our own world, isn't it? I can see why you love it so much." Her expressive features were lit up like rays of sunshine.

Autumn had always understood the lure of the water and why being a fisherman had been his life's passion. His dream job. He'd always believed that this meant they were made for one another. But he couldn't have been more wrong.

"My son loved being out here too." He let out a low chuckle. "Mary wasn't keen on boats. Believe it or not, she never learned to swim, but we gave Zane lessons at two years old. He swam like a minnow. He had the whole crew wrapped around his finger." His voice wobbled. "They called him Little Captain because he used to bark out orders like an adult."

"He sounds like a chip off the old block,"

Autumn said, grinning. "That must have made you proud."

"He was everything to me," Judah said in a muffled voice. He wasn't able to explain his son any better than that. Usually he avoided talking about him because when he did it felt as if he had shards of glass in his throat. Bringing up Zane had caused his soul to ache for all he'd lost in an instant. For whatever reason, the words had come today. He wondered if it was due to Autumn and their long history. And although the pain was still there, at least he could breathe normally. And chuckle. And remember Zane without wanting to smash something into pieces.

"I imagine he was...and will always be. Back in New York I had a friend who lost a child to cancer. I remember her saying that she would always be a mother and her child's life mattered. So she encouraged everyone to talk about her daughter and say her name. That way she wouldn't ever be forgotten."

Judah nodded. "Makes sense. Sometimes people don't want to mention Zane so as not to upset me. But it's way more painful to act like he wasn't here. To erase him like he never existed."

Autumn made a sympathetic sound. "That

must be frustrating. I imagine most parents would want that affirmation."

He kept surprising himself by telling Autumn things he hadn't told a single soul. She had this effect on him unlike anyone else.

All of a sudden the water began churning violently with the boat rocking from side to side. A sudden groundswell caused Autumn to lose her footing and stumble on the slippery deck. Judah reached out and grabbed her parka, pulling her against him to prevent her from falling. He put his arms around her and anchored her to his chest as the boat continued to undulate. Autumn looked up at him with wide eyes. Her hands were on his chest for balance. He felt a little jolt at the contact. For a moment their gazes were locked as everything else around them faded away. She was standing so close to him Judah could see the little caramel flecks in her eyes and the small gold studs in her ears.

"Are you all right?" Judah asked, still holding her tightly. The idea of letting go of her left him with an empty feeling.

"I—I'm fine," she said. "I just lost my balance for a moment."

"I tried to warn you that the waters get choppy out here." Thoughts of her getting

hurt wouldn't stop whirling around his mind. As the boat's captain it was his responsibility to safeguard everyone on board. He didn't want anything to happen to Autumn or the baby, especially not on his watch. And definitely not on his boat.

After making sure the vessel was no longer lurching, Judah let go of her.

"I know, Judah, but I wasn't in any danger," Autumn said. "Please don't worry about me. I'm a big girl."

Despite the chill in the air, a warm sensation spread through his chest. "True, but I'll always want to keep you safe, Autumn. Old habits die hard."

And that was the problem. After all this time and the years that stood between them, Judah still cared about Autumn way more than he wanted to. It was the main reason why being near her wasn't in his best interest. The last time around it had taken a long time to mend his shattered heart. There was no telling what could happen if he opened the door even a crack and let Autumn in. This time he might never recover.

Old habits die hard. That pretty much summed things up. Here she stood on the

deck of Fishful Thinking filled with admiration for Judah. Watching him reel in arctic char, haddock and herring had been an eye-opener about what it took to operate a commercial fishing vessel. Under Judah's direction his crew was a finely oiled machine. The camaraderie they shared was evident in the way they worked so well as a team. Seeing their haul up close served as a reminder that the work of Judah and his crew fed people and supported the seafood industry in Alaska.

Now she knew how Judah had kept his rugged frame in such great shape all these years. There was a lot of physicality in his job, and he was in constant motion when he wasn't driving the vessel. Years ago when she had gone out on the Alaskan with Judah's dad there hadn't been much work involved since it was a pleasure trip, so she hadn't really known how everything operated. By the time they docked back at harbor, Autumn felt as if she'd attended a master class in commercial fishing.

The experience of being out on Kachemak Bay so far from land had been a thrilling adventure, far removed from her daily life. With the wind whipping through her hair and the

heady scent of the Bay filling her nostrils, Autumn had been euphoric. Certain situations in life made a person feel as if they were living life to the fullest. This had been one of them. And that moment where Judah had held her in order to prevent her from stumbling had been heavily charged with electricity. She now knew with a deep certainty that she hadn't been imagining anything at Ida's house.

After they arrived back at the harbor, Autumn said her goodbyes to the crew before making a beeline to Judah.

"I really appreciate you allowing me to go out on Fishful Thinking with you and the crew," Autumn said. She had chosen her words wisely. Today had been a gift— of his time and expertise, as well as Fishful Thinking and the crew. There had been such a strong sense of pride in their work that radiated from all of them. She couldn't remember ever feeling so impressed by a group of people.

Judah nodded. "I hope it helps with your article."

"More than you realize. I have a newfound admiration for your profession."

Judah nodded. "That's nice to hear. I'll pass

it along to the crew." He jerked his chin in the direction of his crew members. "I've got to finish up before I have a mutiny. Take it easy, Autumn."

As she walked toward her truck, fatigue swept over her. She'd done a full day on Judah's boat, and she was beat and hungry. The lunch cooked by the crew on board had been hearty, but she was extra hungry these days as she entered her third trimester. Pretty soon she would be bringing a child into the world, something she hadn't thought possible.

Now that she had gone out on Fishful Thinking with Judah, she really wouldn't have much of a reason to be in contact with him. Along with the interviews she'd been doing, she would now have enough to flesh out an article. She should feel relieved, yet a part of her was lamenting the end of something. It was difficult to put her finger on her emotions, but she thought it might be tied up in the friendship they'd once shared. She missed sharing secrets and finishing each other's sentences. Nothing was as it used to be, but that didn't stop her wanting to see Judah whole again and healed.

Frankly, she didn't know if it was possible. She had always believed that with God any-

thing was possible, but she wasn't even sure if Judah was a man of faith anymore. If she had to guess she would say he wasn't. Loss had rocked his world and shaken his faith, she imagined.

Perhaps it was for the best that she and Judah kept away from one another, she reasoned. Judah made her think of things she hadn't thought of in over a decade. And he made her feel guilty about the secret that had ended their relationship. Back in New York it had been easy to cast her lie of omission to the side and pretend as if it had never happened. But now that she was back in Serenity Peak and close to Judah, the lie was weighing heavily on her every time she gazed into his soulful blue eyes.

Chapter Eight

A loud knock sounded on Judah's front door, causing Delilah to let out a loud bark in response. The door swung open and his nephew, Ryan, strode into the house. With a head of dark hair and sky blue eyes, Ryan turned heads. He had a reputation in Serenity Peak as a charmer. In the past, it had gotten him in a bit of trouble. Ryan was a deputy in town, and he'd spent the last year trying to rework his image. All Judah saw when he looked at him was a good-hearted young man who at twenty-seven years old was still learning and growing.

"Hey, Unc. I heard you weren't out on Fishful Thinking today." Ryan headed straight toward where Judah was reclining in his living room. Delilah trailed behind Ryan, looking up at him as if he owed her a doggy treat.

Judah let out a groan. Gossip spread as fast as tornado winds in small towns. He hated being talked about. "How did you hear about it?" Two days ago he'd aggravated an old shoulder injury and he was taking a few days off due to the throbbing pain.

"I ran into Brody, and he told me you were taking off a few days. It wasn't hard to figure out that you must be out of commission, because you never miss a day of work." Ryan's tone was matter-of-fact. He held up a paper bag. "I brought some reinforcements." The smell of savory meat and grilled food rose to his nostrils. How mad could he be since Ryan had brought food along with him?

Judah winced as he tried to sit up on his couch. "It's my shoulder. I think that I pulled a muscle. I just need to rest it for a few days and use some heating pads and take pain relievers." He didn't bother to tell his nephew that he had been getting cortisone injections in his shoulder for the past few years.

"Let me know if you need any Bengay," Ryan said, bursting into laughter despite his best attempt to keep a straight face. His nephew enjoyed acting as if Judah was as old as Methuselah. He couldn't count the number of times he'd made this joke.

Judah frowned. "Ha ha. You're hilarious."

Ryan placed the bag down on his coffee table and began taking out the food and making plates for both of them. He slid a plate over to Judah along with utensils and a water.

"So I heard Autumn went out on the boat with you a few days ago." Ryan flashed a broad smile. He was the spitting image of Leif when he was in his midtwenties.

Judah let out a groan. "Brody has a big mouth," Judah said.

"I never said it was Brody," Ryan said with a chuckle. "Did you throw your back out showing off for her?"

Judah glared at him. "Did you just come over here to aggravate me?"

"Pretty much. Is she still as gorgeous as ever?" Ryan asked.

"Even more so if that's possible," Judah admitted. "She's writing an article on the fishing community so I did her a favor. End of story."

Ryan had a wistful expression etched on his face. "I had the biggest crush on her when I was a kid."

Both Judah and Autumn had been well aware of his nephew's affection for Autumn. She had viewed his fondness as sweet and heartwarming.

"She's having a baby in a few months."

Ryan drew his dark brows together. "Whoa. I didn't see that plot twist coming."

Neither did I, Judah wanted to say. He bit his tongue, knowing if he did it would only add flames to the fire. He wondered if anyone was whispering about him and Autumn. Not that there was anything going on, but everyone in town knew their history and the gossip mill already knew she'd been out on his boat.

Judah quickly filled him in on her marital status. "She wants to raise her baby here. By herself. Sounds like her ex is completely out of the picture."

Ryan let out a low whistle as he dished out the food on to Styrofoam plates. He settled down into a seat across from Judah. "That's admirable. Raising a baby as a single mother won't be easy. She's going to face a lot of challenges."

"If anyone can rise to the occasion it's Autumn," Judah said forcefully.

Ryan raised a brow. "So, is there any chance the two of you can find your way back to one another? A reunion romance?"

"No!" he said sharply. "That's all water under the bridge. We ended things a long time ago. Or should I say she was the one

who kicked me to the curb." Back then his pride had prevented him from fighting back and questioning her decision. He had been so hurt and wounded by her decision to end things between them. Why hadn't he pressed her for a reason? Even to this day, her decision hadn't made much sense. She'd loved him. Of that he was certain.

"Ouch," Ryan said, quirking his mouth. "I didn't know that."

"It's ancient history," Judah said with a shrug. No matter how many times he tried to convince himself of that fact it still rang hollow. Seeing her again after all these years had brought their relationship back to the forefront.

"Okay, so will you be making an appearance at the festival?" Ryan asked before putting a forkful of food in his mouth.

Serenity Peak would be hosting its annual Midnight Sun festival featuring live music, art, vendors, food trucks and dancing. It had always been the town's ultimate event. The past few years he hadn't attended the celebration. This year would be no different. The last thing he wanted to do was schmooze with people he couldn't trust.

"Probably not," Judah said bluntly. Being

at town events wasn't his thing. He hated the idea of being whispered about and gawked at like he was a character in a sideshow. He didn't feel comfortable being at the center of things. Before the accident he'd loved any and all opportunities to mix and mingle with the townsfolk. But all that had changed in an instant.

"I was hoping it would give you and my dad an opportunity to talk. This impasse between the two of you has gone on too long." Ryan heaved a big sigh. "As you well know, tomorrow isn't promised."

"Ryan, I know you're coming from a good place, but I have my reasons to keep a distance from Leif." His brother had continued to do business with some of the folks who had spread ugly whispers about Mary after the crash. His brother had chosen business and a paycheck over Judah and his family. Although Leif had tried on several occasions to repair their relationship, Judah hadn't been interested. Some fissures couldn't ever be mended. There was still an ache in his chest knowing their estrangement couldn't be mended.

Ryan quirked his mouth. "We miss them too, you know. Zane was my little buddy. Dad

loved him just as much as you love me. I know your whole life was rocked to the core when you lost them, but you're still alive. You still have people who love you."

His nephew's words were humbling. Sometimes he did tend to forget that he wasn't the only one who had suffered a tremendous loss. Ryan and Zane had been incredibly close. The very night of the accident Ryan had taken Zane out for pizza before dropping him back home. Hours later he was gone.

"I really appreciate you sharing that with me," Judah said. "It means a lot. And in case I've never told you, I want to thank you for being such a good role model for Zane. You were like a big brother to him."

Ryan's eyes looked moist, and he forcefully cleared his throat. "I'll never forget him. I just want to make sure you're in a place where you can move forward. Aunt Mary would want that for you. So would Zane."

He knew his wife and son would want healing for him. But at some point he needed to want it for himself.

"I'm doing the best I can, Ry. I really am." Maybe his actions didn't look like much from the outside, but every day he'd been fighting his way through grief. For the first few years

it had seemed as if he was walking through quicksand. Only in the last year had Judah begun to find his way out of the darkness. And even now he still had moments where he struggled to make sense of such a devastating loss. He had crawled through glass to get to where he was today.

"Do you need anything before I head out?" Ryan asked. "You might benefit from a hot shower."

"Can you get me one of those medicated patches on the kitchen counter?" Judah asked. He wasn't due for another cortisone shot for a few weeks and the patches helped him get through an episode.

"Sure thing," Ryan said, grabbing their plates and the bag before heading toward the kitchen. A few minutes later he returned with the patches and handed them over to Judah.

"Nice catching up, Unc," Ryan said as he headed toward the door. "I'd love to see you at the festival...so would Dad."

"But you won't," Judah said after the door closed. He wished that he could simply say yes and make an appearance at the festival, but he couldn't face a town that had turned its back on him when he'd needed them the most.

* * *

The following day, Autumn was at Northern Lights helping Sean out with his inventory. The work wasn't difficult, but she found it incredibly monotonous. After hours of standing, she headed into her brother's office to put her feet up and have a snack. Autumn had found that if she didn't eat something every few hours her energy levels began to dip. So far pregnancy had been kind to her, but she'd begun to notice fatigue throughout the day. She had made an effort to stay hydrated and active to combat her symptoms as Doc Poppy had advised.

A sudden noise caused her to swing her gaze up. Judah stood in the doorway dressed casually in a pair of dark jeans and a hunter green colored sweater. She was surprised to see him here, knowing he was usually on his boat in the early afternoon.

"Hey there. I was looking for Sean. Is he playing hooky today?" Judah asked.

Autumn smiled. "Hi, Judah. He actually had some errands to run with Helene so I'm covering for him." Helene was Sean's wife of almost twenty years. They had gotten married when they were barely twenty-one. Autumn liked to say they were still as giddy about

each other as they'd been in high school. It made Autumn continue to believe that loving relationships were possible if both people put in the work and honored their commitment.

Judah gave her propped up feet a pointed look.

"I've been working really hard all day. I only stopped a few minutes ago."

"Working hard or hardly working?" he asked. The corners of his mouth twitched with laughter.

Autumn put her feet back on solid ground. "Seriously?"

"I was teasing you," he said. "Please put your feet back up and relax. You deserve it."

This, she thought, was the old rapport they had once shared with Judah always joking and laughing. The push and pull of their friendship had led to romance.

"Was that you I saw leaving the clinic this morning?" she asked. "Either that or you have an identical twin." She had beeped as she'd driven past, but Judah hadn't looked in her direction.

Earlier this morning she'd had her prenatal appointment with Doc Poppy. On her way into the parking lot she had gotten a glimpse of Judah driving away.

"Yeah, it was me. I've been off work for a few days due to my shoulder acting up. My doctor took pity on me and gave me a cortisone shot a few weeks early." He rotated his shoulder. "It already feels much better. I've been doing everything at home to make it feel better."

Autumn made a face. "Sounds painful. I'm glad they could help you out."

She hadn't seen Judah since the day on his boat. Autumn still felt grateful for his assistance in allowing her to observe operations on Fishful Thinking. Maybe they could be friends after all. Perhaps she had been overthinking things. Or was influenced by the guilt she felt for holding on to the secret from their shared past. No matter how she tried to bury it, she couldn't ignore the fact that she'd ended their relationship rather than tell him about being infertile. She had broken up with him under false pretenses, which was tantamount to a lie.

"So, how are the articles coming?" he asked as he stepped closer toward the desk.

"I have some holes to fill in, but they're coming along nicely. A few more weeks and I should be done with the entire series. The first article will come out next week." Once

the fishing series was finished, Autumn would write a few articles about coming home to Alaska and a feature on dog musher Ace Reynolds, before taking some time off to welcome the baby and enjoy maternity leave.

"That's great. Sounds like you've made a lot of progress after the interviews." Judah seemed pleased for her which left her feeling encouraged.

"Talking to people who have ties to the fishing community made all the difference." She nibbled on her lip. "When I did the interviews some information came up about your name being tied to the fraud investigation."

Judah bristled. "I really don't want to get into all of that. I do my best to just focus on my work and not get dragged into the muck."

"Why not? If someone's trying to tarnish your reputation don't you want to know who it is?" she pressed.

"Not really," he said with a shrug. "I know I'm honest and hardworking. Furthermore, not a single official has contacted me about this investigation, which lets me know that I'm not under the microscope. As long as no one's trying to take away my business I'm good."

She let out a ragged breath. "That's funny

because when you first found out I was writing a piece for the *Tribune* you seemed mighty concerned that I might be targeting you."

"And you assured me you weren't. End of story," he spit out. "Or so I thought," he muttered. "Now it seems as if you're just poking and prying into stuff that's none of your concern."

She stood up and threw her hands up in the air. "I just don't get it. Everyone I talked to wants to defend you and here you are acting blasé about everything."

"Leave it alone. I never asked for help. I don't need it. I'm good."

Autumn let out a snort. "Of course you didn't because you're enjoying being Judah against the world. You don't need anyone, right? How's that working out for you?" She folded her arms across her middle. At this point they were mere inches from one another. Both of them were speaking in raised voices. The tension between them was palpable. It crackled in the air between them.

Judah took a step closer toward her so there were only a few inches resting between them. A vein pulsed alongside his jaw and his breathing sounded uneven. "Autumn, you actually have no idea what's going on with

me. None! You swept back into town after a twelve-year absence acting like a know-it-all. Trust me, you don't know half as much as you think you do about anything in Serenity Peak, never mind the fishing industry." His nostrils flared and he was breathing heavily. "You see, that's what happens when you're missing in action for over a decade." He curled his lip. "I don't have time for this, especially not today."

Judah stormed away from her, his strides full of anger. Seconds later she heard the back door slam shut with a thunderous bang.

Her whole body was trembling from their encounter. How had things gotten so out of control within seconds? Everything had spiraled downward in an instant. Judah was like a powder keg.

Just then Cecily raced into Sean's office. Her eyes were wide as she looked at Autumn. "Are you all right? I heard shouting."

"Yes, I'm fine," she said in a quivering voice, "but Judah isn't. He stormed out of here like a tornado." She ran a shaky hand through her hair. *What in the world had set him off? Didn't he realize that she'd been trying to help him?*

At this point she was ready to throw in the

towel and stop trying to establish any kind of friendship between them. Why was she trying so hard anyway when Judah clearly wanted a life of isolation? It was almost as if he always picked a fight with her to deliberately alienate her.

"Hey, it's not you," Cecily said, placing her arm around Autumn. "Really, it isn't."

Autumn scoffed. "I think you're wrong about that, sis. Every time I think Judah's turning a corner, he shows me he's a wounded bear with a thorn in his paw. And I'm always the one to set him off." She wasn't going to admit it to her sister, but it really hurt her feelings to have him lash out at her. She ached to get to a place where they were on an even keel, but at some point Autumn needed to let it go.

"I'm not excusing his behavior, but he has every reason to be upset today." Cecily bit her lip. "It's Zane's birthday. He would have been eleven years old today."

Autumn shut her eyes and let out a groan. "Oh, how awful. I had no idea." Of course she didn't. As Judah had made clear, Autumn had been MIA from Serenity Peak for a long time. She was just now getting acclimated and playing catch-up on everything she had

missed. There was no way she could have known, but if she had, Autumn would have kept their conversation light and easy.

"Judah was probably already having an awful day when I went and upset him. I can't imagine what's going through his mind." Why hadn't she kept her mouth shut? In trying to help Judah she'd poked the bear and riled him up.

"I'm guessing it didn't take much to unravel him on a day like this," Cecily said.

"I wish there was something we could do to ease the pain for him," Autumn said. Her heart felt heavy for Judah. No matter their differences, she still cared about him. Even if he didn't want her to, she would continue to do so. Most likely from a distance.

"I know, Autumn, but I don't think Judah is in a place right now to accept any help. He's intent on dealing with all of this pain by himself." Her sister shrugged. "He's been pushing everyone away for years. Some days I really think I'm seeing glimpses of the old Judah, but it never lasts for long."

Cecily was right! Judah didn't want help or a shoulder to lean on. He wanted to be alone to grapple with his emotions. Maybe he needed to honor this day by himself. Perhaps

it should be a day of reflection. She prayed that his memories of Zane would sustain him, not only for today but for all the days to follow.

Lord, please hold Judah in the palm of your hand. Protect him. Nurture him. And guide him until he comes back to You.

Chapter Nine

There weren't many places where Judah could go in Serenity Peak that brought him absolute peace. The Halcyon Mountains were a rare exception. Beautiful and majestic, the peaks boasted the most breathtaking views he had ever seen in his life. If he stood on a certain ridge, Judah could see all of Serenity Peak, as well as Kachemak Bay. Ever since he was a kid, Judah had been hiking these trails and exploring the mountain's hidden gems. The air up here was pristine, and the clouds seemed to be within reach.

"I thought that I might find you here." Sean's voice came from behind him.

Judah had been so deep in his thoughts that he hadn't heard his best friend approaching. Even though Judah often gave off standoffish

vibes, Sean knew better. He understood instinctively that Judah didn't want to be alone today. There was something about this eleventh birthday remembrance that was hitting him particularly hard. Maybe it was because turning eleven had been full of such joy and wonder for Judah. If anyone were to have asked him he would have told them it was his favorite birthday year.

"He loved being up here in the mountains. I wanted to spend some time in a place he adored." Judah shoved his hands into his parka pockets. "I've never seen him quite so happy as when we came out here."

"I get it," Sean said. "It's a nice way to honor him. He was an amazing kid, Judah. Someone special that's for sure. He had a light and a raw energy that dazzled all of us."

"Did you know he could recognize ten different species of birds by the time he was six?" Judah let out a chuckle. "That used to make Mary so proud. Not that it took much. She was his biggest fan."

Silence settled in as they looked out over the valley. Time seemed to stand still here. That quality was comforting to him. He didn't have to worry about everything whirling and speeding past him.

"I blew up at Autumn earlier. I'm feeling pretty torn up about it." Ever since he'd left Northern Lights he had been filled with recriminations. Things had gotten so ugly between them. Even though he'd been annoyed with Autumn poking around in his business, he'd been in a bad way ever since he had woken up. She didn't deserve to be a scapegoat.

The fact that he should be celebrating Zane's eleventh birthday today instead of mourning him caused his soul to ache. It wasn't fair! *Why Zane, God? Why did you pick my son?* The question had been reverberating inside his mind ever since the accident.

"I know. She told me." Sean shook his head. "The two of you have unfinished business, Judah. Maybe you should just hash out the past with her so you can move forward… as friends…acquaintances. Whatever you decide."

"Hash what out? She dumped me. What's there to talk about?" he asked.

Sean shrugged. "I don't know, man. There was always something odd about the breakup if you ask me. She was so into you. And now there just feels like something is fueling this discord between you."

Judah soaked in Sean's words. They made a lot of sense. He had always known there had been words left unspoken between him and Autumn. Pride was a powerful emotion. He'd been so gutted by the breakup he hadn't stuck around to ask any questions. Judah had retreated into his own solitude in order to lick his wounds. Some things never changed. He'd done the same thing after the accident. And what had it gotten him? A whole lot of nothing.

As they walked back down the trail to the bottom, Sean turned to him. "I have something for you." He held up his hands and said, "It's a little bit cheesy, but also really meaningful."

"Okay," Judah said. He had no idea what Sean was talking about, but he had a feeling he was about to find out.

When they got closer to where their vehicles were parked, Judah immediately noticed balloons peeking through the half-lowered windows of Sean's truck.

"Balloons? You bought me balloons?" Judah asked. He looked at Sean and raised an eyebrow.

"Yes," Sean said with a nod. "Eleven bal-

loons to be precise. To celebrate how old he would be today. We can release them into the sky as a remembrance of Zane."

Sean shifted from one foot to the other. "If that's okay with you."

For a moment Judah couldn't respond. He wasn't sure he could get any words out. His throat felt clogged with emotion.

"Or I can just take them back home with me," Sean said. He was suddenly looking sheepish as if he might have made a wrong move.

"No, don't do that," Judah said. "Zane loved balloons. He couldn't get enough of them." Judah chuckled at a memory of his son filling up water balloons on the first day of summer and bombarding his parents with them. This would be the perfect low-key way to celebrate his birthday.

Sean grinned and reached through the window to collect the strings. Judah stepped forward to assist him as he opened the truck's door. Judah stood with Sean as they released each blue balloon into the air, one by one. When they were done, Judah watched as Sean lowered his head and crossed his hands in front of him. More than anything, Judah wanted to follow suit and pray for his son, but

the words wouldn't come. It was frustrating, but he couldn't force things.

His heart was lighter now. "Thanks for putting this together," he said, clapping Sean on the shoulder. "It's not something that I would have ever thought of doing, but it was perfect."

"I can't take the credit for it though. This was all Autumn. It was her idea, Judah. She didn't know Zane, but she wanted to help you celebrate him."

Judah sucked in a shocked breath. *Autumn! Sweet, thoughtful Autumn.* The fact that she had come up with this way to honor his son was touching. Especially after the way he'd lashed out at her earlier. But that was Autumn's nature. She had never harbored grudges and always worked hard at forgiveness. He could learn a lot from the way she lived her life, he realized.

For so long now he had been harboring resentments against all of the townsfolk. Deep down he had always known it was unfair to blame an entire town for the actions of a few. But doing so had served a purpose at the time, allowing him to retreat into his own surroundings so he could mourn and rage

against the unfairness of the bottom falling out of his world.

Autumn extending him grace was an eye-opener. It had him thinking about his own actions and what kind of man he wanted to be. His father's favorite passage came to mind. *And be ye kind one to another, tender-hearted, forgiving one another, even as God for Christ's sake hath forgiven you.* Judah wasn't living up to any of those principles.

For so long now everyone in his life had been stepping up for him. It was high time he took some steps of his own toward healing.

Chapter Ten

Serenity Peak's downtown area was bursting with excitement as crowds gathered to celebrate the Midnight Sun festival. Delicious aromas wafted in the air as people lined up to order from the food trucks and other vendors. Autumn grinned at the shaved ice truck parked by the town green. That was a new one in Alaska. Tents had been set up for pie-eating contests and jewelry making. She tapped her foot to the beat of a band performing live music as townsfolk took to a makeshift dance floor. Everywhere around her there were smiling faces and residents enjoying themselves. She ran into former classmates and a few of her former teachers. It felt really nice to be welcomed back to town with such enthusiasm.

Getting ready for the event had made Autumn feel like a younger version of herself. Every year her family had attended the festival together as a unit. They had made incredible memories that were now indelibly imprinted on her heart. Someday soon her child would be attending and having just as much fun. Yet another moment she could look forward to in her future.

The festival was an all-day affair, going from mid-morning to midnight. Although Autumn knew she wouldn't stay until midnight, she was looking forward to being here and celebrating with the townsfolk.

She made her way over to the table hosted by Northern Lights. Sean, Cecily and her sister-in-law, Helene, were standing there handing out desserts. Sean had decided not to sell any food today. Instead, he was giving away desserts for free. The offer was good for as long as the scrumptious treats lasted. Autumn shook her head at the massive line.

"Your sweets are in high demand," Autumn said as she made her way to the table.

"Tell me about it," Sean said, wiping his brow with his forearm. "We're going to run out soon at this rate."

"*My* confections, thank you very much,"

Cecily said proudly. "Key lime tarts. Wild berry cobbler. Coconut cream puffs. And that's just a sampling." She was practically puffing out her chest. Her sister had been making all of the desserts for the restaurant for the last six months. Sales had almost doubled according to the books.

"You really need to get a side gig going, Cici," Autumn said. "You'd make a small fortune."

"Don't encourage her," Sean said. "Her desserts are the reason sales are up."

"Desserts by Cecily," her sister said. "I can totally see it."

Sean let out a groan as the sisters and Helene laughed. They all knew Cecily wasn't going anywhere although Autumn thought Sean should offer her sister the opportunity to buy a stake in the business.

This was nice. She hadn't hung out with her siblings in a very long time. This was overdue and it reminded her of all the good times from their childhood. It was comforting knowing she could look forward to more moments of togetherness in the years to come.

"As I live and breathe. Look who's here," Cecily said in a raised voice. Autumn followed Cecily's gaze. Judah! He was walking

straight toward them with a look of uncertainty plastered on his face.

Her pulse began to quicken at the sight of him. In a million years she'd never expected Judah to show up at a town event. He had made it quite clear that he wasn't interested in being part of the fabric of Serenity Peak.

"Hey, everyone. How's it going?" Judah asked. "It's a beautiful day for a festival."

Sean and Cecily greeted him warmly as Autumn stepped to the side and focused on handing out desserts. After their argument the other day, she didn't know how to speak to him with such awkwardness sitting between them.

A few moments later Judah walked up beside her. With stubble on his chin, he looked rugged and way too handsome for his own good. After all this time she still felt a little jolt when she laid eyes on him.

"Autumn," Judah said. "Can we talk for a moment?" His blue eyes threatened to bore a hole straight through her. She always found it hard to look away when he gazed into her eyes.

"Sure," she said, bracing for more awkwardness. She walked a few steps away from the

table so they could speak privately. "What's up?" she asked, trying to sound casual.

"I want to apologize for the other day," Judah said. "It wasn't right for me to raise my voice at you or say the things I did." Their gazes locked and Autumn saw the sincerity radiating from his eyes. "Zane's birthday always hits me hard. But that's no excuse for lighting into you."

She ran her hand through her hair, nervously winding a few strands around her fingers. "I can't imagine how painful the birthdays are for you. It's an unfathomable loss."

His intense gaze swept over her. "Sean told me the balloons were your idea. I don't have the words to tell you what that meant to me." His jaw trembled. "I've had such a difficult time trying to mark birthdays and anniversaries, so your gesture was spot-on. I don't think I'll ever forget it."

A warm sensation spread through her chest upon hearing that the balloons had meant something to him. She had been at a loss as to how to help him navigate the day until the idea came to mind.

"I know you've had a rough time of it, Judah. And that breaks my heart for you."

She blinked away tears. "Of course I forgive you. Anyone can have a bad moment."

"I appreciate you being so gracious." He reached out for her hand and squeezed it. Autumn felt a little funny at the way their hands were joined. She was having a hard time ignoring the way his hand made her palm tingle with awareness. And it felt so solid in hers.

"I'm really happy you decided to come today, and I know so many folks who will be thrilled to see you."

Judah made a face. "Let's not get carried away," he said with a chuckle. "I'm just putting my baby toe in the water. I'm not sure that I actually want to talk to anyone. I don't want to lose my reputation as a man of mystery."

Autumn laughed along with him. "It's too late to turn back now."

Being able to laugh with Judah was heartwarming. Although his mood shifts were confusing, she now realized that he was still walking through his grieving process. He was a strong person to have made it through such a terrible loss without completely falling apart. The only real grief Autumn had ever known was related to her infertility diagnosis and the dissolution of her marriage. Being

told she would never conceive a child had been devastating. She had been sad about the divorce, but certain that brighter days were ahead of her. She hoped Judah had things to look forward to in his future so that he could see tomorrow's promise.

"And it's a wrap," Sean called out. "All the desserts are gone."

Cecily and Autumn let out cheers at a job well done while some folks standing in line began to groan with disappointment.

"Always leave them wanting more," Helene said with a grin.

Judah jumped in to help Sean take down the table while Autumn grabbed the Northern Lights sign advertising free desserts. She didn't want anyone to see the poster and think that treats were still available.

As Sean and Helene headed out to locate their kids, Cecily took off to meet up with a few friends which left Autumn and Judah on their own. She was surprised when Judah asked her if she wanted to explore the event together. Autumn wasn't going to say no to Judah's invitation. She was really proud of him for showing up today. Although he didn't seem completely at ease being in this public

setting, attending the event was a huge step in the right direction.

"So, I'm curious, what brought you to the festival?" Autumn asked Judah.

"I figured it was time. This is a step in moving forward. It's something I thought a lot about on Zane's birthday. Am I still angry that some folks in town tried to smear my wife's name? Yes, that won't ever sit well with me. But I love this town. I'm not going to let anyone take that away from me. I've been on the sidelines for too long now." He lifted his shoulders. "It's hard to explain, but something about Zane's birthday caused a shift inside of me."

"I couldn't agree more. You have so much to offer this town."

"Oh, really." Judah's eyes twinkled. "Tell me more. I'm listening." He cupped his hand to his ear.

Autumn felt her cheeks getting flushed. Judah's playful side was coming out and it was causing her stomach to do flip-flops. She didn't want him to think she'd been gushing about him. Autumn swatted at him and said, "I see you still have an overgrown ego. I was just being nice."

"Ouch," Judah said, placing his hand over his heart. "That hurts."

"In all seriousness, Serenity Peak needs you. You're honest and hardworking. You have so much integrity and deep ties to this community. That means something."

"Maybe I should run for mayor," Judah said. The sides of his mouth were twitching just before he broke out into a full-fledged smile.

"Stranger things have happened. What would your campaign slogan be?" she asked.

"Judah Campbell. Fishing for votes," he quipped. They both burst out laughing with neither one letting up. Autumn knew that they were drawing their fair share of curious looks, but she didn't care. For today she was going to put aside all the many reasons why she should steer clear of Judah. She was going to live in the moment and enjoy herself.

"I'd vote for you," she said, flashing him a grin. A look passed between them and all of a sudden the moment was full of a heightened energy that pulsed in the air.

"You two look like you're having way too much fun." Violet, accompanied by her son, Chase, sauntered up to them. Chase held a huge piece of fried dough smothered in cinnamon sugar in his hands. The mere sight of the sweet treat made Autumn's mouth water.

"It's great to see you, buddy," Judah said, reaching down and putting his hand on Chase's shoulder.

"You too," Chase said, looking up at him with a shy smile. "I missed you."

Autumn thought her heart might melt as Chase placed his little arms around Judah.

"I missed you too," Judah said as he hugged Chase back. "You've gotten so big I barely recognize you."

"I've been eating my vegetables. Even spinach," Chase said somberly as the adults laughed.

"We're headed over to the art tent," Violet said. "Picasso here wants to make a sand art masterpiece. We'll probably run into you later on."

"Have fun," Autumn said, waving.

"Call me," Violet said, wagging her eyebrows at Autumn behind Judah's back.

Autumn knew Violet was no doubt imagining all sorts of things about her and Judah, none of which were true. They were really just two people who were taking delicate steps at reestablishing a friendship. If she occasionally experienced belly flips or goosebumps in his presence it was simply due to their fractured past.

"Do you still like fried dough?" Judah asked. "I remember how you used to love it."

"Are you kidding me? It took every ounce of self-control I have not to snatch it from Chase and inhale it." She shook her head. "These pregnancy cravings are no joke. The other night I wanted peanut butter and marshmallows." She chuckled. "And I don't even like marshmallows."

"I say we go in search of fried dough. My treat," Judah offered. "You can even get seconds."

"How can I say no to that?" Autumn asked. She was thoroughly enjoying herself with Judah. So many memories of their shared past were coming back to her. How many times had they enjoyed this very festival as a couple? They had walked hand in hand, danced under the moonlight and cheered as the town parade passed by. Although so much had changed between them, Autumn still felt a connection to Judah. Perhaps they could really be friends after all.

As they walked around the festival, Autumn and Judah were greeted with enthusiasm and warmth. Autumn noticed plenty of curious glances in their direction. She imagined folks were thinking back to the days

when they'd been in love and scratching their heads at seeing them together. Most were probably just happy to see Judah participating in a community event since he'd been missing in action for years.

They stood in a short line for the fried dough where she was able to engage Judah in light chitchat. He had never been a big talker, so Autumn carried most of the conversation. Judah paid for two orders of the fried dough and they both dug in with gusto. Although it was just as delicious as she remembered, the treat was giving her a bellyache.

"I think my eyes were bigger than my stomach," Autumn said as a tight feeling spread across her abdomen. "I can't eat anymore."

"Are you all right? I seem to remember you always going for seconds on fried dough," Judah responded.

"I'm fine. Too much of a good thing," she said, scrunching up her nose. So much of the time she was fearful of something going wrong in her pregnancy. She didn't want to get paranoid about slight stomach discomfort. Doc Poppy had just given her a glowing report just days ago so she shouldn't worry. It felt a little bit like indigestion.

Judah reached for her remaining portion. "Don't mind if I do," he said, taking a huge bite.

Autumn laughed at the way he devoured the treat with such enthusiasm. He resembled a little kid. "You have some sugar on your face." She reached out and brushed it away, her fingers tingling as soon as she made contact with his skin. She was so close to him she could see the slight stubble on his chin and the little scar by his mouth. She remembered the day he'd received that scar. They had been kids hanging out in the woods and Judah had tangled with a rabid fox. She remembered watching as he got stitched up and received a rabies shot without releasing a single tear.

The lively beats of jazz music filled the air. Autumn pulled Judah by the sleeve and walked toward the platform where the band was performing. She began to clap to the upbeat rhythms as Judah stood a few feet away watching her. Suddenly, Autumn stopped in her tracks. Leif, Judah's brother, was walking straight toward them with his son, Ryan, by his side. Autumn let out a startled sound once she noticed their approach. Just when Judah seemed to be in a good place! She didn't want

anything or anyone to spoil these precious moments.

Judah and Leif were on a collision course and seconds away from crossing paths. And there wasn't a thing Autumn could do to stop it from happening.

Judah hadn't imagined he would be enjoying himself so much at the festival. For the most part it wasn't awkward running into old friends and acquaintances he hadn't seen in quite some time. Everyone truly seemed happy to see him again. He was glad he'd made the effort to attend rather than hole up by himself at home. Autumn was good company, pleasant and humorous. He couldn't help but notice the way she lovingly cradled her stomach from time to time. She had so much to look forward to, he thought. If he could, Judah would go back in time and relive Zane's first few years and the wonder of having a new baby in the house. Those were precious years.

Autumn had waited a long time to have a baby, he realized. Judah didn't have the nerve to ask her, but he wondered why she'd decided to have a baby after all these years. Especially in a flailing marriage. He knew she would be an amazing mother, but there

would be challenges ahead of her. *It's none of your business!* he reminded himself. She was living her life the way she saw fit and he admired her courage.

Suddenly, Autumn seemed to be frozen, staring at a spot in the distance.

"What's the matter?" he asked, following her gaze.

Leif! And Ryan. They were heading toward them from the opposite direction, engaged in an animated conversation. Neither one had yet spotted him. His brother was the last person he wanted to see. He should have known Leif would show up at the festival. There was nothing he liked better than being in the thick of things.

He abruptly turned toward Autumn. "I think I've had enough of the festival."

"Judah, come on. You can't keep this up," Autumn said, grasping his wrist. "This town isn't big enough for you to not speak to one another."

Judah clenched his jaw. "It's been four years, and I've been managing just fine."

She let out an indelicate snort. "I highly doubt that."

He frowned at her. "Believe what you want."

"Isn't it time you dealt with the situation

head-on?" Autumn pressed. "You don't have to be best friends, but this isn't moving forward. Isn't that what you told me earlier? That coming here today was about making progress."

Judah could see Leif continuing to walk in his direction. He stopped a few feet away from him. Judah's eyes were drawn to his nephew who was shifting from one foot to the other. Ryan glanced back and forth between Judah and his father. "Hey, Uncle Judah. Hi, Autumn. It's been a long time."

Autumn stepped toward Ryan and placed her arms around his neck, drawing him in for a hug. "I can't believe you're all grown up. And a deputy!"

"Welcome back to Serenity Peak. And congratulations on the baby," Ryan said. Before Judah knew it was happening, the two of them had walked a discreet distance away. Judah sucked his teeth. Clearly they had done so in order to allow him and Leif some privacy.

"I think it's time we talked." His brother's words came out of his mouth like a challenge. Judah immediately bristled.

"Oh, really. I thought that I made it clear that we had nothing to discuss." Judah spit out the words.

Leif took a few steps closer to him. "So you plan to go on like this for the rest of our lives? Ignoring me. Not speaking."

"Why should I? You didn't have my back when I needed you the most." Saying the words out loud caused a twisting sensation in his gut. After the accident he'd been caught up in a maelstrom of grief and pain and sadness. When he'd heard the cruel whispers about Mary being under the influence of pills the night of the accident it had brought him to his knees. He had never imagined that the people in Serenity Peak he'd known all his life could be so vicious. At one point in time Mary had been addicted to painkillers due to a chronic injury, but she had gotten clean well before Zane came into the world.

Leif scoffed. "That's not true. You've got it all twisted. Judah, grief has blinded you to reality. I never turned my back on you. I simply didn't cut off relationships with all of the folks you suspected spread rumors."

"Exactly," Judah said, breathing heavily. "I've never quite understood how you justified maintaining those friendships and business relationships."

"The key word is suspected," Leif said. "I know you were in a world of pain, but you

were lashing out at everyone and anyone. It's true that a few folks were spreading terrible gossip, but it wasn't the entire town. And it was wrong of you to place blame in every direction. You didn't cut anyone an ounce of slack."

Leif's words slammed him in the face. Was his brother right? Had he taken his agony out on everyone in Serenity Peak? He had been in such deep grief four years ago. Judah hadn't known whether he was coming or going. His mind raced to find a response, but none came. A big part of him wanted to break the heavy chains he was carrying around. Anger. Resentment. Bitterness. At some point he had to acknowledge the toll these toxic emotions were taking on him as well as others.

"Why don't you admit why you're really angry at me?" Leif's voice was low and steady. Compassion flickered in his eyes.

"What are you talking about?" Judah asked.

Leif's gaze never wavered. A tremor ran alongside his jaw. "The night of the accident. That's why you've cut me out of your life. It's the reason you won't talk to me. You blame me for the crash, don't you?"

Chapter Eleven

For the last few minutes Judah had been stone silent. The encounter between him and Leif had been tense and emotional. Both of their bodies had been rigid and unyielding. They'd reminded her of two cowboys at the O.K. Corral, with neither one giving an inch to the other. Autumn hadn't meant to eavesdrop, but she'd heard Leif's voice as it carried. *You blame me for the crash.* The words had caused Autumn to shudder. What was Leif talking about?

Moments later Judah walked away from the conversation. The expression etched on his face as he walked past her had been one of shock and pain. Autumn followed behind him, knowing instinctively that he needed someone by his side. She might be over-

stepping, but she followed after him, trying hard to keep up with his long strides. Judah quickly reached the perimeter of the town square, away from most of the action.

"Can you slow down? Pregnant lady here," she called out. "I'm not a speed walker, especially after eating that fried dough. It's sitting on my stomach like a stone."

Judah stopped walking and looked over his shoulder at her. "You don't have to babysit me. I know this isn't exactly the fun you were expecting today."

Autumn sank down onto a bench in the town square. Judah walked back to stand next to her. "It's all right," Autumn said. "I would feel a lot better if the two of you had mended your issues, but I'm guessing that didn't happen."

"No, it didn't," he acknowledged. "But I walked away because I'm trying to process something he said to me."

She shook her head. "I never would have imagined that you and Leif would be estranged. Growing up it was rare to see one of you without the other. Don't you want to get that close bond back?" she asked. "One of the bright spots of coming back home has been the way my relationship with Cecily has strengthened. We're getting closer every day."

"Things happen, Autumn. Grief colors everything." He let out a hissing sound. "My dad would be so hurt if he was alive. I feel ashamed. He prided himself on family coming first as well as his faith. I haven't had God in my life for a while now."

Autumn knew Judah was spot-on about his dad. Kurt Campbell had been the patriarch of a loving and faith-filled family. Not only had he taught Judah everything he knew about being a fisherman, he had shown him the path to becoming a good man, rooted in faith and love.

Where had Judah's faith gone? If God was in his life, she didn't think his struggles would be so profound. Leaning on the Lord and seeking His counsel would have benefited Judah.

"It's understandable that you would question your faith after such a profound loss, but I think you need to ask yourself if you need Him in your life." Autumn wanted to be gentle and not sound judgmental. This was Judah's journey after all. She wasn't going to tell him how to live his life but she knew he would be more grounded by His presence.

"I still have a hard time processing that in one instant my whole world came crashing

down around me. I've accepted it and I've walked through the grief stages, but I still wonder where was God?"

Judah's question was a deep one that she knew many struggled with after tragedies.

"I don't want to overstep, but what did Leif mean when he said you blame him for the accident?" For Autumn those words had been a bombshell. What wasn't Judah saying?

He sat down next to her and looked at the ground as he fiddled with his fingers. "The night of the accident we were over at Leif's house celebrating Ryan joining law enforcement. It was getting late and Zane was really tired. Mary had to work early the next morning so she was itching to get home." He let out a ragged sigh. "Leif wanted me to stay longer. We were looking through old photo albums and reminiscing about the past. Mary left with Zane while I stayed behind. Leif was going to take me home later on. Then the random snow and ice came…twenty minutes after they left I got the call about the crash. By the time I arrived…it was too late. They were both gone." Judah's face looked ashen and his jaw trembled.

"Oh, Judah. I'm so sorry. A living nightmare." She placed her hand over his and held it there.

"I've never really thought about it, but I guess maybe I have been blaming Leif. And I'm wrong for doing so. For the most part I've been feeling guilty about not driving my family home myself that night, but if it hadn't been for my brother—"

"You wouldn't have lost your family," Autumn said, finishing the thought for him.

"He begged me to stay that night and I did." Judah let out a brittle laugh. "I can't believe I've been holding on to this for all this time. Blaming Leif. It wasn't his fault. We were just taking a deep dive into the past with all those pictures of our family." He winced. "I never imagined that night would end in unthinkable tragedy."

"Judah, it's no one's fault. I wish you could understand that and stop thinking someone has to be responsible."

"I'm trying, Autumn. Right now I'm probably closer to accepting that reality than I've been in four years. And I know that Leif and I need to talk, just as soon as I figure out what to say to him."

"'I'm sorry' is a good start," she said. "From what I saw Leif is eager to get back on track with you. I don't think it will take much."

Judah shoved his hand through his hair.

"I'll find a way. And knowing my brother, he'll never let me live this down. But it'll be worth it if we can find a way forward."

Autumn could tell Judah was ready to take this first big step. Tears filled her eyes at the idea of reconciliation between the brothers.

"Autumn, I didn't mean to make you cry," Judah said as he peered at her face.

"Everything makes me tear up these days," she admitted, dabbing at her eyes with the hem of her coat. "I'm really overjoyed that you plan to make things right with Leif." Judah's realization that he was wrong signified progress. He had managed to see the situation from Leif's point of view. He'd gotten out of his own head long enough to view the situation objectively.

A huge grin crept over his face. "I think my nephew is going to be over the moon. He's been bugging me about the situation for a long time."

"He's a wonderful young man who clearly loves his family. I had a chance to talk to him earlier and I was really impressed." Autumn was a firm believer that where there was love anything was possible. She felt incredibly hopeful about being back in Serenity Peak. Now, more than ever she needed reas-

surance that she'd made the right decision in packing up her life in New York City to come back to Alaska.

"I'll keep you posted," Judah said, shoving his hands in his pockets. The weather was getting chillier by the moment with temperatures dropping. "In the meantime, it's almost sunset. The bonfire should be starting soon if you want to check it out."

"Of course I do," Autumn responded. She hadn't even realized it had gotten so late, but the sky was beginning to darken. This time of year sunset was at approximately five-thirty. Because she had been away for so many years it still took some getting used to when the sun began to fade from view.

They ran into Sean, Helene and Cecily, as well as Violet, Chase and Sky. She had been hoping they would cross paths with Leif again so Judah could begin their reconciliation. But, as with all things, she knew it would happen in God's time.

The mood amongst the townsfolk was celebratory. Kids were holding light-up wands and wearing glow-in-the-dark necklaces. S'mores were being made on the fire as the aroma of melted chocolate wafted in the air.

With the stars shining in a velvet sky and

the moon illuminating the area, Autumn couldn't remember an Alaskan night quite like this one. Hope shimmered all around her. Happiness and fellowship. She couldn't explain why but it seemed as if anything was possible at this moment. Had someone told her a year ago that she would be back in Serenity Peak preparing for the birth of her first child that she would be raising alone, Autumn wouldn't have believed them. But, as she looked around the throng of people surrounding her, Autumn had a strong feeling she was meant to be here.

Judah had scored a comfy seat for her by the bonfire. By the time things got started, the area was jam-packed with townsfolk. Judah had to squeeze next to her in order to sit down. He was sitting so close to her that their arms were touching. Despite the fact that she was wearing a long-sleeved parka, Autumn shivered when Judah's arm brushed against hers. She felt a little flustered at the realization that she might be in way over her head with Judah Campbell.

Her head was telling her that Judah was off-limits, but her heart didn't seem to be listening. She needed to shake this off. He was in her past, not her future.

Judah leaned toward her, asking in a low voice, "How are you doing? Are you comfortable? I can go get you a water if you want," he offered.

His thoughtfulness had always endeared him to her. Judah was a caretaker. He was the type of man who always made sure that everyone in his sphere was taken care of. It was one of the reasons she'd fallen so hard for him. Even though Autumn felt confident in her new life in Serenity Peak, she also felt vulnerable at the moment. Being with Judah made her think of all the dreams they had once shared… marriage, kids, the white picket fence.

"I'm actually feeling really wiped out," she blurted out. "I think I'm going to head home now."

Judah's eyes widened. She thought there was a hint of disappointment on his face. "Oh, no. And miss the bonfire?"

"There's always next year," she said, standing up. As soon as the words came out of her mouth she realized that this time next year she would have a baby to take care of. Her life would be very different. Bringing a baby to a bonfire might be a stretch.

"Do you need me to walk you to your truck?" Judah asked, beginning to stand up.

"No!" she said in a raised voice. That was the last thing she needed or wanted at the moment. "I'll be fine. Goodnight," she said, quickly gathering her purse and beating a fast path away from Judah and the bonfire.

As soon as she got inside the truck, Autumn turned the ignition on and let the vehicle run until the interior warmed up. Her thoughts were all over the place and her pulse was skittering wildly. She raised her hands to her cheeks. Despite the fierce chill in the air she was flushed.

Back at the bonfire her mind had taken her to an unexpected place. The desire to kiss Judah had swept through her to the point where she'd had to walk away rather than do something foolish. A kiss would have been disastrous. And perhaps unwelcomed. They were just at the brink of becoming friends again, which meant more to her than she'd ever imagined. When it came to Judah she felt like a helpless moth drawn to a bright flame. Whenever they spent time together she found herself wanting more of him. More conversation. More laughs. More Judah. She needed to tamp down these emotions and focus on her reality—this baby she would soon be bringing into the world and her career.

There was no future for her and Judah. Autumn had burned those bridges a long time ago.

As soon as Autumn took off, Judah immediately felt a letdown in his spirits. Try as he might to enjoy the festivities, his thoughts kept veering back to Autumn. She had left the bonfire in a very abrupt manner, causing him to wonder if anything was wrong. Had he done something or said something to upset her? Was she not feeling well? Ever since Autumn had come back to Alaska Judah hadn't been able to keep her out of his mind.

It's okay to care about an ex, a little voice buzzed in his ear. *You're rebuilding a friendship and that's healthy.*

As the bonfire wound down and the crowd began to disperse, Sean cut through the crowd straight to Judah. Without skipping a beat, Sean asked, "Hey, can we talk for a minute?" Strain was evident on his face. Tiny stress lines stretched across his forehead.

"Sure, buddy. What's going on?" he asked. His first thought was about Autumn. Had something happened to her on the drive home? His heart began beating like a drum inside his chest. He knew this was a holdover

from the accident four years ago. He was always waiting for impending disaster.

Sean motioned him aside. "First off, I'm so happy to see you here. It's awesome knowing you decided to take such a huge step today. Kudos."

"But?" Judah asked. He'd known Sean way too long not to know there was a *but* coming.

Sean's hands were at his sides but Judah noticed they were clenched. "What's going on with you and my sister?"

Judah sputtered. "Going on? What do you mean?"

"The two of you were hanging out all day laughing and carrying on. Then you were all cozied up at the bonfire. You obviously said something to upset her. She lit out of here like she was being chased by a grizzly bear."

The fierce expression on Sean's face caught him by surprise. It was clear Sean wasn't playing around. He meant business.

Judah held up his hands. "First of all, there's nothing going on between us other than friendship. She was gracious enough to pal around with me today. In case you forgot, I'm a little out of practice with schmoozing at town events."

"So there's nothing romantic going on?"

Sean appeared to be waiting on pins and needles for his reply.

"No, there isn't," he said without hesitation. *Why did he feel as if he wasn't being completely honest?* Technically, there wasn't anything going on, but there had been loaded moments between them where he'd felt flickers of awareness. Maybe he was simply imagining things. There was absolutely no reason to say anything to Sean about those moments, especially since he and Autumn hadn't come close to crossing any lines.

"Okay, I'm sorry for grilling you and jumping to conclusions," Sean said. "It's just that she's had a hard time lately with the divorce and moving back to Serenity Peak. She doesn't let on, but she's a nervous wreck about this pregnancy. They say divorce, having a baby and relocating are three of the most stressful events in a person's life." He ran a hand across his jaw. "Autumn is undergoing all three at once."

"I get it," he said with a nod. And he did. Autumn had a lot on her plate. She was under a great deal of stress. But he had done nothing to add to her anxiety. Matter of fact, he had assisted her in finding local fishermen to interview for her article even though he'd wanted to stay out of it.

"She's pretty vulnerable right now and I don't want to see her get hurt again," Sean continued. "That husband of hers put her through a lot."

For a moment Judah was going to let the comment slide until a little bubble of anger began to rise up inside him. What was Sean accusing him of doing? Hurt roared through him. He and Sean had been friends for most of their lives. Did he even know him at all?

"And you think I'm going to do something to hurt her?" he asked. At this point Judah wasn't even trying to keep anger out of his tone.

"Judah, I'm just trying to protect Autumn. I didn't mean to cast any aspersions on you." Even though Sean's voice was filled with remorse, Judah was still heated. Not once had he ever done a single thing to hurt Autumn. And he never would.

"In case you forgot, Autumn was the one who ended our relationship," Judah said. "She hurt me, Sean, not the other way around. I know she's your sister, but please don't act like I'm the bad guy. I would have walked through fire for that woman."

"I know, Judah. Hey, c'mon. Let's talk this out," Sean said as Judah stormed off.

Although Sean called after him Judah didn't turn back. He didn't want to stay and say something he might later regret. So much for venturing out into the community today. Two steps forward, three steps back. Maybe he should have just stayed home the way he'd been doing for the last four years. Now, he'd gotten into it with Sean, who had stuck beside him through the worst of times.

As a result of his discussion with Sean, he had yet another reason to stay away from Autumn. His best friend had just made it perfectly clear that he wasn't comfortable with them spending time together. Sean had gotten things wrong though. Judah was fairly certain that Autumn was the one who had the power to hurt him rather than the other way around.

He was more determined than ever not to allow that to happen.

Chapter Twelve

A week had passed during which Autumn hadn't laid eyes on Judah once. Nor had he texted her or called. *Ha!* She was being a bit ridiculous. It wasn't as if they had been burning up the phone lines or texting prior to this moment. And hadn't she been the one to abruptly take off from the festival? There was no telling what Judah thought of her disappearing act. As long as he didn't realize why she'd left. She would be mortified if he knew where her thoughts had drifted that night.

It didn't feel right not to hear his voice or the low rumble of his laughter. Over the past few weeks she had gotten used to him being around. He hadn't been in her life for more than a decade, yet now she missed him. If she was being honest with herself, there had

been many times when she was living in New York City that she'd pined for Judah. A little voice in her head had always told her to deal with it. Their entire relationship had ended because of her choices, so she'd never allowed herself the luxury of feeling sorry for herself for long.

"You look nice. Where are you off to?" Cecily asked, giving her the once over.

In order to cheer herself up, Autumn had decided to dress up a little bit by wearing a long skirt, a silk top and her black wool coat. She planned to do a little baby shopping after her interview with Bob Agler, a retired fisherman. Bob laughingly referred to himself as an old-timer. She was meeting him at Humbled in half an hour. Once she was finished with this interview, Autumn thought she would have enough to finish the second article.

"I'm heading over to Humbled for my next interview." She rubbed her hands together. "To be honest, I'm really looking forward to sampling more of the menu over there. Everything is so delicious." She winced as pain spread across her abdomen.

Cecily reached out and grasped her by the arm. "Hey. What just happened? Are you okay?"

"I—I think so. Maybe just Braxton-Hicks contractions." As Doc Poppy had explained these contractions were the body's way of preparing for labor down the road. They didn't mean a person was actually in labor but they could be intense.

Cecily scrunched up her face. "Are you sure about that? You're barely six months along."

"Doc Poppy warned me about them. I'll definitely call her if they intensify, but I'm praying they don't. This baby needs more time in the oven," she said, chuckling.

Cecily laughed along with her. "Well, I'm heading into Northern Lights for a shift. I'm really excited to make mini Baked Alaskas today."

Autumn loved her sister's enthusiasm about her craft. She'd never seen her so excited about going to the restaurant.

"I'll love you forever if you save me some," Autumn said. Her sweet tooth had been activated by her pregnancy. After a few years of floundering, Cecily had found her life's passion.

"Done," Cecily said as she sailed out the door.

Ten minutes later Autumn was on the way

to town as a light flurry of snow fell from the sky. A moose crossed the road twenty feet ahead of her. She lightly pumped the brakes so the truck wouldn't skid on the snow. Sean's truck had tire chains for safety, but driving carefully had been drummed into her growing up in Alaska. Autumn watched as the majestic animal made it across the road.

She smiled as she continued driving. How many people could say they crossed paths with an actual moose on their way to work? This, she thought, was a slice of life from Alaskan living. Being here was invigorating to her senses.

By the time she reached Humbled, Bob was already sitting at a table waiting for her. He stood up to greet her and held out a bouquet of forget-me-not flowers.

"Nice to meet you, Autumn. I remember you running around town in your younger years. Welcome back," he said with a grin.

"Thank you. I appreciate you taking the time to meet up with me."

With a shaggy mane of gray hair and a beard to match, Bob cut a striking figure. He was wearing a bow tie along with a button-down sweater. She had the feeling he'd gotten decked out for this interview.

"I'm grateful to you for writing this piece. Oftentimes we fishermen tend to be forgotten even though we're woven into the fabric of everyday Alaskan life. What we do is important."

"I couldn't agree with you more." She raised the flowers to her nose and inhaled the lovely scent. "Thank you for the flowers. How did you get them this time of year?"

He grinned at her. His green eyes sparkled. "I have a greenhouse at my home. It allows me to cultivate vegetables and flowers all year long."

For the next hour and a half, they chatted while sipping tea and nibbling on a variety of treats. Autumn's interview with Bob was informative and lively. The older man's personality was infectious. His stories about being a commercial fisherman were full of highs and lows, as well as comical moments.

"Fishing isn't just a job, Autumn. It's a way of life,"

Molly, Humbled's owner, walked up to their table just as they were finishing up. She placed her arms around Bob and said, "Hey, Grandpa. Do you need anything else?"

He lovingly patted her hand. "No, Molly-girl. We're doing just fine."

"This is your granddaughter?" Autumn asked, surprised at the connection between the two. Sometimes it seemed as if she was relearning everything about Serenity Peak all over again.

"She sure is," Bob said. He reached for Molly's hand and looked up at her. "Prettiest girl in Serenity Peak."

"Aww, you're too sweet, gramps," Molly said, her cheeks blushing.

Autumn thought that Molly and Bob might just be the most adorable twosome in town. Maybe even in all of Alaska.

As they said their goodbyes Bob reached for Autumn's hand and pressed his lips to it in an old-fashioned courtly gesture. "Until we meet again." He walked off with Molly by his side.

Autumn sat back down for a few minutes to finish her notes. When she stood up to leave she swung her large purse around so fast it caused her to stumble. Strong hands caught her before she fell. When she swung her gaze up to thank her rescuer, she saw Judah standing there.

"Judah!" she said, unable to hide her surprise. "Th-thanks for the catch. You're making a habit out of saving me."

"You're very welcome," he said. He jerked his chin in the direction of her bag. "Be careful. Your purse weighs more than you do."

"I know," she said with a smile. "I tend to overstuff my bags until they weigh a ton."

He held up a little white bag. "I came for the blueberry muffin. If you haven't tried them they're amazing."

"I'll try one next time." Autumn looked around the café. "This place is wonderful. If I didn't have errands to run, I'd happily sit here all day and try out all the different teas. Are you off today?"

Judah appeared to be looking around at everything but her. For some reason he wasn't making eye contact. "Yeah, I've been going out on the boat every day for the last week. I took today off just to get a break."

Why did it seem as if they were dancing around each other? Up to this point they had enjoyed a relatively natural ease in each other's company. Something felt completely off and she was struggling to figure it out.

All of a sudden, she didn't feel so well. Whereas a few minutes ago she'd had a slight chill, she now was experiencing hot flashes. Nausea rose up in her throat. Oh, no. She felt like she might get sick.

"Is it hot in here or is it me?" she asked. Autumn felt beads of sweat pooling on her forehead. She began to fan herself as waves of queasiness rolled through her. All of a sudden fear gripped her. Something didn't feel right. Her body began to sway to the point where Autumn worried she might fall over.

Judah gently gripped her arm in order to steady her. "What's wrong, Autumn? You don't look so good."

"Judah, I think that I need some air," she gasped. "Please, I need to go outside."

"Okay, let's go." He took her arm and gently guided her outside.

"I feel a little light-headed and nauseous. I'm feeling like I might throw up." She placed her hand low on her belly in the hopes of feeling some movement. If she could feel the baby kick then she wouldn't be so frightened. She winced as a painful cramp swept through her abdomen. *What was happening? This didn't feel right.* "I—I think something's wrong. I'm cramping." Fear had her in its grip and she choked out the words. Hot tears splashed on her cheeks.

How many nights had she prayed to make it through this pregnancy and to deliver a healthy baby? *Dear God, please don't for-*

sake me or my child. Please shelter my baby until I can safely deliver him or her into this world.

"Okay, don't worry. I've got you, Autumn. Let's get you to the doctor." He placed his arm around her waist and pulled her against his side so that she could place all of her weight on him.

Autumn looked up at him as she tightly clutched his side. "Judah! I'm scared. I think that I might be losing the baby."

Autumn's anguished cries were tugging at Judah's heartstrings as he broke every speed limit to transport her to the medical clinic. There hadn't been many times in his life when he had felt so helpless. Although this was very different from the crash that had taken Zane and Mary from him, he was struggling with similar emotions. Fear was leading him as well as the knowledge that at least now he had the ability to help someone he deeply cared about.

Seeing Autumn in so much pain wrecked him. He'd lost a child and he knew the utter devastation it wrought. Autumn might just snap in two under the strain if things didn't end well. She was living for this baby, her

sweet blessing. If it was taken away from her it would rock her entire world. This might very well be her last chance at motherhood.

Please, Lord. Help Autumn. Give her and the baby strength enough to make it through this trial. I know You haven't heard from me in a while, but I am here now humbly asking for help.

The prayer rose up out of nowhere and surprised Judah. Where had those words come from? He hadn't been to church in four years and he never prayed. Losing his family had caused him to step away from his faith. He was still angry at God for taking away his loved ones. Not just Zane and Mary but his beloved father, Kurt. The losses had piled up one after the other, dragging him into an abyss of sorrow.

When they pulled into the parking lot, Judah put his truck in Park right by the entrance. He turned off the ignition and raced around to the passenger side door. With a quick motion, he jerked the door open and lifted Autumn out and into his arms. She didn't utter a word of protest. Autumn laced her arms around his neck and buried her face against his chest. She continued to make

whimpering sounds that threatened every ounce of composure he had.

When he reached the entrance, Judah pushed the clinic door open with his elbow and made his way over the threshold.

"Help! We need some help here," Judah called out.

Staff members, followed closely by Dr. Poppy, raced to the waiting area.

"Autumn!" Poppy exclaimed as soon as she spotted her in his arms. "What happened?"

One of the nurses brought a wheelchair and placed it in front of them. Judah gently lowered her into the chair.

Autumn was groaning even louder at this point and clutching her stomach. She didn't even lift up her head to meet Poppy's gaze. "I'm cramping and nauseous. I feel hot and then cold."

"She's sick," Judah said curtly. "You need to check her out now." His voice sounded almost as frantic as he felt. Why weren't they taking her to the examination room? If Autumn was losing the baby time was of the essence.

"Excuse us, Judah," Poppy said, "but we need to assess the situation."

Autumn was tightly holding his hand. He was afraid to let go of her, but he knew the

sooner he loosened his grip the faster Autumn would be examined. One of the staff wheeled her toward the back. Autumn turned and sent him a look filled with fear and anxiety. More than anything Judah wanted to reassure her that everything was going to be all right, but he couldn't shake his own fears.

What if Autumn's baby didn't make it? She would shatter into a million little pieces.

What if something happened to Autumn? He'd lost so much in his life. He wouldn't survive losing her as well.

Poppy patted his shoulder. "I promise we'll take good care of her. Will you be waiting here?" she asked.

Judah ran his hand over his face. "Yes, I'm not going anywhere. I'll be right here in the waiting room. Can you tell me if she and the baby are going to be all right?"

Poppy shook her head. "I'm sorry, but we have to examine her and run some tests before we'll know anything. Try not to worry too much in the meantime, Judah."

That, he realized, was an impossible task. His mind was whirling with anxiety. Judah sank down onto a couch and reached into his pocket for his cell phone. He needed to let Autumn's family know what was going on.

Judah quickly dialed Sean's phone number. He let out a sigh as the call went to voice mail. He looked through his contacts and found Cecily's number. He thought it was best to tell her the news so she could convey it in person to their family members.

When Cecily answered, Judah quickly told her as much as he was able to about the situation. He wished that he had more of an update to share with them.

"Poppy told me to hold tight until she can provide an update," Judah explained.

"This doesn't sound good," Cecily said. "I'll tell my parents and I'll try to get hold of Sean. Pray, Judah. Autumn and the baby need to be lifted up in prayer."

"Thanks, Cecily. I'll be in touch as soon as I know anything." Judah ended the call without saying how fervently he had been praying since the onset of Autumn's medical crisis.

For the next hour Judah paced around the waiting room, idly flipped through magazines and fielded phone calls from Autumn's family. Although they wanted to come down to the clinic, Judah advised them to stay put until the doctor provided an update. When the door opened, and the doctor began strid-

ing down the hall Judah froze. His heart was racing wildly.

Lord, please let Poppy deliver good news about Autumn and the baby.

When Poppy was within a few feet of him, a smile broke out on her face. "Autumn and the baby are going to be just fine," she said. Judah let out the ragged breath he'd been holding. All the oxygen flew out of his lungs at once.

"She's much better now that we've given her an IV. Since she hasn't been able to keep anything down we suspected food poisoning and the exam and initial tests confirm it," Poppy explained.

Food poisoning! It was rough on the body, but much less scary than where his mind had taken him. He couldn't put into words how the doctor's words made him feel. It was almost as if the weight of the world had suddenly been lifted off his shoulders.

"You can come in now and see her if you like," Poppy suggested. "I'll be back in a few minutes to check on her."

Judah walked into the room, eager to see Autumn with his own eyes. She was sitting up in the hospital bed wearing a plain blue gown. Although her complexion was a bit

ashen, she looked pretty good considering what she'd been through. At the sound of his footsteps, Autumn swung her gaze toward the door.

"Hey there," Judah said as he reached her side. He jammed his hands in his pockets and shifted from one foot to the other.

"Hi," Autumn said in a soft voice. "Thanks for sticking around. It appears that I must have eaten something that made me violently ill." She wrinkled her nose and ran her hands across her abdomen. "I can't remember ever feeling such awful belly pains."

"Poppy gave me the update. You gave me quite a scare," he said. He had wanted so badly to take away her pain. That knowledge unnerved him. He was in way over his head now. And his heart was telling him it was too late to backtrack.

"I'm sorry. I was pretty petrified myself."

Seeing Autumn in so much physical agony had been difficult for Judah to witness. Her cries had done a number on his insides. He'd wanted her to lean on him so he could give her all his strength.

"Feeling better?" he asked.

"So much better," she said with a sigh. "I was so afraid that the baby was going to be

in danger…or come early. Once Poppy confirmed that it was food poisoning I felt incredibly relieved."

"And the baby?" he asked. Even though Poppy had reassured him, he needed to hear it again from Autumn's lips.

"The baby seems to be fine with a strong heartbeat, but Doc is going to come back and do a sonogram just to make sure," Autumn explained. "Judah, you don't have to stay if this is dredging up painful memories for you. That's the very last thing I'd ever want to do."

He looked down for a moment as he struggled with finding the right words. "I hate medical clinics and hospital settings. I just do. That probably won't ever change. But today was different. I was actually able to help you, Autumn." He dragged his gaze up to look at her. "After the accident I rushed to the hospital, but there was nothing I could do but stare at the clinical white walls until the doctors came out and told me the terrible news. I was never able to help my family and it was the most hopeless feeling I've ever known."

Compassion flared in Autumn's eyes. He knew she understood what he'd been through which helped him get the words out.

"Don't get me wrong, I was scared for you

and the baby, but knowing you're going to be fine restored me in some way. A part of me has always blamed myself for the accident that killed my family. I wasn't there to protect them and that gutted me. I should have been driving, not Mary. If I had been with them that night things would have been different."

Autumn made a fretful sound. "Oh, Judah. There wasn't anything you could have done to prevent the accident. It's impossible to turn back time and fix things. Life doesn't give us that gift."

For so long now everyone close to him had been saying the very same thing, but it hadn't resonated until now. Part of his grief had been rooted in guilt. Finally, he was in a place where he could clearly see he wasn't to blame. Accidents were by nature unpredictable and chaotic. And in order to move forward he had to accept that he couldn't change the events of that tragic night.

"It's been a long time coming, but I realize that now," he admitted. "It's finally sinking in."

Because of you, he wanted to say. So much of his personal growth as of late could be tied to Autumn's return to town. He was opening up and letting his guard down. He was real-

izing that he needed to be a part of the Serenity Peak community. Being at the Midnight Sun festival had shown him that. No man *was* an island. He required God in his life. And Autumn. Sweet, beautiful Autumn. His first love. His friend. A woman he couldn't get out of his mind. Or his heart.

Just as Judah opened his mouth to let her know how deeply he cared about her, the door opened with a sharp click, putting an abrupt halt to his near confession.

Chapter Thirteen

The door swung open and Doc Poppy reentered the examination room. Autumn had the distinct feeling that Judah had been on the verge of telling her something important. But whatever he'd wanted to say had been swallowed up by the doctor's arrival.

Judah's presence was reassuring. She didn't know what she would have done if he hadn't been at Humbled when she'd fallen ill. It was nice watching his evolution from a man shrouded in pain and loss to one who was now pushing past grief to make a life for himself and to care for others.

"I'm back. Sonogram time," Poppy called out. "Let's see what this little one is up to in there."

Judah looked back and forth between them.

"Should I leave and give you some privacy?" he asked. The sheepish expression stamped on his face was comical, Autumn thought. He really was such a sweetheart.

"There's nothing invasive about this," Poppy responded. "I'm just putting some gel on her stomach before waving the wand around her abdomen so we can get a clear view of the baby. Nice and easy."

Judah turned to look at Autumn. "I'd like you to stay if it's not too much trouble," she said. She hated putting him on the spot, but Judah's presence gave her strength. He'd been so calm and reassuring during her medical crisis.

"Let's do this," Judah said, sending her an encouraging nod.

Within seconds Poppy had everything set up. Autumn sat back patiently as gel was spread on her abdomen and the process began. A whooshing sound filled the air as Poppy pointed to a small shape on the screen. She began to point out body parts. Head. Spine. Fingers. A pulsing heartbeat.

Tears streamed down Autumn's face, and she made no attempt to wipe them away. These were born out of joy and she honestly couldn't remember the last time that had hap-

pened. The last few hours had brought her so much fear and anxiety, as well as physical discomfort. Relief washed over her. Suddenly, all was right in her world.

"I can't believe I'm actually seeing my little peanut," Autumn said. This, she thought, was the embodiment of all the dreams she'd nurtured about bringing a life into the world.

"I can tell you the gender if you want to know," Poppy said, smiling at her. "It's your choice. Some people like to be surprised."

"Please tell me," Autumn instructed. "No more surprises for me. After what I went through today I want to know who's in there." She let out a nervous giggle. Either way, all she wanted was a healthy child.

"It's a boy," Poppy announced.

Autumn let out a little squeal. She couldn't take her eyes off the screen. Her beautiful baby boy! He was safe and sound. *Thank you, Lord, for answering my prayers.*

"Congratulations," Judah said, reaching out and squeezing her hand.

"So I'll print a copy of the ultrasound for you," Poppy said as she wiped the gel off Autumn's abdomen. "I'd like to see you next week just to follow up with you. For the next

few days just relax and hydrate. You'll be back to normal in a few days."

Judah left the room so Autumn could get changed into her street clothes and ditch the hospital gown. A short while later they were in Judah's truck, and he was driving her home. Cecily and Sean had already picked up her vehicle from Fifth Street. When they pulled up, Cecily's house was ablaze with lights.

"Looks like people are waiting on you," Judah said. "It's lit up like a Christmas tree." He wondered if Sean was inside. They still hadn't spoken since the festival.

"That's sweet of them. Thanks for telling my family not to come check on me at the clinic. My parents don't need that kind of stress. I hate that I worried everyone," Autumn said. "But it's also comforting to know I'm not alone."

He reached out and grazed his palm across her cheek. "You were really brave, Autumn. I know it must have been scary in the moment, but you handled everything like a champ."

She heaved a tremendous sigh. "I was really scared, but you guided me through the worst parts of the whole ordeal. I can't thank you enough."

"I wouldn't have wanted to be anywhere else," he murmured. "I'm so happy that the two of you are fine."

Looking into Autumn's eyes was like tumbling down a rabbit hole. He could see a wealth of emotion radiating from their depths. There was nothing he wanted more in this moment than to kiss her. Despite all of his past doubts, he couldn't think of a single reason why he shouldn't. *Seize the moment.*

He moved closer then dipped his head down and placed his lips on hers. Judah tenderly placed his mouth over hers, enjoying the sweet taste of her. Her lips tasted like spun sugar. The moment their lips touched Judah felt sparks flying all around them. Her lovely floral scent rose to his nostrils. She placed her arms around his neck and pulled him closer, drawing him further into the kiss. Judah wanted the embrace to go on and on until the stars were stamped from the sky.

She whispered his name against his lips just before they broke apart. Judah leaned his forehead against Autumn's for a few beats. They were still so closely connected he could hear the steady pulsing of her heart. He placed one last kiss on her temple before

saying, "You should get some rest. It's been a long day."

Her hands were still clutching the collar of his parka. When she let go, Judah wanted to reel her back in. He wanted to hold Autumn in his arms and protect her from anything that might cause harm to her. Because once they drew apart, he knew the doubts would creep back in.

He quickly stepped down from the truck and made his way to the passenger side. Once he opened the door, Judah held out his hand and helped Autumn out. Although under normal circumstances he would walk her to the door, Judah didn't want to exacerbate the situation with Sean. For all he knew, his best friend could be upset that Judah had been the one to take her to the clinic.

"Night, Judah," Autumn said in a low voice.

"Night," he said, turning on his heel and heading back to the truck. For a few moments he sat and watched Autumn as she walked to the door and let herself in. For a moment he'd had the impression she had wanted one last kiss before they parted ways. Her beautiful face had been turned upward toward him. Judah didn't know how to explain it, but stepping outside the truck into the chilly night

air had woken him up a bit. He had been in a bit of a dreamy state when he had initiated the kiss.

On the drive back to his place, Judah kept thinking that kissing Autumn had been one of the most foolish things he could have done. Not that their embrace hadn't been fantastic. Autumn had responded with such tenderness and longing. Smooching Autumn had felt so right in the moment, but it hadn't taken long for doubt to creep in. Autumn wasn't the type of woman to kiss as a spur of the moment whim. And now, he wondered if he was giving out mixed signals.

They were friends and nothing more, despite the way she stirred up old feelings inside of him. Romance only complicated things. He didn't think he could handle a full-fledged relationship with Autumn. He questioned whether he could ever fully trust her not to crush his heart again. In their past he had been over the moon for her, and it was unlike anything he had ever felt for anyone else.

So many years had gone by since they'd been in love. It was a long time to be apart from someone. Over the years Autumn had blossomed into a wiser and more confident

woman. Witnessing her being so excited about welcoming her baby boy into the world had touched his heart in ways he couldn't even explain. Back at the clinic he'd watched as Autumn's baby flashed on the screen. Such a tiny blessing. A perfect creation. Yet he had experienced a mix of emotions. He'd been ecstatic that Autumn's medical crisis had been something easily treatable. Her joy had been effusive. Yet it had been hard to see the baby boy on the screen. He and Mary had sat in a doctor's office and viewed their baby on the same type of screen. They had both been overjoyed by the sight of their healthy, robust baby boy.

How could Autumn ever truly understand that he was grappling with his emotions about her little blessing? She would be terribly hurt. It made him feel awful, but he couldn't pretend that his feelings didn't exist.

Being around her was wonderful, but terrifying at the same time. She had shattered his heart once before and he couldn't trust that she wouldn't break it all over again.

As soon she stepped inside the house Autumn was swept up in the loving arms of her family. Her parents were the first ones to step

forward and wrap her in a tight embrace. Raw emotion radiated from them in waves.

"We're so relieved to see you," her mother said. "We didn't want to think the worst, but when Cecily called us we were beside ourselves."

"We sent up a lot of prayers," her dad told her. His voice cracked as he barely got the words out.

"And got down on our knees." Her mother crossed her hands in prayerlike fashion. "It's such a blessing to know our daughter and grandbaby are doing well."

"Come sit down. You shouldn't be on your feet," her father said, guiding her toward the living room.

Cecily and Sean looked on with wide grins as their parents fussed over her. Autumn didn't balk at all the tender love and care they were showing her. It felt nice to be looked after even though she was an adult now and ready to mother her own child.

"Let her up for air," Sean said. "You're smothering her."

A half an hour later her parents and Sean headed home after reminding Autumn to get a good night's rest and drink plenty of water. As soon as they left Cecily led her to the

kitchen for a nice cup of decaf green tea and some crackers.

"Hopefully you'll be able to keep this down," Cecily said. "Make sure to eat the crackers slowly." Autumn was seeing such a nurturing side of her sister. She would make a wonderful mother herself.

"So you and Judah, huh," Cecily said. She wiggled her brows in Autumn's direction.

"Not so fast. We're just friends," Autumn said. But did friends make out in trucks? She didn't think so.

"So you haven't kissed at all?" her sister asked, her voice filled with disappointment.

"Just once," she admitted. "Tonight actually."

Cecily let out a squeal of delight. "I knew something was brewing. The two of you have that whole meant-to-be vibe."

Autumn bit her lip. "I'm not sure that's true. It's complicated. Judah acted a bit aloof after we kissed. And it's not as if we declared any feelings for one another." She shrugged. "It's a bit up in the air."

"But you do feel something for him, right?" Cecily leaned across the counter using both elbows. She was waiting with bated breath for Autumn's answer.

"Yes," she said, nodding. "There's so much I'm feeling for him, but it just seems like our past is still casting this shadow over us."

"What do you mean? There's really nothing standing in your way."

"Oh, Cecily, that's not true." She took a deep breath. "I never wanted to end things with Judah in the first place."

Cecily's eyes widened. "Then why did you? At the time you made it seem as if you'd outgrown him."

"That wasn't the case. Not at all. I only broke up with him after I was told that I couldn't bear children."

Cecily let out a gasp and raised a hand to her neck. "What are you talking about?"

"My endometriosis diagnosis was twelve years ago. Because I had so many polyps I was told by my gynecologist that it would be impossible for me to conceive a child." Tears streamed down her face. She let out a little hiccup. "I knew how much Judah wanted children. He talked about raising a houseful of kids all the time. Whenever he was around kids he lit up like sunshine. How could I take that away from him? I made a sacrifice so he could live the life of his dreams."

Cecily couldn't hide her shock. "Why

didn't you tell me? I would have told you not to do it. You could have adopted or fostered. Or you could have just told him the truth and dealt with it head-on."

How many times over the years had she told herself the same exact things? Back then her mind hadn't been in that headspace. She'd been lost and confused and grieving the loss of what might have been.

"Yes, I know that now," she acknowledged. "But at the time I was so broken after being given that news. It felt as if my entire life was crumbling right along with Judah's. We had so many hopes and dreams that revolved around getting married and having children. I knew he was thinking of proposing to me." She twisted her fingers around and around. "It seemed as if I was ruining everything we'd planned. And I couldn't have stood it if he stayed with me out of pity. So I set him free."

She let out a sob filled with regret and despair. Her past actions were indefensible.

Cecily came around the kitchen island and put her arms around Autumn. "Oh, sweetie. You were so young and uncertain. You did what you thought was right at the time. But

if you and Judah want to start fresh, that's still possible."

"There's no way we could ever be together until I come clean with Judah. And even then, I have no idea if he can ever forgive me."

Cecily patted her back. "Don't give up hope. Wait and see if the two of you are on the same page about your feelings. If so, you can find a way to tell Judah the truth. If he cares for you as I think he does, he'll forgive you."

Autumn sniffed back tears. Cecily was right. She didn't even know for certain where Judah's heart lay. For him, their kiss might have been nothing special or just a way to pass the time. Either way, she knew the truth was important. This lie of omission had festered for way too long already. It would eat her alive if she kept quiet. She had come back to Serenity Peak for a fresh start and to live her life in peace and comfort. That was still her goal. Being honest with Judah would establish a strong foundation for the future.

Lord, please help me find a way to speak the truth. Give me the courage to follow through with my intentions. And if Judah can't understand my motivations, grant me the grace to understand his feelings.

* * *

Judah looked out over Kachemak Bay and breathed in a contented breath. In all the world there couldn't be a more stunning view than Serenity Peak Harbor. The sun was dipping below the horizon, casting an orange glow in its wake. Being a fisherman wasn't an easy profession by any means, but Judah loved it. His body was bone-tired, but his mind felt free of all the things that had been weighing him down for the past few years. That was the power of the Bay. It was soul soothing and life affirming. Today it had allowed him to think about his future…and Autumn.

In a few minutes he would be meeting up with Leif, at Judah's invitation. He'd reached out to his brother yesterday in an attempt to clear the air between them and they'd arranged for Leif to come down to the boat. His nerves were on edge in anticipation of their upcoming discussion. *What if they couldn't bridge the gap?*

"Thanks, boss."

"See you tomorrow."

"Take it easy, captain." His crew called out to him before they gathered up their belongings. Judah watched as his crew dispersed

and headed home to eat and sleep. They would return in the wee hours of the morning to do it all over again. It was exhausting but rewarding work. There wasn't a single crew member who didn't pull their weight. That single fact made him proud.

He stayed behind to clean the boat and spray down the holds. He stripped off his GORE-TEX jacket, bibs and rubber boots, packing them away for tomorrow's work day before putting on his winter parka. A quick glance at his watch was interrupted by the sound of footsteps on the dock. His brother was right on time!

Judah looked up and Leif was standing a few feet away from him. Sometimes when he looked at his brother it was almost like looking into a mirror. The resemblance was uncanny. Growing up they had always been mistaken for twins. Irish twins—born less than a year apart—their mother had always said.

"Need some help?" Leif offered, moving closer.

"Thanks, but I'm pretty much done," Judah said. He shouldn't be nervous, but he was. This is Leif, he reminded himself. You know each other inside and out.

Leif swept his gaze around the boat. "It's been a long time since I've been here. You run a tight ship," he said. "Dad would get a kick out of that."

Judah smiled. *You run a tight ship.* That had always been their father's favorite expression and the highest compliment one could ever receive. Hearing those words come out of Leif's mouth highlighted one of the things that would always bind them together. They were family. And somehow, out of blindness, he had forgotten the raw power of those connections.

"So, you asked me to meet you here." His gaze narrowed. "You either want to talk or you're going to throw me overboard. Which is it?"

"I'm sorry." He swallowed hard. Apologizing wasn't difficult but there was so much he needed to say. *Where did he even start?* "I was a fool to cut you out of my life, Leif. There's so much I want to say, but it might take me forever to get it all off my chest. You were right. I didn't realize how much I was holding onto until the festival. On some level I've been blaming you for asking me to stay that night." He shoved his hands into his pockets. "It allowed me to think that maybe

I could have saved them if only I had gone home with Mary and Zane. And it placed the blame on you rather than on me, because living with the guilt has been almost too much to bear."

"There's absolutely nothing to feel guilty about," Leif said. "I wish you could accept that as the truth."

"My head knows that on some level, but my heart tells a different story."

Leif stood quietly and listened. "We've lost a lot of time, Judah. I don't want to dwell on fault or blame. Tomorrow isn't promised. All I really care about is that we're in a good place moving forward. I've missed you."

"I'll do my part to make that happen," Judah promised. "I've missed having you around."

"I know what you've been through…what you've lost. You've been knocked down, Judah, but you got up. You didn't give in to despair. I think you're pretty brave," Leif said, tearing up. "God isn't through with you yet. He has great plans for you."

Judah took a step toward Leif, easily closing the distance between them. He grabbed his brother by the shoulders and pulled him into a bear hug. The heartfelt embrace went

on for a long time. Judah didn't want to let go and he sensed Leif was of the same mind. By the time they pulled apart both had moisture pooling in their eyes.

Leif cleared his throat. "So…you and Autumn looked mighty cozy at the festival. Anything going on there?" Leif raised an eyebrow.

Judah couldn't act cavalier with Leif. His brother knew him too well for him to pull that off. "I have feelings for her, Leif. From the moment our paths crossed again, I've been pulled in her direction like a magnet. She's just as gorgeous and lively as she was when we were together. And she might be the most interesting woman I've ever known."

"And she's having a baby?" Leif asked. "Ryan mentioned it."

Judah smiled. "Yes. A boy. And she couldn't be any more excited about welcoming a child into the world."

Leif knitted his brows together. "Is that a complication for you?"

He weighed his words carefully. His feelings had been all over the place. "Honestly, I wasn't sure. I was with her when she found out that she was having a boy. I was torn between excitement and fear." A sigh slipped

past his lips. "That sounds awful, but Zane's death is still raw. Maybe it always will be."

"It doesn't sound awful. Just honest."

"We kissed last week, but neither of us has said anything about where we go from here. For all I know she doesn't feel the same way that I do." That thought gutted him. Maybe he was reading everything wrong.

Leif chuckled. "Judging from what I saw at the festival you don't need to worry. She's smitten."

Although Leif's assessment made him stand a little taller, he was still unsure. "I've been wondering if I can trust her which might not be fair. We were much younger then and if she wasn't certain about me, can I really hold it against her?"

"Sounds like you're pretty stuck on her," Leif said with a knowing look. "Those old feelings are still there. Don't put roadblocks in your way."

Judah shifted from one foot to the other and ran a weary hand across his face. His brother was right. "I did a lot of thinking today when I was out on the boat. I've spent the last four years steeped in grief and pain. I cut you out of my life as well as God. Not to mention the townsfolk. Having a second

chance with Autumn is my rainbow after the storm. I don't want to blow it."

"So what are you going to do about it?" his brother asked.

Leif knew how to challenge Judah like no one else on earth.

"I'm going to tell her what's resting on my heart," Judah said. A burst of confidence flooded him. Up until now he'd been filled with so many doubts and insecurities.

Leif held up his hand for Judah to high-five. As the brothers celebrated Judah's decision to be open and honest with Autumn, he couldn't help but feel that his life was changing for the better. Finally, he was coming out of the shadows and embracing the sunlight.

Chapter Fourteen

Autumn woke up to a beautiful Alaskan morning. The sky was the color of forget-me-nots, the state flower of Alaska. The sun was dazzling in a sky almost devoid of clouds. She was on her way to Northern Lights to pick up Cecily. The thought of running into Judah there crossed her mind, but he was most likely fishing today. A smile tugged at her lips at the memory of the day she'd spent out on the water with Judah and his crew. She would love to go out on the Bay with him again, although she wasn't confident it would happen.

She wasn't quite sure what to think about Judah. He had done a little bit of a disappearing act on her and it was confusing. Ever since the night they had kissed, he'd been

radio silent. Autumn had been left to wonder if he was avoiding her. They had bonded so beautifully during her medical ordeal. He had been so tender and supportive.

Had she said or done something to push him away? Did he regret kissing her?

It was hard not to feel hurt that he hadn't checked in on her. Had she been imagining them growing closer to the point where both of them were feeling more than friendship? Surely a kiss meant something. But perhaps it had caused Judah to run for the hills.

She was trying to stop fretting about Judah. It was time to shift her focus to practical matters. She still needed so many items for the baby's arrival. A crib. Diapers. A bassinet. Cecily had offered to go with her into town so they could do a little baby shopping. The day of her medical crisis she'd never made it to the shops, so in her mind she was way overdue some retail therapy.

When she pulled up outside the restaurant Autumn put the truck in Park then texted Cecily to let her know she'd arrived. She knew if she went inside it would only prolong their departure since the customers who frequented Northern Lights tended to be chatty. It would take her forever to get out of there.

A strong gust of wind swept inside the truck as the passenger side door swung open. Instead of Cecily it was Judah stepping up into the passenger side seat.

"Hey there, beautiful," Judah said with a wide grin.

"Judah! What are you doing here?" She wasn't even annoyed at him anymore for leaving her hanging after their kiss. With just one look at his handsome face Autumn forgot all about the way she'd been feeling for the past few days. Chills were racing down the back of her neck at his close proximity.

"I have a surprise for you!" His blue eyes sparkled. He resembled a little kid at the moment with the gleeful expression stamped on his face.

"Really?" she asked. "More surprising than popping into my ride when I was expecting my sister?" She shook her head in disbelief. Although he had been on her mind a lot, she hadn't expected this sudden turn of events.

He looked at her earnestly. "I know you had plans with Cecily, but there's something really cool I need to show you. Please don't be mad at her. This is all me. She just went along with the plan."

A secret plan? This really wasn't Judah's

style. He wasn't an impulsive person. Or at least the old version of Judah hadn't been. The man sitting next to her in the passenger seat was full of surprises.

"Okay, so where to?" Autumn was stepping out on a limb of faith and trusting Judah. What did she have to lose? She would have to postpone her baby shopping for another time.

Judah proceeded to give her step-by-step directions. A short while later they were on the back roads leading away from town and toward the mountains. Even though her mind was whirling with ideas about their final destination, Autumn took time to soak in the view. Serenity Peak's mountains and wildlife sightings were a far cry from the skyscrapers and throngs of people in New York City.

All of a sudden Autumn knew exactly where they were headed. Sugar Works. They had just driven past the hot springs, so the only other big location in this area was the Drummonds' property. She wondered if Violet was in on this as well.

"What do you have up your sleeve?" She darted a quick glance in his direction when she slowed the car down at a bear crossing sign.

He made a turning the key motion near his

lips. "I'm not saying a word until we get there. There aren't many happy surprises in life, so why not savor the anticipation?"

"When you put it like that," Autumn said, "I'll just focus on the road and enjoy not knowing what's happening."

The low rumble of Judah's laugher filled the interior of the truck. By this time Autumn wasn't even listening to Judah's directions. She knew how to get to Sugar Works by heart. When she turned in to the lane leading to the property, Judah told her exactly where to go. As she drove up to the red barn a sign announcing "Abel's Place" greeted them.

"Curiouser and curiouser," Autumn said. She placed the car in Park and turned toward Judah. "So…we're here. Want to clue me in on what you're up to?"

"Sure thing, but I need to show you," Judah said, jerking his chin in the direction of the barn.

"You didn't get me a puppy did you?" Although she loved furry four-legged friends, Autumn didn't think the timing was right for her to bring a dog into her life. She would be up to her elbows in dirty diapers and baby food.

"No, I didn't get you a puppy," Judah said.

"Let's get out of the truck before your imagination really starts to run wild."

Once they exited the truck, Abel came walking out of the barn. He was wearing a white apron, a long T-shirt, jeans and workman's gloves.

"Hey, Abel. How's it going?" Judah called out to the older man.

"Pretty well. I've been waiting for the two of you to get here," Abel said as he enveloped Autumn in a hug.

"It's good to see you, Abel, even though I'm in the dark as to what we're doing here," Autumn said as she looked back and forth between the two men. "Anyone care to tell me?"

"Well, come on inside the barn and all will be revealed," Abel said. His eyes were twinkling with merriment. He seemed quite pleased with himself.

Judah pulled the barn door open and ushered her inside. Once Autumn entered, the smell of wood shavings permeated the air. Everywhere she looked were examples of Abel's woodworking skills. A beautiful mahogany chair. A jewelry box. A small dresser.

Abel led them toward the corner where an object sat covered with a large tarp.

"I'll let you do the honors," Abel said, nod-

ding toward Judah, who quickly went to stand beside the covered object.

"Autumn, this is a gift for you and the baby. Crafted with love." Judah ripped the tarp away, revealing a stunning maple-colored crib. The wood sparkled and glistened. The craftsmanship was immaculate. Along the headboard were grooves in the shape of clouds.

Autumn stood without moving a muscle, transfixed by the site of the magnificent crib. After a few moments she walked over and lovingly ran her hand across the headboard. "This is for me?" she asked. She couldn't believe it!

"It is. And the baby of course," Judah said with a smile. "I asked Abel about making a crib for you, but it wouldn't have been ready for quite some time. Coincidentally, he happened to be working on one that he was willing to sell to me. I actually suggested some of the little details on the headboard. I thought little clouds would help him sleep better."

"This is such a beautiful surprise," she gushed. "Abel, thank you for creating something so stunning. I feel incredibly blessed that my baby boy will be sleeping in this work of art."

"All the thanks should go to Judah," Abel

said. "He was determined to make sure you received the perfect crib for your baby." He chuckled. "He hounded me a bit to make sure I was on schedule. Okay, if you'll excuse me, I need to head over to give a tour of the property." Before they knew it, Abel had sailed through the barn doors, leaving them alone.

Autumn was awash in gratitude. She hadn't been expecting such a magnificent gesture "How can I ever thank you, Judah? This truly means so much to me. It's really exquisite."

"You don't need to thank me. Consider it a baby gift and a welcome back to Serenity Peak gift all rolled into one."

"I'm grateful, Judah. It may very well be the most wonderful blessing I've ever received. Other than the baby of course." She was getting choked up at the idea that Judah had arranged something so special for her and the baby. And here she had been wondering if he cared about her. Surely this wondrous offering meant something.

"Can you hold the barn door open for me? I should get this packed up."

"Sure thing," Autumn said, striding over to the doors and swinging them wide open.

Judah picked up the medium-size crib and carried it to the truck, then placed it down on

the ground while Autumn pulled the hatch down. Within a few minutes the crib was safely secured in the back of the truck.

Autumn gazed at the gift. She still couldn't believe that Judah had been so thoughtful. "I hope you know that I might never stop thanking you for the crib."

"You and the baby deserve everything good this world has to offer. I'm just happy that I was able to help you in some way."

She wanted to know where they stood. Was the crib a kind gesture from a friend…or something more? What was the point in holding her tongue? At least this way she would know.

"I was surprised to see you earlier at Northern Lights. I had the impression you were avoiding me. I could be wrong, but it felt like you had mixed emotions about the kiss we shared." She let out the breath she'd been holding. A sense of relief flooded her. It felt good to get this off her chest.

"It wasn't the kiss. Our past is complicated. I'm still a work in progress in case you hadn't noticed. You have the baby as your main priority, as he should be. There's a lot of moving pieces, Autumn. But I care for you…deeply. Ever since you came back to town you've never been far from my thoughts."

"That's good to know," she murmured. Happiness gave her wings. She felt as if she could soar at this very moment.

"So as not to leave any doubt about how I feel about smooching you…" Judah reached out and placed his hands on the sides of Autumn's neck, pulling her close. He leaned down and put his lips over hers, tenderly showing her what her heart already knew.

Autumn kissed him back with equal measure, resting her hand over his thumping heart. She wondered if it always beat so fast or was this a result of their embrace? The smell of birch syrup drifted on the wind as the kiss soared and crested. Judah ran his hands through her hair and after they pulled apart he continued to rain kisses on her temple, cheeks and by her earlobe.

The other embrace had been wonderful, but this one signified something she'd needed to know. Judah had feelings for her and kissing her wasn't something he questioned any longer. Being swept away by Judah really was like coming home again. He had always been the big love of her life and now she knew without a shadow of a doubt that they were rekindling their romance. She didn't know if this relationship would withstand the test

of time, but she was beginning to believe it might have staying power.

Everything in her life was falling into place, yet her lie of omission still stood between them. Judah deserved to know everything she had withheld from him in the past. She opened her mouth but the words wouldn't come. A new life with Judah was within reach, but opening up to him could cost her everything.

"Ready to head back to town?" Judah asked as his fingers stroked her earlobe.

"I'm ready," she answered, locking gazes with Judah. There was so much radiating from his eyes that mirrored her own feelings—joy, wonder and hope.

Please, God, she prayed. *Let the shadows of the past fade away so that we can build a solid foundation for a future.*

As happy as she was, Autumn couldn't quiet the loud whisper in her head on the ride back to town. It reminded her that until she spoke complete truth to Judah, everything they were building sat on shaky ground that could easily tumble down around her.

As far as Judah was concerned, life was pretty good. Earlier this morning he'd gone to

church with Autumn. It was the first time he had been back in four years. He had surprised himself by singing along to every hymn and thoroughly enjoying himself. All this time he hadn't made the connection that God not being present in his life was responsible for the gaping hole at his center. Attending Sunday service had served as a healing balm. He still had work to do, but he was walking a righteous path.

Now he was grabbing lunch with Leif and Sean at Northern Lights before meeting up with Autumn later on to watch a movie.

"So how are things going with Serenity Peak's newest It Couple?" Leif asked.

"I can't complain," Judah said. "Everything's going smoothly. We're falling back into familiar rhythms which is uncanny considering it's been a while."

"Pretty smooth move with the crib," Sean said with a nod of approval. "Autumn can't stop talking about it. Abel really outdid himself. And so did you, Judah." Sean held out his hand so he could fist bump Judah.

Judah and Sean had managed to talk things through with Judah acknowledging that he and Autumn were more than friends. He'd promised Sean that no matter what happened

he would never hurt Autumn. He loved her too much. Judah hadn't said those words yet to Autumn, but he knew it was time. Sometimes when they were together Judah wanted so badly to profess his love to her, but he always held back. A part of him wondered if the past didn't still have him in its grip. Was he afraid of Autumn hurting him all over again?

Fear thou not, for I am with thee. The passage from Isaiah washed over him with the strength of a thousand suns. Going forward, this would be his mantra. He wasn't going to let fear rob him of his future. He needed to believe in his and Autumn's potential. It was limitless.

Judah drummed his fingers on the table. "I want to make Autumn happy. Seeing her smile is my happy place."

Leif and Sean began groaning loudly. "You've got it bad," Leif said. "That was like a cheesy greeting card."

Sean was chuckling. "Seeing you like this is hilarious."

Judah didn't mind the ribbing. "I'm happy. If that makes me corny then so be it. Autumn doesn't seem to mind."

"You tell 'em," Cecily said as she walked up with a tray of desserts. "I'm testing out

some new recipes so I wanted the three of you to be the first to try them."

Sean rubbed his hands together. "Mmm. You don't have to ask me twice."

"You're in for a treat, Leif," Judah said.

"We've got a chocolate Alaskan moose tart, a pecan cinnamon pound cake and key lime cupcakes," Cecily explained as she placed the servings in front of them. "When you get a moment, let me know which one is your favorite and least favorite."

Leif's eyes widened as he dug into the pound cake. He closed his eyes and said, "Oh, this is incredible. Marry me, Cecily!" he said, placing his hand over his heart.

Cecily giggled. "That good, huh? You're going to have to get in line, Leif Campbell. Half of the single men in town are proposing once they've tasted my desserts. Including your son."

All three men burst out laughing. As Cecily headed back toward the kitchen they continued to enjoy their lunch and the dessert samples.

After finishing lunch, Judah headed back to his house to check in on Delilah and take her for a long walk. The weather forecast for this evening predicted a small storm later this

evening. Judah made sure to put more salt down around his walkway and steps. Before heading over to meet up with Autumn, he fed the Irish Setter and made sure she had plenty of water to tide her over. "I'll see you later, girl. Next time I'll bring you with me, okay?"

As he headed over to Cecily's house Judah's mind began to whirl regarding all the things he didn't know about Autumn. *How did she take her coffee in the morning? Did she want a dog of her own one day? Was her favorite color still pink?*

It was exciting being on this journey of discovery with Autumn. Little by little they would peel back the layers until there wasn't anything they didn't know about one another. Pretty soon they would be finishing each other's sentences like back in the day. God had blessed them by reuniting him and Autumn. He wasn't going to take it for granted because he knew people didn't usually get second chances.

Chapter Fifteen

Autumn walked around the kitchen making sure she had everything set for this evening. A hearty beef stew was cooking in her Crock-Pot while sourdough bread baked in the oven. The aroma wafting around the house was mouthwatering.

Sweet, wonderful Judah. She had so much to be thankful for, with the baby and Judah being at the top of her list. She enjoyed spending time with him. They were at ease in each other's presence. Judah had allowed God back into his life and she knew it had altered his outlook. Being able to lean on the Lord in times of turmoil was a game changer.

She was more optimistic about her future than she could ever remember. And Judah was a huge part of it all.

Reality check! They couldn't walk off into the sunset any time soon. Her lie still stood between them. She had conveniently pushed it to the back of her mind for weeks now, but doing so didn't change anything. Judah still didn't know that she had ended things with him in a misguided attempt to spare him a life without children. He had no clue that she had dealt with an infertility diagnosis.

What difference does it make now? a little voice buzzed in her ear. *He never has to know. Just stuff it down into a little black hole.*

But *she* would know. And if she did end up with Judah in a permanent way, that lie of omission would burn a whole straight through her heart. There was no doubt about it. She wouldn't be able to live with herself.

How many times had she bashed herself for going down that road in the first place? Judah trusted her and he had no idea that she didn't deserve his faith in her. Why hadn't she listened to Violet twelve years ago when she had begged Autumn to tell Judah the truth? Her heart had been in the right place, but not divulging everything to Judah had been the wrong decision. And tonight she would have to face it head-on. It was time to do what was right.

When Judah walked into the house an hour later, Autumn was a bundle of nerves. She had no way of knowing how this night would end. Either in tears or in triumph.

Judah sniffed the air. "Something smells incredible. You Hines women sure know your way around a kitchen," Judah said.

"I can't take much of the credit for the beef stew. The Crock-Pot is doing all the work."

He placed his arm around her waist and brought her close so that their bodies were touching. Judah leaned in and kissed her. It was short and sweet, but full of tenderness.

"I missed you."

She shook her head and chuckled. "How is that possible? We went to church together this morning."

"I don't know, but it's the truth," Judah said. "I promise."

"If I'm being completely honest, I missed you too," Autumn admitted.

"The good thing is," Judah said, "there's absolutely no reason why we have to miss each other ever again."

Autumn nodded in agreement. Her throat suddenly felt as dry as a desert.

"Let's eat," she suggested, leading Judah toward the table. She had already set the table

and added utensils, floral placemats and her sister's best china, as well as crystal glasses.

Judah let out an appreciative whistle. "You really went all out."

"Why don't you sit down while I get our bowls," she said, then headed back to the kitchen for the beef stew and the sourdough bread. When she returned Autumn placed the food on the table before joining hands with Judah and saying grace.

They ate in companionable silence, interrupted only by Judah's compliments about the meal. Autumn ate slowly, knowing that her moment of reckoning was quickly approaching. As they finished the food, Autumn picked up the plates and brought them to the kitchen. Although she had tried to keep Judah seated, he ended up following her to the kitchen and helping her fill the dishwasher with the dirty dishes.

After finishing up they settled in to the TV room to watch the movie. Autumn was so nervous about talking to Judah that she had completely forgotten what movie they had decided to watch. All she knew was that it was a thriller starring Sandra Bullock. They got comfy on the couch with two canned sodas.

Autumn couldn't enjoy herself. It felt wrong to pretend as if nothing was wrong when in reality so much was resting under the surface. But now it was all bubbling up. She couldn't bury it any longer.

"Judah, we need to talk," Autumn blurted before she could chicken out.

Judah's jaw went slack. "I don't think any man in history has been happy to hear those words. This must be important if you're pre-empting our viewing of *Maximum Speed*." He smiled when he said it so she knew he was joking, but she didn't have the strength to joke back.

"Before I say anything else, I just want to let you know that I love you."

Autumn's voice sounded strong and sure when she professed her love to him. Was this what she wanted to talk to him about? If so, he would be the happiest man on earth.

Love! Autumn's words sent him to the stratosphere. He didn't think his feet were even touching the ground anymore. Judah was soaring. Flying to the moon. The woman of his dreams loved him! If he wasn't worried about looking like a dork he would do a jig right here and now.

Thank you, Lord, for answering my most fervent prayer.

"I lo—" he began to say before she cut him off.

"No, don't say it, Judah! You need to know something first. Something important." Her voice sounded sharp and filled with urgency. Considering the circumstances, it felt off somehow.

"Nothing's more important than telling you how I feel." He leaned in and placed a searing kiss on her lips. Autumn broke off the kiss and took a step away from him. She bowed her head so he couldn't look into her eyes. At the moment Judah was flying blind. He had no idea what was going on with Autumn. He was caught up in all these conflicting signals she was sending out. She loved him but her expression looked like she was all doom and gloom.

Judah reached out and tilted her chin up. "Hey. What is it? Talk to me."

Her lips were trembling. "I lied to you twelve years ago, Judah."

Judah swallowed hard. He didn't say anything. Autumn needed to explain what she was talking about. Suddenly it seemed as if all the air had left his lungs. His entire body

froze. Here it was. The thing that would get in the way of their happiness. By this time, he was sitting up straight on the couch. Not a single muscle in his body was relaxed.

"When I broke up with you it wasn't because I didn't love you. It was because I did." Her body shuddered. "A doctor told me I wouldn't be able to bear any children. That rocked me to my core. It felt as if our entire future was in ruins. I knew you wanted kids more than anything."

"No," he said hoarsely, "I wanted *you* more than anything."

"I kept thinking about all of our conversations about the future and how they revolved around having kids together. It was so hard to imagine you giving up that dream for me."

"But I would have," Judah responded. "Without question."

She bit her lip. "I didn't think you should have had to make that sacrifice."

Judah was hearing the words coming out of Autumn's mouth, but he wasn't understanding any of it. Infertility? A medical issue. She hadn't told him a single thing about this diagnosis at the time. Why would she have withheld that information from him?

"But you're pregnant now. You're not in-

fertile," he said woodenly. This didn't seem real. She couldn't have done this ridiculous thing. Autumn wasn't capable of such a deception. Or of making such a random decision that had affected them both.

"I had surgery for my medical condition a few years ago," she continued. "Endometriosis. When the polyps were removed it allowed me to conceive. I wasn't given that option back then. It made a world of difference for me."

Judah lowered his head into his hands. If he'd been standing his legs might have buckled underneath him. All this time he had been waiting for the other shoe to drop and now it had. This, he thought, was why he'd never completely trusted Autumn. He'd known deep down that she was going to hurt him. And here it was. A bomb from the past that she had just detonated.

Everything had blown up in his face. What they'd been building had been torn apart in one moment.

"Judah, I know this is a lot to absorb, but I had to tell you."

He scoffed. "You *had* to tell me? Twelve years later?"

"Moving away from Alaska allowed me to stuff it down so I didn't have to think about it.

I've always regretted it. You have no idea how much I've wished I'd taken another route." Tears ran down her face, but he tried his hardest not to be moved by her emotion. He was the one who had been lied to for all this time. She wasn't going to make herself the victim!

"But you didn't. You broke my heart." He stood up, fueled by the need to keep some physical distance between them. It felt painful to even look at Autumn.

"Other than having this baby," Autumn said, pressing her hands against her belly, "you're the one dream I've held in my heart. I knew if we had any hopes of a future together—and I so hope we do—that I needed to be honest with you. It's been a long time coming, but my heart has always been in the right place."

At this point he had heard enough. Nothing coming from Autumn's lips was resonating with him. It was all just white noise. His own heart ached too much for him to bear. This was soul crushing.

"I've got to get out of here." He spit the words out of his mouth.

Judah staggered out of the room and headed down the hall. He reached for his jacket on the peg and jammed his arms through the

sleeves. He quickly followed suit with his boots, stuffing his feet inside with jerky movements.

"Please, Judah. Don't go. Not like this," Autumn pleaded. "I know you're furious with me, but I'm here to talk this through. However long it takes."

He turned back toward her. "I'm not angry. Frankly, I'm too stunned to feel anything other than shock and disappointment. You basically changed the course of my life and never gave me any say in the matter. You decided my future. *Our* future." He let out a brittle laugh. "And you clearly didn't trust me enough to know I would have stuck by your side come what may. Because that would have been my choice. To love you wholly and unconditionally. I could have dealt with your diagnosis with grace and we could have explored other options. Face it, Autumn. You didn't believe in me or us. Moving forward, how in the world could I ever feel secure that you wouldn't bail on me again?"

Judah heard Autumn let out a sob as he wrenched the front door open and headed out into the Alaskan night. Snow was falling at a fast clip and he could barely make his way toward his truck between the moisture in his

eyes and the fluffy white stuff. His breathing was heavier than normal. Everything had slipped away from him in an instant. After so much suffering in his past, he'd truly believed that he was headed toward happiness. But his joy had been fleeting.

Autumn wasn't the woman he'd believed her to be. She was nothing more than a figment of his imagination.

Autumn watched from the front window as Judah drove away from her. Maybe for the last time. She couldn't imagine anyone forgiving something so grievous. As his taillights blazed red against the falling snow, Autumn pressed her hand against her mouth to stop herself from crying out again. She didn't want to get too upset due to the baby, even though it felt as if her world was crashing and burning all around her. From all the reading she had done about having a baby, Autumn had learned that babies could absorb their mother's emotions. She needed to take deep breaths.

Judah had been completely knocked off-kilter by her confession. At some point it seemed as if he had just shut down. It had all been too much for him to carry on his shoulders.

He hadn't yelled or raged at her.

He hadn't even raised his voice.

Maybe it would have been better if he had. Anger faded over time, but shock and disgust lingered. She had never felt more ashamed of herself in her life. Viewing the situation through Judah's eyes had been devastating. Although she wished that it was possible to go back in time and fix things, life didn't work that way. All she could do was try and make amends with Judah.

But how? What could she possibly do to repair the damage she'd caused? She didn't truly believe any more words could be spoken. She'd done her best to explain her rationale for having gone down that destructive path in the first place. She had been dealing with so many emotions that she hadn't been able to handle. Fear. Sorrow. Shock over her infertility diagnosis. And above all, an unwillingness for Judah to have to sacrifice his dreams for her. Of course she now knew her actions had been misguided, but it was too late to turn back the tide. Judah was right. There had been a domino effect as the result of her lie. In the end, there was nothing she could say to him that would justify her actions.

For now, she could pray and find com-

fort in Him. No matter what she'd done, He would never forsake her. Autumn knelt down on the floor. She crossed her hands in prayer-like fashion and closed her eyes.

God, please show me the way. Let me be a salve for Judah's pain. Even if he can't forgive me, allow me to help him as he continues his journey toward healing.

The snow was coming down now fast and furiously as Judah headed home. The storm had started hours earlier than expected. He could barely see five feet ahead of him on the road. Visibility was poor and his truck was skidding all over the place. He pulled the truck over to the side of the road, knowing his emotions combined with the hazardous conditions were a bad combination. In a perfect world he wouldn't be driving right now.

He idled his truck and looked outside his window, trying to monitor the situation as best he could. The ache inside him wasn't fiery or explosive. He felt completely depleted. All he'd wanted was to spend a simple night with the woman he loved. Watching movies. Eating popcorn. Instead he had been taken on a wild roller-coaster ride that made him question everything. It hurt so badly to

know she hadn't trusted him. What had he ever done to make her doubt him?

Judah laid his head on the steering wheel and let out an agonized sigh. Autumn had come back into his life and brought him so much joy. Because of her, Judah had found his way back to his faith.

What if something happened to Autumn? The thought crashed over him like a powerful wave. He had learned through losing Mary and Zane that one never knew when someone might be taken in an instant. He had left her without saying goodbye. Judah hadn't wanted to look in her eyes. Maybe a part of him had known he would have headed straight back into her arms if he did so.

A moment of clarity struck him. Judah had loved this woman for most of his life. This was their second chance to get things right. He knew the universe rarely handed out do-overs. And he'd lost so much in his life already that could never be replaced. Despite the fact that he felt stunned by her admission, Judah knew he wanted to walk through the rest of his days with Autumn by his side. She made him a better man. When she was with him Judah felt hopeful. She had given him way more than she'd taken.

He knew with a deep certainty that everything she'd done had been born out of love for him. Misguided. Foolish. Shortsighted. But genuinely from the heart.

He needed to see Autumn, to talk things through with her. And he didn't want to wait until morning to see her beautiful face. Tomorrow wasn't a given for anyone. The distance between his location and Cecily's house was less than if he headed home. And this storm wasn't letting up anytime soon. Judah carefully got off the shoulder of the road and turned his truck around so that he was now traveling in the direction he'd just come from.

What should have been a twenty-minute ride took nearly an hour as Judah white-knuckled his way down the slippery, snow-packed road. The entire way he was praying for safe travels. When he finally pulled up in front of the house, Judah was happy to see a few lights were still blazing inside. With his heart in his throat, Judah trudged up to the front door and banged on it a few times in rapid succession. He was impatient to see Autumn. Eager to take her in his arms and put this whole matter to rest.

When the door swung open, Autumn was standing there with a stunned look stamped

on her face. "Judah! You're back. Come on inside."

Covered in snow and chilled to the bone, Judah walked into the house. The cozy warmth enveloped him, making him wish he'd never left in the first place.

"Did something happen with the storm?" Autumn asked as she began helping him take his parka off. "Sit down," she instructed. "Let me help with your boots."

Judah sank down on to a wooden chair as Autumn tugged at his boots until they came off.

"So what happened?" Autumn asked, looking up at him. "It's bad out there."

Judah rubbed his hands together. "It got so nasty that I had to pull off the road."

"Oh no. That's terrible," Autumn said, letting out a fretful sound.

"Actually it wasn't as bad as it sounds. Being there gave me time to think. I don't want to squander our second chance. I don't intend to lose you a second time. I love you, Autumn. I never imagined I would love anyone again after losing Mary. But then you came crashing back into my life, reminding me at every turn that I have a lot of living ahead of me."

"Judah. Are you saying that you forgive me?" Autumn asked. Her voice trembled.

He pulled her down so she was perched on his lap. "Of course I forgive you. You're human. And I know you must've been struggling with the news you received. But now you're owning it." He winked at her. "It took you twelve years to get around to it, but you did it."

Autumn covered her face and let out a groan. "Don't remind me," she wailed.

"I'm sorry. Bad joke. It struck me when I was in the truck that you didn't have to tell me a thing. I would have never known. You could have shoved it all under the rug."

She shook her head. "No, I couldn't do that. It would have tainted our future, Judah. I couldn't take that risk."

He reached up and grazed her cheek with his thumb. "That's why I love you so much. You never take the easy path in whatever you do, whether it's writing an ambitious article or facing your past mistakes. Or starting over in your hometown."

"As a pregnant lady no less," she said, pointing to her belly.

"A brave pregnant lady," Judah said, squeezing her hand.

"I've been thinking a lot about what I did," Autumn said. "I'm just now realizing that I wasn't as sure of us as I thought I was. If I had been secure I would have trusted you to stand by my side through my infertility diagnosis. I would have known that I was enough, just me. Somehow I thought you needed me as a package deal along with babies."

"How could you ever think that, Autumn?" He reached out and grazed the side of her face with his palm. "I loved you wholeheartedly. Completely. If it had been up to me, we would have walked through life together. I loved Mary, but you were the great love of my life. My other half. I would have chosen you time and again."

She blinked away tears. "Oh, Judah. I loved you then and I love you now. I'm so grateful for your grace in forgiving me."

"My motives are a bit selfish. I want to be with you, Autumn, for the long haul. I don't want there to be anything standing between us," Judah said. "Not the past. Not things left unspoken. Nothing."

"I know that I can trust you, Judah, with anything. It's something I should have known back then, but I didn't."

"It's okay. From now on we're just going

to think of it as something that happened on our journey. We can't dwell on it."

"I'm so happy I came back home to Serenity Peak." She placed her arms around his neck and pressed a kiss against his cheek.

"I'm so happy you're mine," Judah said, leaning in for another sweet kiss. Autumn happily obliged.

Happiness was theirs for the taking. There were no obstacles standing in their way now. A glorious future stretched out before them. With faith, hope and an abundance of love, Autumn and Judah would make their second chance love story last a lifetime.

Epilogue

The sun was shining brilliantly on a warm September day in Serenity Peak. Autumn and Judah had driven out to the hot springs for an end of summer picnic and to celebrate the birth of the baby boy she'd decided to name River. Judah had agreed that it was a strong and powerful name. Over the past few months, all of the most important things had come into sharp focus for them. Love. Forgiveness. Hope. New beginnings.

Both her and Judah's families were soundly in their corner as their relationship continued to blossom. For Autumn it demonstrated the strong ties that bound families together. She would never stop treasuring her beautiful family. Or Judah.

Autumn shook her head. "Sometimes it

feels like none of this can be real. How did all of my dreams come true at the same time?"

"Because you're worthy of every happiness this world has to offer." He leaned over and kissed her. "And I'm going to make sure the blessings keep coming."

"My editor told me this morning that my articles are some of the most read on the *Tribune*'s website," Autumn said. She was bursting with pride over how well her work was being received by the public. Her piece on the hardworking fishermen in Alaska was a nice contrast to her hard hitting article about fraud in the industry. Once fraud charges had been levied against two fishing operations in the Kenai Peninsula, Autumn had been able to conclude the series with a bang. It gave her confidence to continue to write the stories of her heart and to dig deep to unearth the truth when necessary.

Thankfully, the rumors about Judah had fizzled out once arrests had been made. He no longer felt as if he was the subject of whispers and finger pointing.

"I'm proud of you, Autumn. I know it wasn't easy packing up your whole life and coming back to Serenity Peak. But you followed your heart and it led you straight back to me."

"You've made me very happy, Judah. I came back home for the sake of this little guy," she said, touching River's little toes as he slept, "but you were the icing on the cake. An unexpected blessing."

"Ditto. I thought that I was going to be walking through life alone until you opened my heart up again. You dared me to start living again."

"You did all the heavy lifting." She reached out and caressed his cheek. "The courage you've shown in moving forward is awe-inspiring." Moisture pooled in her eyes. "You could have walled yourself up for the rest of your days. But you chose to live again…and love. I'm so blessed to be the recipient of this big old heart." She placed her palm on his chest, right over his thumping heart.

He entwined her hand with his own. "Truth is, you've always owned a large chunk of my heart. Life took us both in other directions. God gave me Mary and Zane. He blessed you with River. And now He is making a way for us. That's pretty spectacular."

She squeezed his hand. "God is good, my love. And so are you. You're a very special man. I'm glad you're my person."

"Right back at you." He leaned over and

placed a kiss on her lips. "I'm not sure any of this would have happened without you. And River. You showed me that I was still a man of faith and that I deserved to be part of the living. That knowledge transformed me."

"You didn't ever lose your faith, Judah. You simply got sidetracked. By loss and grief. By the storms of life that crashed over you. I'm so sorry you had to endure all of that pain."

"It brought me to my knees, but something inside of me never gave up. Even when I wanted to hide away from the world and wallow, I still got a thrill out of fishing and visiting Ida…and you. When I first saw you stranded in the rainstorm it was as if my entire body was jolted back to life."

"You came to my rescue that day and every day since then, Judah Campbell."

"We rescued each other, sweetheart. If not for you I would still be stuck in the past and licking my wounds. You brought me back into the world. And for that I'll always be grateful."

For a few moments they sat in companionable silence as they enjoyed the balmy weather and the beauty of their lovingly created family.

"I have something to ask you," Autumn said, looking deeply into Judah's eyes.

Judah let out a groan. "Uh-oh. The last time you said those words to me you were on assignment and wanted my help. What is it this time?" He made a face, which earned him a slight push from Autumn.

"Be nice. This is serious business," Autumn said in a solemn tone.

Judah's expression turned on a dime into a somber one. "Okay, I'm listening," he said.

She reached out and linked their hands. "I, Autumn Hines, want to humbly ask you to do me the honor of becoming my husband." She reached out and placed a finger on his lips. "Shh. Before you say a word, there are a few things I'd like to tell you. We loved and we lost one another. We've loved other people between then and now. But I've always held on to a piece of you, Judah. I buried it so deeply inside of me that I didn't even realize it myself until I came back home. Having you in my life…and River's is a dream come true. I'm happier than I've ever been and that's because of you, my sweet Judah. That was all part of the journey that led us to each other."

"Autumn, the answer is yes," Judah said in an exuberant voice. "It seems as if I've waited a lifetime for this moment. I've lived enough life to know that we have to seize happiness

when it's within reach." He cupped her face in his hands. "I can't wait to start our journey and grow old together. I want to walk through this life with you, sweetheart."

Autumn leaned in and placed her arms around Judah's neck. "And maybe we can give River a sibling…or two."

Judah threw back his head in laughter. "If God blesses us with more kids that will be amazing. The more the merrier," Judah said. "But if it's only just the three of us, I'll be the happiest man in Alaska."

Autumn turned her face up toward Judah. "And I'll be the happiest woman because of what you've brought to my life." He kissed her then—tenderly, lovingly—whispering, "Forever" as his lips brushed against hers.

Peace. Love. Forgiveness. They had found their blissful happily ever after right here in Serenity Peak. For now and for always, they would be at each other's side.

* * * * *

If you enjoyed this story, look for these other books by Belle Calhoune:

Hiding in Alaska
Their Alaskan Past
An Alaskan Christmas Promise

Dear Reader

Welcome to Serenity Peak, Alaska. There's something so thrilling about introducing a new town to readers. There are so many possibilities to explore and stories to be told. It's all a fresh slate. I've left a few breadcrumbs in this book about possible future lead characters who'll have their own love stories.

I hope you enjoyed Autumn and Judah's love story. Judah is a man who has lost his entire world through a terrible accident. Steeped in grief and bitterness, it's hard for him to find a path forward. Autumn returns to Serenity Peak in the hopes of creating a new life for herself and the baby she's carrying. As a single mother she's facing challenges that might make her journey all the more difficult. When the two reunite there is a connection that they both feel even though they resist the attraction.

There are a few themes—forgiveness, resilience, grace—that run through this book. I enjoyed writing Autumn and Judah—two flawed characters who deserve a shot at happily ever after.

As always I'm thrilled to be a part of the

Harlequin Love Inspired author team. I love writing inspirational romance and crafting happily ever afters. You can find me on my Author Belle Calhoune Facebook page and join my newsletter on bellecalhoune.com.

Blessings,
Belle

Get 4 FREE REWARDS!

We'll send you 2 FREE Books plus 2 FREE Mystery Gifts.

FREE Value Over **$20**

Both the **Love Inspired®** and **Love Inspired® Suspense** series feature compelling novels filled with inspirational romance, faith, forgiveness and hope.

YES! Please send me 2 FREE novels from the Love Inspired or Love Inspired Suspense series and my 2 FREE gifts (gifts are worth about $10 retail). After receiving them, if I don't wish to receive any more books, I can return the shipping statement marked "cancel." If I don't cancel, I will receive 6 brand-new Love Inspired Larger-Print books or Love Inspired Suspense Larger-Print books every month and be billed just $6.49 each in the U.S. or $6.74 each in Canada. That is a savings of at least 16% off the cover price. It's quite a bargain! Shipping and handling is just 50¢ per book in the U.S. and $1.25 per book in Canada.* I understand that accepting the 2 free books and gifts places me under no obligation to buy anything. I can always return a shipment and cancel at any time by calling the number below. The free books and gifts are mine to keep no matter what I decide.

Choose one: ☐ **Love Inspired**   ☐ **Love Inspired Suspense**
            Larger-Print   **Larger-Print**
            (122/322 IDN GRHK)   (107/307 IDN GRHK)

Name (please print)

Address   Apt. #

City   State/Province   Zip/Postal Code

Email: Please check this box ☐ if you would like to receive newsletters and promotional emails from Harlequin Enterprises ULC and its affiliates. You can unsubscribe anytime.

> **Mail to the Harlequin Reader Service:**
> **IN U.S.A.:** P.O. Box 1341, Buffalo, NY 14240-8531
> **IN CANADA:** P.O. Box 603, Fort Erie, Ontario L2A 5X3

Want to try 2 free books from another series? Call 1-800-873-8635 or visit www.ReaderService.com.

*Terms and prices subject to change without notice. Prices do not include sales taxes, which will be charged (if applicable) based on your state or country of residence. Canadian residents will be charged applicable taxes. Offer not valid in Quebec. This offer is limited to one order per household. Books received may not be as shown. Not valid for current subscribers to the Love Inspired or Love Inspired Suspense series. All orders subject to approval. Credit or debit balances in a customer's account(s) may be offset by any other outstanding balance owed by or to the customer. Please allow 4 to 6 weeks for delivery. Offer available while quantities last.

Your Privacy—Your information is being collected by Harlequin Enterprises ULC, operating as Harlequin Reader Service. For a complete summary of the information we collect, how we use this information and to whom it is disclosed, please visit our privacy notice located at corporate.harlequin.com/privacy-policy. From time to time we may also exchange your personal information with reputable third parties. If you wish to opt out of this sharing of your personal information, please visit readerservice.com/consumerschoice or call 1-800-873-8635. **Notice to California Residents**—Under California law, you have specific rights to control and access your data. For more information on these rights and how to exercise them, visit corporate.harlequin.com/california-privacy.

LIRLIS22R3

Get 4 FREE REWARDS!

We'll send you 2 FREE Books <u>plus</u> 2 FREE Mystery Gifts.

FREE Value Over **$20**

Both the **Harlequin® Special Edition** and **Harlequin® Heartwarming™** series feature compelling novels filled with stories of love and strength where the bonds of friendship, family and community unite.

YES! Please send me 2 FREE novels from the Harlequin Special Edition or Harlequin Heartwarming series and my 2 FREE gifts (gifts are worth about $10 retail). After receiving them, if I don't wish to receive any more books, I can return the shipping statement marked "cancel." If I don't cancel, I will receive 6 brand-new Harlequin Special Edition books every month and be billed just $5.49 each in the U.S. or $6.24 each in Canada, a savings of at least 12% off the cover price, or 4 brand-new Harlequin Heartwarming Larger-Print books every month and be billed just $6.24 each in the U.S. or $6.74 each in Canada, a savings of at least 19% off the cover price. It's quite a bargain! Shipping and handling is just 50¢ per book in the U.S. and $1.25 per book in Canada.* I understand that accepting the 2 free books and gifts places me under no obligation to buy anything. I can always return a shipment and cancel at any time by calling the number below. The free books and gifts are mine to keep no matter what I decide.

Choose one: ☐ **Harlequin Special Edition**
(235/335 HDN GRJV)
☐ **Harlequin Heartwarming**
Larger-Print
(161/361 HDN GRJV)

Name (please print)

Address   Apt. #

City   State/Province   Zip/Postal Code

Email: Please check this box ☐ if you would like to receive newsletters and promotional emails from Harlequin Enterprises ULC and its affiliates. You can unsubscribe anytime.

Mail to the **Harlequin Reader Service:**
IN U.S.A.: P.O. Box 1341, Buffalo, NY 14240-8531
IN CANADA: P.O. Box 603, Fort Erie, Ontario L2A 5X3

Want to try 2 free books from another series? Call 1-800-873-8635 or visit www.ReaderService.com.

COMING NEXT MONTH FROM
Love Inspired

THEIR AMISH SECRET
Amish Country Matches • by Patricia Johns
Putting the past behind her is all single Amish mother Claire Glick wants. But when old love Joel Beiler shows up on her doorstep in the middle of a harrowing storm, it could jeopardize everything she's worked for—including her best-kept secret...

THE QUILTER'S SCANDALOUS PAST
by Patrice Lewis
Esther Yoder's family must sell their mercantile store, and when an out-of-town buyer expresses interest, Esther is thrilled. Then she learns the buyer is Joseph Kemp—the man responsible for ruining her reputation. Can she set aside her feelings for the sake of the deal?

THE RANCHER'S SANCTUARY
K-9 Companions • by Linda Goodnight
With zero ranching experience, greenhorn Nathan Garrison has six months to reopen an abandoned guest ranch—or lose it forever. So he hires scarred cowgirl Monroe Matheson to show him the ropes. As they work together, will secrets from the past ruin their chance at love?

THE BABY INHERITANCE
Lazy M Ranch • by Tina Radcliffe
Life changes forever when rancher Drew Morgan inherits his best friend's baby. But when he learns professor Sadie Ross is also part of the deal, things get complicated. Neither one of them is ready for domestic bliss, but sweet baby Mae might change their minds...

MOTHER FOR A MONTH
by Zoey Marie Jackson
Career-weary Sienna King yearns to become a mother, and opportunity knocks when know-it-all reporter Joel Armstrong comes to her with an unusual proposal. Putting aside their differences, they must work together to care for his infant nephew, but what happens when their pretend family starts to feel real?

THE NANNY NEXT DOOR
Second Chance Blessings • by Jenna Mindel
Grieving widower Jackson Taylor moves to small-town Michigan for the sake of his girls. When he hires his attractive next-door neighbor, Maddie Williams, to be their nanny, it could be more than he bargained for as the line between personal and professional starts to blur...

LOOK FOR THESE AND OTHER LOVE INSPIRED BOOKS WHEREVER BOOKS ARE SOLD, INCLUDING MOST BOOKSTORES, SUPERMARKETS, DISCOUNT STORES AND DRUGSTORES.

LICNM0323

HARLEQUIN
PLUS

Try the best multimedia subscription service for romance readers like you!

Read, Watch and Play.

Experience the easiest way to get the romance content you crave.

Start your **FREE TRIAL** at
www.harlequinplus.com/freetrial.